LEGALITY

LEGALITY

AND LEGITIMACY

———

Carl Schmitt

translated and edited by Jeffrey Seitzer

with an introduction by John P. McCormick

Duke University Press Durham & London

2004

To Janet Smith

CONTENTS

———

Legality and Legitimacy

I

The System of Legality of the
Parliamentary Legislative State

II

The Three Extraordinary Lawgivers
of the Weimar Constitution

TRANSLATOR'S PREFACE

———

Much of the current interest in Carl Schmitt centers on his contribution to political theory during the Weimar Republic. However, Schmitt was by training and by inclination a legal theorist, a fact reflected in his work from this period. Not only does he focus on issues where politics and law naturally intersect, such as those involving the nature and limits of constitutional government; but his mode of argumentation is also decidedly "legal" even in those essays that do not address legal questions directly. The legal cast of Schmitt's political theory, moreover, is deeply steeped in the Continental, particularly German, legal tradition, which deviates in important respects from the Anglo-American one.

Because Schmitt was primarily writing for a German audience, and one with some knowledge of German law, he could assume that the reader had a sufficient understanding of the distinctive features of this tradition as well as of how the Weimar Constitution constituted both a continuation and a departure from it. Also, writing in the midst of a political crisis, Schmitt could assume that the reader was familiar with major political, social, and economic developments and with the main currents of thought, including his own, on how to respond to the pressing problems of the Weimar Republic.

In preparing the translation, however, I assumed that the intended reader does not have in-depth knowledge in all of these areas. Compensating for the abstractness of Schmitt's presentation, I have included explanatory notes discussing aspects of the Weimar context, which provide an unstated background to the work. My aim in doing so is not to argue for or against Schmitt's position, but rather to provide readers with information that may aid them in understanding and evaluating Schmitt's argument. The translator's notes are placed in brackets to distinguish them from Schmitt's.

Among the explanatory notes are a number concerning the translation of particular terms. Given the frequent references to the institutions of government, both in Schmitt's text and in my notes, it is best to address issues regarding the translation of these terms at the outset. Some terms appear commonly in English and are thus best left in the original German. This is clearly the case, for example, with the term *Reich* ("empire" or "imperial"), referring to national level of government and its institutions, which Americans would term "federal," and *Kaiser*, or emperor. Other terms offer additional reasons for special treatment. Because in English the terms *Reich* and *Bund* might both be translated as "federal," even though they refer to different institutions in distinct time periods, I have decided to leave the following terms in the original German: *Reichstag* (federal parliament), *Bundesrat* (federal chamber in the Reich and post–World War II periods), and *Reichsrat* (federal chamber in the Weimar period). Another advantage in doing so is that this will distinguish general references to parliaments from specific references to the German legislature. Two of the Weimar system's high courts, the *Staatsgerichtshof* (state court) and the *Reichsgericht* (high court for civil and criminal cases), have no clear English equivalents. Since they are often left in the original German, the same is done here as well. I translate the other institutions of the national government, the *Reichspräsident, Reichskanzler,* and *Reichsregierung* as President, Chancellor, and Reich government, respectively. Finally, the term *Land* might be rendered "state," as in the fifty American states. But the German term *Staat* is also translatable as "state" and has a rich history of its own; Schmitt, along with many others, is inclined to deny the status of a state to a *Land* (plural, *Länder*). To avoid potential confusion, therefore, Land (unitalicized) will be left in the original German.

I have also made some minor changes in the text of Schmitt's work and added some additional materials. In regard to the former, I have replaced Schmitt's often long and sometimes sketchy references in the main body of the text with an author-date system of citation. In the corresponding bibliography, I have attempted whenever possible to verify Schmitt's references, render them more complete, and, in some cases, identify more accessible editions of the works cited. This should help the reader interested in consulting Schmitt's sources. However, readers should be aware that I was not able to identify all of Schmitt's quotations and verify or supplement all of his sources.

For the convenience of the reader who would like to follow the original text, I have included page breaks from the original 1932 edition as well as from the 1958 second edition, which is frequently used by scholars. Each set of page breaks appears in brackets, with the year of publication before the page number, each separated by a slash. For example, the beginning of page 43 from the original edition is marked as [1932/43], and the start of page 300 of the second edition is marked as [1958/300].

A translation of Schmitt's untitled commentary on *Legality and Legitimacy* from the second edition is included in this volume as an afterword. These comments are potentially significant because Schmitt discusses his motivation for writing the work, its reception in Weimar, and the way the current German constitution, the Basic Law, addresses some of his primary concerns. Two further additions are an index to Schmitt's text and an appendix with translations of the articles of the Weimar Constitution that Schmitt cites.

Many persons contributed to the completion of this book. Miriam Angress, Valerie Millholland, and Pam Morrison patiently shepherded the project through various stages of the publication process. Paul Betz, John McCormick, George Schwab, and two anonymous reviewers shared their helpful reactions to the entire manuscript. Susanne Degenhert, Rainer Forst, Oliver Lepsius, Chris Thornhill, Eric Warshaw, and Michael Wieczorrek helped with a number of difficult terms, while the Holcombe Academic Translation Trust provided generous financial assistance. Finally, Janet Smith and Ethan McGinnis Seitzer supplied timely and much needed distractions.

IDENTIFYING OR EXPLOITING THE
PARADOXES OF CONSTITUTIONAL
DEMOCRACY?

———

An Introduction to Carl Schmitt's
Legality and Legitimacy

JOHN P. McCORMICK

Carl Schmitt's *Legality and Legitimacy* is an invaluable arti-
fact from the most notorious crisis in the history of constitutional democracy.[1] It is also a critical yet often overlooked con-
duit in a century-long debate over the legitimacy of the rule
of law that raises perennial issues concerning the stability of
parliamentary government. Schmitt composed and published
the book in 1932 as Germany's Weimar Republic (1919–33) stag-
gered through its final crisis—one characterized by devastating economic depression and often violent political disorder.[2]
Schmitt, who has since become recognized as the last century's
foremost reactionary thinker,[3] dissected the Weimar Constitution, identifying it as both the source of the near-civil-war circumstances plaguing the Republic and as a possible solution to
them as well. He claimed that while the parliamentary, liberal,
and legalistic aspects of the 1919 constitution may have exacerbated Germany's problems, the presidential, democratic, and
popularly legitimate component might actually solve them.
  Whether Schmitt's prescriptions proved to be simply inadequate to the severity of the crisis or intentionally and successfully accelerated the Republic's demise in 1933 has been a controversial question for years.[4] Certainly, Schmitt's subsequent
endorsement of National Socialism has made the case difficult
for those who portray him as merely a diagnostician of the immediate circumstances, whose practical intention, if he had

one at all, was to save the Republic. No matter what Schmitt's motives in 1932 may have been, the ideas of *Legality and Legitimacy* were intimately entwined with political reality because he advised powerful conservative cabinet ministers, most notably the aristocrats Kurt von Schleicher and Franz von Papen. Indeed, it is quite possible that one or both conveyed Schmitt's thoughts to President Paul von Hindenburg; we know for sure that the aides of Schleicher and Papen were citing *Legality and Legitimacy* in support of various political and legal strategies throughout the last year of the Republic.[5]

Beyond the immediate Weimar context, *Legality and Legitimacy* holds a critical place in intellectual debates over the ability of liberal- or social-democratic regimes to secure substantive legitimacy through legal procedures. If legitimacy requires compliance with authority on grounds other than the mere threat of sanction or the simple force of habit, then why do people obey the law? Max Weber first raised the issue at the start of the Weimar Republic in the "Economy and Social Norms" and "Sociology of Law" sections of his posthumously published *Economy and Society*.[6] Weber left ultimately unsubstantiated his claim that rational-legal authority stood alongside traditional and charismatic authority as an independent type of legitimacy.[7] The status of legal authority was rendered even more precarious by Weber's professed doubts over the efficacy or even continued existence of rational-formal law as the nineteenth-century state governed by the liberal rule of law, the *Rechtsstaat*, was eclipsed by the administrative or welfare state, the *Sozialstaat*.[8] Finally, in his later writings Weber ascribed superior democratic legitimacy to a directly elected president over the party-dominated and bureaucracy-dependent parliament.[9] Hence Germany's greatest social scientist and leading public intellectual, who had himself contributed to the framing of the Weimar Constitution, bequeathed to the nation's first attempt at a constitutional parliamentary democracy these serious hesitations over its analytical consistency and historical possibility.[10] These hesitations would not be lost on Carl Schmitt.

The potentially problematic relationship of legality and legitimacy continued to haunt German political thought throughout Germany's second attempt at constitutional democracy, the Federal Republic. It persistently emerged in all of the major works of its greatest political philosopher and social theorist, Jürgen Habermas,[11] until finally occupying the central place in his recent magnum opus, *Beyond Facts and Norms*.[12] Habermas would go to great lengths to show that the substance of rational-legal legitimacy consists in the *participation* of citizens in the formulation of legal and constitutional norms, and not in, as Weber suggested, their "belief in" such norms or, as Schmitt averred, their collective acclamation or rejection of them. Habermas has often found Schmitt lurking behind arguments that, on the one hand, insist on the homogeneous concrete will of a demos that preexists and takes priority over legal or constitutional arrangements,[13] or that, on the other hand, posits a purely formalistic apparatus that does not take into account the moral-practical reason institutionalized in and carried out by legal procedures.[14]

More generally, Schmitt's *Legality and Legitimacy* raises many questions that often prove awkward for liberals, constitutionalists, and even democrats who understand themselves to be committed to the rule of law. To count off a minor litany of such questions: When does law reflect the popular will to the extent that those over whom it is exercised can be said to have authored or at least consented to it? Is it when law is elevated to unchangeable or remotely accessible constitutional norms? Or do statutes produced by a parliament satisfy such conditions? If so, can simple majorities lay claim to a general will or are supermajorities required to do so? If the content of law is decided by a majority of the people's representatives, is it consensually binding on as much as 49 percent of the population, or does it merely serve the 51 percent's coercion of them? On what grounds could any vote short of parliamentary unanimity meet the standards of legitimacy? Moreover, percentages notwithstanding, the party compromise and bargaining that plainly characterize the legislative formulation of law suggest little connection with a general will. Might not the proclamations of a more unitary institution like the president, generally elected, better reflect a broader popular will?

Schmitt poses some deeper, even existential problems for liberal democracy as well. A rule-of-law regime founded on completely formal or procedural standards, for example, allows parties that are avowed enemies of the law to help formulate and apply that law—thereby opening the way for its abuse.

Furthermore, law placed in the service of democratically responsive policies of regulation and redistribution necessarily descends into arbitrariness and incoherence. Schmitt suggests that the new legal policies of the latest party or interest-group coalition that formulated them constitute a kind of revolution approximating an illegitimate assault on the very structure of state and society. All of these problems can be solved, Schmitt claims, by admitting that there are preconstitutional and prelegal substantive values or concrete decisions to which appeals might be directed when the formal rules of a liberal- or social-democratic regime collide or appear vulnerable. If such substantive criteria indeed prove available, then these, and not the law itself, as liberals hope, are the source of the regime's legitimacy.

Granted the profundity of these questions, it is fairly astounding that *Legality and Legitimacy* has not appeared in English before now. Consider its place as (1) first-person testimony to historical disaster or a blueprint for it, (2) a crucial link between intellectual figures as widely influential as Weber and Habermas, and (3) an inconvenient reminder of the difficult relationship of democracy and the law. Jeffrey Seitzer's excellent translation now makes available to Anglophone audiences this work that most blatantly exposed and perhaps most shamelessly exploited the apparent paradox of legality and legitimacy in twentieth-century political theory and practice. In the book itself Schmitt asserted that the problem of legality and legitimacy must be interrogated both "historically and conceptually" (LL 15). My ensuing remarks in this introduction are organized precisely along these lines.

The Conservative Stab in the Back?
Schmitt and the Sabotage of the Republic

The collapse of the Weimar Republic is often understood as a case of antidemocratic forces exploiting formal legal and constitutional procedures for their own advantage. National Socialism, so the story goes, gained success in Germany by garnering sufficient popular support through legal means so as to seize, suspend, and destroy the very legislative apparatus that brought them to power. In other words, the Nazis gained power "legally," just as Schmitt in *Legality and Legitimacy* prophesied that they or the Communists would. More generally, this thesis supposedly illustrates the inherent weakness of regimes based on the rule of law. Notwithstanding its powerful resonance in narratives about the viability of constitutional democracy in the twentieth century, this may in fact be a gross mischaracterization of the historical record.[15] In this brief sketch of the context of *Legality and Legitimacy*, I hope to draw attention to extralegal machinations that contributed as much or more to the demise of the Weimar Republic than the fragile nature of the rule of law.

While ultimately a devastating year for the Republic,[16] 1932 was a profitable one for the forty-four-year-old Carl Schmitt. The book-length version of *The Concept of the Political*, first published in essay form in 1927, appeared early in the year.[17] The "friend-enemy" theory of politics and the state that it espoused garnered significant attention and was reviewed widely in the scholarly and popular presses. Schmitt held an academic position at the Handelhochschule, a school of administration and management, in Berlin. Even if it was not the appointment in a prestigious law school to which the ambitious lawyer aspired, it did allow him to reside in the capital. Thus situated, Schmitt could continue to advise government officials on political and legal matters, as he had been serving the cabinet of Chancellor Heinrich Brüning. But, as the events of the year unfolded, Schmitt would be drawn more deeply into current affairs and would interact more intimately with statesmen than he ever had before.

In April, President Hindenburg, the former Field Marshall of the Army, was returned to office in a two-round electoral victory over Adolf Hitler. But Hitler, head of the National Socialist Party (NSDAP), garnered a surprising 37 percent of the vote. Combined with its already intimidating physical presence—the party's Storm Troopers (SA) and Security Forces (SS) outnumbered the German army more than four to one—the new electoral muscle of the NSDAP was disquieting for the conservatives attempting to govern the nation in these days of economic depression and political unrest. For several years, conservative elites at various levels of the Reich had been playing a dangerous game: they generally looked the other way as the Nazis beat down the more hated Communists and attempted to intimidate the rival Social Democratic elements in the country—sometimes even encouraging such activity. But now the NSDAP proved to be a power in its own right. On May 30, in the first effort at appeasing the party, conservative ministers ousted Brüning, who was unpopular with the Nazis, and began relaxing restrictions on the party's paramilitary wings, the SA and SS. The ministerial cabal also hoped that Brüning's dismissal would lead to a new, more wide-ranging, pan-conservative governing coalition.

When that did not materialize, the new Chancellor, Franz von Papen, attempted to solve both the Nazi and Communist threats by using the emergency-decree powers granted to President Hindenburg by Article 48 of the Weimar Constitution. The first Weimar President, Friedrich Ebert, ruled through emergency decree to address economic crises and armed revolt in the early years of the Republic. By 1932, most of the elites around Hindenburg wished to use such decrees simply to institute their preferred policies, which were at odds with those of many of the duly elected members of the *Reichstag*. Papen, along with Interior Minister Wilhelm von Gayl, would have liked to have suspended parliament indefinitely and amended the constitution to empower an aristocratic upper house and restrict the franchise in significant ways. The influential Defense Minister, General Kurt von Schleicher, feared that such drastic measures would convert an already violent social situation into all-out civil war. After all, over one and a half million people were enlisted in paramilitary groups of one kind or another spanning the political spectrum. To avoid a revolution, Schleicher and his aides, Colonel Erich Marcks and Colonel Eugen Ott—with whom Schmitt consulted fairly closely— favored the use of Hindenburg's emergency powers in less overtly drastic but still legally questionable and parliament-circumventing ways.

These were the circumstances in which Schmitt wrote *Legality and Legitimacy* in the spring of 1932. Given his affiliation with the ruling conservative clique, it is not surprising to find Schmitt arguing in favor of wide presidential latitude under Article 48. Schmitt asserts that the lack of clarity in the constitution concerning jurisdictional authority, the contradictions that it manifests between liberalism and democracy, and its professed directly democratic spirit all justify presidential supersession over every other aspect of the document. With a parliamentary election looming in midsummer, Schmitt published parts of the monograph as a journal article in advance of the rest of the book.[18] These sections criticize the principle of "equal chance," whereby all parties are eligible to gain seats in the parliament and thereby contribute to the creation of law—or to obstruct it, as was too often the case in the Republic. The article theoretically justifies, if not specifically endorses, an executive ban on parties like the Communists and the National Socialists who profess enmity toward the constitution and the legislative process itself. How we understand this article and the subsequent book is crucial for how we understand Schmitt's actions in this period and where we should situate him politically: was he trying to destroy the republic, or was he trying to save it? Schmitt argues that even the most formally neutral constitution cannot espouse neutrality toward its own existence; no constitution can with consistency facilitate its own destruction. Is this commonsense advice or an anticonstitutional subterfuge? Schmitt excerpted other parts of the book in progress two weeks later, explicitly warning against any further electoral gains for the "still immature" National Socialist Party.[19]

Schmitt's political advisees did not, however, pursue the strategy of banning the antiparliamentary parties as the election approached. Still trying to placate the Nazis, whose electoral appeal they hoped to diminish and/or whose favor as potential coalition partners they hoped to curry, the Papen cabinet struck left. On July 20, eleven days before the Reichstag election, the *Land* or state of Prussia was placed under martial law, its duly elected Social Democratic government removed, and the statewide ban on National Socialist paramilitary activity lifted. The pretense for this emergency action was the Social Democratic government's purportedly extralegal and ineffectual attempts to maintain order, although the number of dead (approaching 100) and the number of injured (exceeding 1,000) that resulted from the unleashing of the ss and the sa put the lie to that. Prussia, unlike the wider Reich, had been governed by prorepublican forces, including moderate and progressive officials—in other words, exactly the governing coalition that the Brüning cabinet had maintained before being undermined and recently dismissed by the conservative ministerial clique. Clearly, Papen attempted in the nation's largest state (Prussia amounted to roughly two-thirds of Germany as a whole) the kind of authoritarian coup that he and his cabal had already perpetrated against Brüning at the national level. The Prussian government challenged the Reich's authority to act in this manner, and a constitutional court case was slated for October, to be heard by a tribunal before which the greatest legal minds in Germany, Carl Schmitt included, would appear.[20] In any case, Papen's machinations failed: the Nazis neither lost electoral support nor became coalition partners of the conservatives.

On July 31, the NSDAP received almost 38 percent of the vote and the Communists nearly 15 percent, affording them a combined veto power over any parliamentary coalition that might be formed against them. When the Reichstag convened on September 12, Papen circumvented a Nazi-Communist no-confidence vote by dissolving the parliament. The constitution called for new elections in sixty days, but Schleicher lobbied Hindenburg for an extended postponement so that the cabinet's economic policies could take effect, perhaps yielding a better electoral showing for the conservatives down the road. Schmitt suggested to Schleicher's aides that such a recourse would violate the letter of the law but nevertheless might be justified on substantive constitutional grounds. In any case, here as later, Hindenburg, no friend to liberal or social democracy, either in fear of indictment proceedings or serious about his oath to uphold the constitution, resisted the idea of resorting to overt constitutional abrogations such as the postponement of elections.

In the meantime, the courtroom drama that would display the political and legal fissures of the Republic took place in Leipzig under the name *Prussia v. the Reich*. Prominent jurists such as Schmitt, Hermann Heller, and Gerhard Anschütz appeared in person and Hans Kelsen submitted written commentaries. Schmitt's *Legality and Legitimacy* was published in time to be cited frequently at the trial—and was surprisingly invoked in the opening remarks of the Social Democratic plaintiffs to justify the Prussian government's restrictive policies toward the Nazis. In his own statements before the court, Schmitt justified the Reich's actions against the Prussian government on the premise that the Prussian state government behaved toward the Nazis as merely one party dominating another, and not as an objective, independent, and therefore legitimate authority. In *Legality and Legitimacy* Schmitt seems to distinguish the constitutionally enabled, presidentially facilitated actions of the conservative clique with whom Schmitt was affiliated at the national level from the merely strategic-party behavior he attributes to their political rivals in the parliament. Critics like Heller and Kelsen were not convinced that Schmitt could successfully prove along similar lines in the subnational Prussian context that the Social Democratic government was *not* a democratically *legitimate* authority but merely a strategically *legal* one. The case was resolved on October 25 with a rather indecisive ruling: the court reinstalled the Social Democratic government, but it also upheld Papen's status as emergency "Reich's commissar" in the Land, answerable only to President Hindenburg. At this point the Prussian government's authority had sufficiently eroded and the Nazi presence had significantly solidified so as to render the judgment moot.

Despite the fact that the Nazis endured serious setbacks in the national elections of November 6, the Papen cabinet was still split on the appropriate course of action. Chancellor Papen wanted Hindenburg to suspend parliament, ban the extremist parties, and draw up a new constitution. Schleicher, with the support of Schmitt's friend Johannes Popitz, harbored hopes for a parliamentary coalition drawn from the proworker, anticapitalist wings of *all* the major parties across the political spectrum.[21] Hindenburg gave Schleicher a chance, confirming him as chancellor on December 3, but his anticipated parliamentary support did not materialize, especially among conservatives scared off by the redistributive implications of Schleicher's proposals.[22]

Now desperate, Schleicher asked Hindenburg to dissolve the parliament. But the president, assured by Papen that the Nazis could be contained, appointed Hitler Chancellor on January 30, 1933. Any hope that the Republic might survive this disastrous decision was lost with the Reichstag fire of February 27. The pretext of an imminent Communist revolution gave the Nazis an occasion to combine terrorist tactics and legal maneuvers in a suspension of constitutional rights and elimination of all effective political opposition. The Enabling

Act of March 23, 1933, was passed by the parliament under the cloud of extraprocedural and socially repressive Nazi measures. By the end of March 1933, Papen had recruited Schmitt to help attend to the legal details of the Nazi coordination of power. The Republic was finished.

Schmitt's National Socialist career has been well documented: he soon enrolled in the party, acquiesced in the academic purges of leftists and Jews, publicly justified the circumstances surrounding the Röhm purge and the accompanying murder of Schleicher and his wife, accepted the position of Prussian Attorney General, expressed vitriolic anti-Semitism in his published work, fell from favor with the regime in 1936, and refused to submit to the stipulations of official rehabilitation after the war. For our purposes here, the question is whether the book *Legality and Legitimacy* warned against an outcome—the collapse of the Republic—that Schmitt seemed initially to oppose (even if he later benefited from it professionally) or whether he actually encouraged that outcome. During 1932, Schmitt was much closer to Schleicher than to Papen: thus it might be fair to suppose that he, like his patron, was not as radically antiparliament, anti-rule-of-law, and proauthoritarian as Papen. Schleicher's general orientation and Schmitt's public statements at the time suggest that the suspension of parliamentary institutions might be justified only because the concrete "circumstances" rendered the parliament unworkable (see LL 27). And, certainly, if Schmitt was in favor of specific amendments to the constitution or a wholesale scrapping of the document, then why did he not say so, as Papen did?

These are serious points, ones that the reader should keep in mind when interpreting the main text of *Legality and Legitimacy*. However, the commentary that follows in the next section is motivated by the following alternative considerations. Beyond the demands of concrete circumstances, *Legality and Legitimacy* traces an analytical and historical logic that may point to the permanent obsolescence and necessary elimination of the parliamentary provisions in the Weimar Constitution. As for the absence of a specific plan to subvert, change, or overthrow the constitution, Schmitt, like Schleicher, may have only eschewed such programmatic statements because they would have precipitated a civil war from which his side might not have emerged victorious. Indeed, I suggest that *Legality and Legitimacy* justifies presidential decrees that would have a permanent and not just temporary force of law: Schmitt argues that the increasing bureaucratization of society gives presidential decrees a more stable and enduring quality than parliamentary statutes that merely reflect transitory legislative majorities.

Therefore, Schmitt may offer no concrete plans for revisions because presidential discretion, guided by an oligarchic cabinet, is itself a vehicle of substantive constitutional reform. At the very least, the book may be "passively" complicit with a permanent abolition of the separation of powers presupposed by the rule of law because Schmitt sets no limits on the president's power to issue decrees, especially in the capacity to indefinitely postpone parliamentary *and* presidential elections. Readers may wish to form their own opinion of this controversial text without prior influence, specifically regarding its author's intentions toward the fate of the Weimar Republic in 1932. Thus they might skip the following critical summary of the book, returning to this section of the introduction only after reading the body of Schmitt's *Legality and Legitimacy*— or, if they so choose, perhaps not at all.

The Scope of "Legitimate" Extralegality

Like many of Schmitt's books, *Legality and Legitimacy* is short and forceful, filled with statements of analytical brilliance standing alongside illogical assertions; it is characterized by rhetorical magnificence accompanying snide *Schadenfreude*. After the war, Schmitt consistently maintained that the work was merely an objective analysis of the immediate crisis of 1932, significantly downplaying the prescriptive and certainly the polemical aspects of the book.[23] But these aspects, as much as the historical significance and substantive content of *Legality and Legitimacy*, help make the work compelling even today.

A NOVEL TYPOLOGY OF REGIMES Schmitt begins the book by defining the "parliamentary legislative state" (LL 7). The legislative state assumes that the "community will" is expressed in sets of norms, specifically, norms established by a parliament.

But these norms cannot take just any shape: they must be impersonal, general, and preestablished, that is, they take conditional semantic form ("if x, then y"), refrain from targeting specific individuals or groups, and seldomly apply to circumstances retroactively. Institutionally, the legislative state assumes a strict separation between the law and its application, and therefore between the parliament and the administration, the legislative and the executive. As Schmitt describes it, since the nineteenth century, these characteristics of the legislative state have been associated with the configuration known as the Rechtsstaat (LL 7).

Because there is no personal authority in this system, only norms, Schmitt claims that the legislative state assumes away the issue of "obedience" (LL 8). The legacy of Weber's somewhat shallow defense of legality as a form of legitimacy is palpable here. Ignoring all Kantian justifications of obedience to law as a form of self-rule, Schmitt avers that contemporary legality does not account for *why* authority is obeyed. The component with which he started, "community will" embodied in norms, has withdrawn from his account to such an extent that legal norms now appear free-floating, almost spectral, certainly unconnected with real human beings. Law disconnected from both those who make it and those over whom it is applied might easily be identified as illegitimate.

In Schmitt's account of legitimacy, obedience is affiliated most closely with personal authority alone: in Weberian terms, presumably a traditionally legitimated ruling family or a charismatically legitimated exemplary character. But, throughout the book, Schmitt adds to the idea of "consent," which in the Weberian paradigm separates legitimate domination from naked domination, a distinctively Hobbesian twist that brings both back into close proximity: Schmitt formulates consent not in the active terms of compliance but rather in the negative connotation of a "right to resistance." Legitimacy depends not on the overt compliance of those over whom authority is exercised but rather on their choice not to resist such authority. This particular phrase—"right to resistance"—raises a specter that "consent" alone does not: the presence of violence that hovers over a legitimate system. It raises the issue of the circumstances under which the terms of legitimacy have been called off and armed conflict ensues or resumes.

Tellingly, Schmitt also leaves out of this account of legality early in the book something that Weber at least acknowledged might be the source of independent legitimacy for the law: its rationality. According to Weber's thin definition, adherence to the necessary logical construction and appropriate application process of norms is nevertheless a potential source of the legitimacy of law. This formal definition of legal rationality does not account for any substantive rationality that might reside in statutes that are produced through parliamentary deliberation and public criticism. Even if such a state of affairs was beyond the realm of possibilities in Weimar,[24] Schmitt only mentions very late in the chapter the substantive grounds that previously justified parliament and the Rechtsstaat: the guarantee of "right and reason through a process distinguished by discussion and publicity" (LL 28). In the context of *Legality and Legitimacy*, legality possesses neither procedurally formal nor moral-practical rationality.

During his discussion of the legislative state early in the work, Schmitt abandons as obsolete the classical typology of regimes—democracy, aristocracy, and monarchy—and replaces it with the distinctions among legislative, jurisdiction, and governmental/administrative states. The classical regime-types were determined by the class or person that dominated them—hence according to concrete authority—while the new are determined by the manner in which they formulate and apply law.[25] In the jurisdiction state, judges make law. They do not apply to a case preexisting law created by another institution but rather create, in the moment of their decision, law that other subordinate institutions, perhaps even a parliament, subsequently acknowledge as correct (LL 9). The governmental and administrative states are decree-states in which decrees emanate, respectively, from either the personal will of a head of state or a bureaucratic official (LL 9).

Schmitt intimates that the jurisdiction state might be a Rechtsstaat since it is defined in some relationship with law, and he later muses that any of the states mentioned could be demarcated in this way (LL 19). According to this very loose definition of a Rechtsstaat, monarchical or administrative decrees could be deemed just as "legal" as laws passed by a parliament. Schmitt's motives become apparent as he begins merging decrees with laws in this manner over the course

of the book, thus subverting the conventional definition of the Rechtsstaat that presupposes a decree/law distinction. In Anglo-American terms, this distinction conforms with the difference between the rule of men and rule of law: any person can dictate arbitrary decrees, but only a parliament, being representative of the nation and having deliberated extensively, can issue rational laws. But Schmitt draws on noted liberal jurist Richard Thoma to suggest that the contemporary legislative state, identified explicitly as a Rechtsstaat because it is engaged in the dictating of decrees as much as the issuing of laws, is really a mixture of all the types of regimes mentioned above and not an independent type of its own (LL 9). Then, having raised doubts about the conceptual qualifications of the legislative state in relationship to the Rechtsstaat model, Schmitt immediately announces that he is uninterested in ideal types anyway, especially when such types do not conform to factual reality.

But an insidious point has been made: Schmitt suggests that the Rechtsstaat ideal generally identified with the legislative state—a closed system of discretely formulated legal norms, administered by a separation between the legislature and the executive—is a fiction in the contemporary circumstances of a "turn toward the total state" (LL 11). Schmitt here refers to the two alternatives for states emerging in the early twentieth century: the weak "quantitative" total state, a welfare state or Sozialstaat, and the strong "qualitative" total state that most closely resembles Mussolini's Italian state.[26] The former state is drawn into society by myriad special interests, thus depleting the state's vitality, while the latter sets its own terms of engagement with society, thus retaining its vigor and integrity. The quantitative total state presides over the subversion of the separation of power and the deformalization of law as groups ask for more specific regulations, especially redistributive policies, that expand the administration in an unprecedented manner.[27] Drawing on Weber's studies of bureaucracy, Schmitt raises the specter that the administrative decrees associated with the total state represent the ascendance of the administrative over the legislative state (LL 11). In fact, he adds that the radical nature of this era of great transformation is especially conducive to the further development of the administrative state and the decline of the legislative state, as well as ruling out the jurisdiction state, the latter two being appropriate for more stable times (LL 11–12).[28]

LEGITIMACY REDEFINED Shifting back to analytical from historical analysis, Schmitt decisively inflates into a full-blown contradiction what might have been a mere weakness in Weber's theoretical formulations. If Weber cast legality as a thin form of legitimacy, Schmitt specifically invokes Weber to render it the very *antithesis* of legitimacy: in the legislative state, " '*legality*' . . . has the meaning and purpose of making superfluous and negating the legitimacy of either the monarch or the people's plebiscitarian will as well as of every authority and governing power" (LL 14). Note that Schmitt chooses as antagonists for legality one example that represents traditional legitimacy and another that represents charismatic legitimacy. One could expect that Schmitt's readership might tolerate the legal supersession of the traditional *Kaiserreich* by the Republic, but not of the charismatically charged will of the people that was intended to take the Kaiser's place and was institutionalized in the 1919 Constitution. According to Schmitt's logic here, legality *thwarted* rather than facilitated the transfer of sovereignty from the monarch to the people in Germany's first democracy.[29]

Further discrediting legality as a concept, Schmitt draws on the commonsense opposition between what is "merely formal" and what is "legitimate," as well as pointing up what he takes to be the absurd fact that something as substantively significant as a coup d'état may be described in strictly legal terms. A regime may vote itself out of existence legally but never legitimately. Therefore, what is strictly legal is seldom what is really important. In this context, Schmitt may even hint at his own designs in offering an alternative example: "a parliamentary dissolution might substantively conform to the spirit of the constitution, and yet not be legal" (LL 14). In other words parts of a constitution may be legally violated so as to save it legitimately. But we have yet to conceive what aspect of the Weimar Constitution Schmitt might be trying to save.

In this example, Schmitt defends a logic in which something becomes its opposite—an unconstitutional act in fact proves to be constitutionally faithful—in response to what he deems the perversities of logic often resorted to in defense of strict legality. He claims that the opening up of "the legal process to all conceivable aspirations, goals, and movements, even the most radical and revolutionary, enabling them to achieve their aim without violence or disruption[, is] a legal process that establishes order while at the same time it functions in a completely 'value-neutral' way. . . . The distinctive rationalism of the system of legality is obviously recast into its opposite" (LL 15). In other words, open legality invites the triumph of absolute illegality. These are the germs of the "inherent weakness of the rule of law" thesis mentioned in the section above, an issue to which I will return below.

Recall that Weber ultimately reduced the concept of legal legitimacy to a scenario where subjects "believed" in the law. But since belief and rational demonstration are not always reconcilable this definition undermines what makes law an independent source of legitimacy: rationality. This formulation allows Schmitt to relativize rationality's potential as a universal standard into a mere opinion or cultural disposition characteristic of a particular time and place. Schmitt claims that belief *in* rationality, perhaps plausible in the eighteenth and nineteenth centuries, has today evaporated: "The legislative state seems to be something higher and ideal so long as the belief in the rationality and ideality of its normativism is still vibrant in times and in peoples that remain able to cultivate a (typically Cartesian) belief in *idées générales*" (LL 15). But, as Schmitt first suggested in his study of parliamentarism ten years earlier and reiterates in *Legality and Legitimacy*, in contemporary circumstances, belief in *will* is reasserting itself over belief in *reason*.

To be sure, Schmitt softens these charges somewhat by declaring that he himself is not a steadfast opponent of the statute-making process as such: parliaments issuing general norms that officials then enforce is an acceptable state of affairs when there is in place an acknowledged higher authority such as a constitutional monarch, but not when a parliament pretends to fill such a role itself (LL 19). Thus the nineteenth-century German constitutional monarchy was an acceptable legislative state, whereas the Weimar parliamentary system is not (LL 19).[30]

Schmitt proceeds to devote several pages to a rehabilitation

of the German bureaucracy from charges of extreme rationalism and technicism, perhaps to lay the foundations of a
new antilegal administrative state (LL 15–17). He rejects many
of Weber's assumptions about bureaucracy and German bureaucracy, in particular, but eagerly retains Weber's infamous
remark about the functional narrowing of parliament into a
forum for the training of leaders (LL 15–17).[31] The Reichstag's
abuse of the bureaucracy has benefited neither, but Schmitt
intimates that the latter might be redeemed in a new state configuration (LL 18).

Moving from the bureaucracy to the military—the two pillars of the old constitutional monarchy and, potentially, of
an emerging presidentialist democracy—Schmitt discusses the
demise of the German army in terms of a disarming of the
German *people*. It is this space vacated by the monarchy—
space in which the bureaucracy has been exploited by the parliament and the army dishonored by foreign powers—that the
figure of the President makes its first significant appearance in
the work. Schmitt declares that the president, selected by "the
entire German people," now has the role of coordinating the
army and the bureaucracy (LL 18). Schmitt depicts the President
as the sole weapon available to a German people illegitimately
relieved of their arms.[32]

PARLIAMENTARY GOVERNMENT DISCREDITED Having con-
structed this institutional-ideological framework, Schmitt
goes on to establish a fairly crude opposition between statutory
regulations and fundamental rights: he associates one with the
transitory whim of a parliamentary majority and the other
with a quasi-sacred preconstitutional will (LL 21, 27). Of course,
both can be and have been conceived of as different instances
of the present popular will within a democratic arrangement
that merely sets different levels of accessibility to itself depending on the gravity of the issues involved.[33] But this justification for supermajoritarian positions is too formal, and likely,
as we will see, too popularly participatory for Schmitt. Distinctions between constitutional amendments and statutory
laws must be made by a decision rather than along the lines
of formal rules. In this spirit, Schmitt diagnoses a sort of liberal false consciousness whereby the supremacy of statutes, in-

tended to achieve justice and secure freedom, actually entails a threat to rights, rights that he associates explicitly with, once again, the right to resistance: "Only through the acceptance of these pairings [law and statute, justice and legality, substance and process] was it possible to subordinate oneself to the rule of law precisely in the name of freedom, remove the right to resistance from the catalogue of liberty rights, and grant to the statute the previously noted unconditional priority" (LL 22). Of course, the only infringements on rights actually perpetuated by the Weimar Reichstag were the regulatory and redistributive policies that conservatives interpreted as unacceptable violations of quasi-sacred property rights. Certainly the attempt to ban paramilitary groups, or at least disarm them, ought not to be equated with a violation of the basic right to resistance, as Schmitt does here (and conservatives intoxicated with weapons do in other liberal democratic regimes) (LL 24).

But Schmitt wishes to raise a phantom of parliamentary tyranny—in a context where parliament cannot get anything done![34] Schmitt transforms the actual crisis of Weimar parliamentarism—the fact of a weak legislative institution virtually incapable of reaching agreement—into the threatening instrument of an irrational will of some numerically superior party. Of course, he does not mention the past track record or even the present possibility of parliamentary practices of consensus formation and deliberation that do not, without unprecedented self-contradiction, infringe on the very guarantees and rights that facilitate the lawmaking process.

On the contrary, Schmitt's strategy seems to entail a switch from a *dishonest* to an *admitted* relinquishing of the right to resistance: in other words, an exchange of a surreptitious submission to parliamentary statutes for an acknowledged submission to the plebiscitarianly representative President. The one is a subjection to a particularistic, legalistically empowered party, the latter, a subjection to the general, democratically legitimate will. An irony of Schmitt's concern here, still relevant today, is that those social forces most aligned with corporate and military power, therefore those with the best means to "resist," are the ones most concerned with the right to resistance against liberal or progressive government policies.

For Schmitt, the "'value-neutral,' functionalist and formal concept of law" (LL 28) facilitates the legislative state's self-obsolescence since it provides no substantive ground by which to judge the intentions or aims of the different political parties. Thus this staunch anti-parliamentarian is himself concerned that parliament will be seized by parties who have unparliamentary intentions: "Whoever controls 51 percent would be able legally to render the remaining 49 percent illegal . . . and to treat partisan opponents like common criminals, who are then perhaps reduced to kicking their boots against the locked door" (LL 33). Under such circumstances, the majority becomes "the state itself" (LL 35); their ability to behave in this manner is the political "premium" or "surplus" of holding power (LL 35).

In this context, Schmitt raises the threat of the parliament issuing emergency statutes, a right he wishes to reserve for executive decrees because the latter are, according to him, more closely bound to the democratic will (LL 33). But throughout the essay he does not demonstrate *why* this is true: is it because of the general election that selects the President, or is it some unmeasurable relationship between the office of the President and the people established in the constitution? Along these lines, therefore, it is alarming that while Schmitt criticizes the constitution for allowing majorities to tyrannize minorities, he discredits any specific or formally legal way one might guard against such an outcome, instead deeming the only acceptable limitation on parliament to be the prudence of an executive, itself formally unlimited and practically unrestrained.

Schmitt expresses suspiciousness of formal procedures throughout the book, even if these are the best means for making institutions accountable. For instance, he disdains the notion that one can solve the problem of protecting the rights of minorities by making the requirements for constitutional amending more difficult—such as by raising the threshold from 50 to 65 percent of a vote. This increase does not define "the quality and dignity of the additional quantum" (LL 42). Merely rendering the requirement formally "more difficult" gives rise to more *quantitative* reasoning over the issue of minorities and majorities and the criteria for constitutional emendation and not necessarily a *qualitative* confrontation with them. Schmitt's unqualified antiformalism renders his own positive valuations fairly metaphysical—most specifically, his advocacy of democracy.

DEMOCRATIC HOMOGENEITY Schmitt issues the challenge that real democrats ought to admit that the will of the people as a whole more closely approximates justice than that of some party in parliament: "[T]he homogeneous people have all the characteristics that a guarantee of the justice and reasonableness of the people's expressed will cannot renounce. No democracy exists without the presupposition that the people are good and, consequently, that their will is sufficient" (LL 27–28). Of course, democratic theory does not assume, on *ontological* grounds, that the people at large are just; rather, it assumes that the results of their participation, interaction, discussion, and then decision are usually what is for the best. Instead of a process of will formation, Schmitt's definition emphasizes a static will that renders the rectitude and efficacy of the popular will absurdly unlikely.

Moreover, he is simply wrong to state that "every democracy rests on the presupposition of the indivisibly similar, entire, unified people" (LL 29). There are many theories of democracy that allow for pluralism among parties, diversity among individuals, negotiation among classes, and so on; but Schmitt defines democracy in such a way so as to exclude such theories from the parameters of democratic theory. However, one must conclude that only under the standard of such assertions about democracy can right-wing, elitist, nostalgic monarchists like Schmitt present themselves as "democrats" or "populists." Constitutional democracy is established precisely to set limits such that elites like Schmitt's advisees could *not* associate their interests or idea of the good with the "homogeneous will" of the people writ large. The kind of right-vanguardism that Schmitt pursues through the dubious constitutional powers of the presidency would prove to be one of the chief hallmarks of fascism.

Expanding his critique of constitutional neutrality to moral neutrality, Schmitt proceeds to engage in the classic tarring with a nihilist brush those who would hold open-mindedness as a political value: "There is no middle road between the principled value neutrality of the functionalist system of legality and the principled value emphasis of the substantive constitutional guarantees. The functionalism of the weighted majorities would at least be a reasonable 'compromise.' In regard to the question of neutrality or nonneutrality, whoever intends to remain neutral has already decided in favor of neutrality. Value assertion and value neutrality are mutually exclusive. Compared to a seriously intended value assertion and affirmation, conscientious value neutrality means denial of values" (LL 49). The passage could come out of the writings of postwar conservatives who were purportedly reacting against the nihilism of the fascists and the Nazis.[35] In this fighting mood against relativism, Schmitt professes admiration for liberals like Thoma who are willing to identify "fascism and bolshevism" as political enemies of law, freedom and the value neutrality that Thoma holds to be a substantive value. On the other hand, Schmitt criticizes legalists like Anschütz who push value neutrality "to the point of system suicide. Anything is legal, without presuppositions or conditions, that is passed by way of simple statutes or those amending the constitution" (LL 50). The problem is that when carefully interrogated, the "substantive values" generally harbored by authoritarians and conservatives like Schmitt, Hindenburg, Schleicher, and Papen is the preservation of the privilege of sociopolitical elites. Perhaps unsurprisingly, as we will see, *Legality and Legitimacy* ultimately moves in this direction as well.

Thus Schmitt caricatures the legislative state that he has identified with Weimar parliamentarism as a crude tyranny of the majority that is overly aggressive when redistributing property through "substantive law regulations" but excessively weak when allowing all parties access to its lawmaking process through "value-free neutrality." Schmitt avers that this legal-parliamentary part of the constitution stands in opposition to the part with no "substantive law regulations of significant scope, but rather . . . a fundamental rights section that guarantees the bourgeois sphere of civil and political freedom in general and, as such, stands opposed to an organizational part regulating the process of state will formation" (LL 59). This other part of the constitution would therefore both protect bourgeois property rights and defend the essence of the constitution—the conservative definitions of freedom and security. According to Schmitt's description here, the Weimar Constitution is either a Rechtsstaat without a king or a Sozial-

staat without Bolshevik self-confidence. Any alternative between these poles is either insufficient to the requirements of
the times or analytically self-contradictory: there are, Schmitt
observes, "states with a constitution limited to organizational-
procedural regulations and general liberty rights" and those
with "constitutions containing extensive entrenchments and
guarantees in the form of substantive law," but they "contradict
one another in principle, both structurally and organizationally" (LL 60). In other words, no one constitution can guarantee
freedom *and* equality.

MERGING NORMAL AND EXCEPTIONAL SITUATIONS But
Schmitt does not leave matters there. In Mephistophelean
fashion, he begins to propose to the advocates of material legal
guarantees the possibility that these are best provided by the
substantive part of the constitution and not the parliamentary
aspect, which is purely formal (LL 57). After all, transitory parliamentary majorities cannot supply reliable concrete policies
for effective, long-term regulation and redistribution, for these
can be repealed with a change of the electoral-political wind.
This possibility reveals the existence of what Schmitt calls a
division in the constitution between "an extraordinary higher
lawmaker and simple lower one" (LL 62), between superior and
subordinate lawmakers (LL 62–63). The parliamentary legislative state simply runs according to "a different internal logic"
than plebiscitary democracy (LL 63). Schmitt fairly readily ad-
mits that the constitution does not *explicitly* elevate the latter
over the former. He concedes that this hierarchy must be deci-
phered rather esoterically through the obstacles posed by prevailing legalist fictions and the petty political compromises
that characterized the framing of the constitution (LL 63). In
fact, Schmitt describes this tension between the two constitutions, "higher" and "lower," as a civil war between one aspect
of the document that is anachronistic, transitory, dangerous,
and self-contradictory and one that is vibrant, democratic, effi-
cient, and permanent (LL 61).
   If it is not textually explicit, how does Schmitt determine
the supremacy of the presidential over the parliamentary aspect of the constitution? He appeals to the Rousseauian logic
supposedly undergirding every democracy, a logic according
to which representatives must "fall silent" when "the repre-

sented themselves speak," especially in emergencies: Schmitt concludes that "the plebiscitary process is always stronger" (LL 64). The people are more directly and thereby more faithfully represented by the President than the parliament. But this view of democracy, shared not only with Rousseau but with Lenin as well, inevitably privileges elites.[36] Plebiscitarianism is, after all, a nominal celebration of the people that actually perpetuates their wholesale disempowerment; it constitutes the creation of an informational vacuum into which "well-intended" elites can easily step: "[O]ne provides threshold requirements and limitations for parliament, though not for the direct expressions of the people's will itself, about which one has known since ancient times that the people cannot discuss and deliberate" (LL 68). Elite discretion and not formal rules will fill in the blanks left in efforts to determine the popular will, absent their articulation of it themselves.

A major obstacle to Schmitt's attempt to elevate presidential emergency decrees issued under Article 48 over parliamentary statutes is the fact that the two are explicitly distinguished in the constitution. The Reichstag makes statutes of potentially enduring value while the president issues *Maßnahmen* or measures of expressly limited duration.

Schmitt's response to this difficulty is the suggestion that since parliamentary statutes have become more like measures in recent history, conversely, it is not unreasonable to conceive democratically legitimated presidential measures as law (LL 65). In terms that recall "the exception" from his *Political Theology* written a decade before, Schmitt declares that the extraordinary circumstances lend decrees more than normative equality with statutes; decrees have acquired a normative superiority such that "law" now means a measure and not a statute (LL 66). The spiritual undertones that characterized *Political Theology* reemerge when Schmitt remarks that the material or concrete quality of presidential decrees mean that "the extraordinary lawmaker can create accomplished facts in opposition to the ordinary legislature," which issues only abstract norms (LL 72). In other words, the President possesses a world-making, God-like fiat of exceptional legislative authority. At this point, a certain narrative becomes discernible in the work: Schmitt's story of a popularly representing executive emerging to reform a state that had been undermined by parliamentary profligacy sounds like an epic in which a Caesarist hero redeems a decayed and corrupted city. To say the least, this is a far cry from Schmitt's subsequent claims that the work reflects only pure, analytical rigor.

Obviously, Schmitt's elevation of emergency measures to the status of law merges the lawmaking and law-applying tasks kept separated theoretically and institutionally in the Rechtsstaat. Since the parliament has already reduced statutes to measures in economic regulation and redistribution, Schmitt intimates that the President might as well exert more legitimate decree-issuing power that will restore the force of law squandered by the parliament. After all, the presidency more appropriately reflects and directs the will of the people. Ordinary party-pluralist or leftist Sozialstaat practice based on bargaining, compromise, and, optimally, deliberation aimed at societal self-transformation is hereby seized by Schmitt for the purposes of an exceptional, right-wing imposition of order by unilateral action on the part of the executive branch. Schmitt implies that most administrative measures issued by the Sozialstaat merely reflect the intentions of the particular party or interest group that lobbied for them; on the contrary, those issued by the President will purportedly reflect the will of the whole people. Again, however, as the book proceeds, Schmitt consistently reveals this to be a theory of democracy that disempowers the people. According to Schmitt's logic, if the people attempt to actually *participate* politically, they will be merely represented by parties that supposedly threaten popular unity. If they simply *acclaim* the President and his policies, however, they can be represented, embodied, as a whole, because *he* is a whole: "For the extraordinary lawmaker of Article 48, the distinction between statute and statutory application, legislative and executive, is neither legally nor factually an obstacle. The extraordinary lawmaker combines both in his person" (LL 74).[37]

FROM RULE OF LAW TO RULE BY DECREE Either attempting to allay the fear of his critics or simply out of sheer cynicism, Schmitt points to a case where presidential emergency measures restrict the activity of the NSDAP. This is an example where "the President is free to intervene in the entire system of existing statutory norms and use it for his own purposes"

(LL 74). In fact, as the coup of July 20 demonstrates, emergency presidential action was more generally used to the *advantage* of the Nazis against associations and parties on the left. Ultimately, however, these considerations do not really matter, because Schmitt adamantly asserts that the President's emergency powers are unlimited. As to whether the President's use of such power is an institutional innovation, Schmitt suggests that the precedent to set aside several "fundamental rights" was not established by the executive but rather by the parliament through its novel redistributive policies. Thus the President is simply dealing with difficult circumstances created by parliamentary abuses by perhaps resorting to the suspension of *all* rights if the emergency requires it (LL 69–70). Schmitt subtly invokes 1848 as the significant date after which the Rechtsstaat was undermined by the expansion of "administrative law adjudication"; in other words, in the wake of the mid-nineteenth-century revolutions, working-class parties subsequently bureaucratized lawmaking through demands for property redistribution and economic regulation (LL 76). The President is merely reforming a system already made corrupt by the left.

In doing so, Schmitt suggests that the President will merely practice more honestly and efficiently what liberals and the left have been doing with deleterious results for the regime for some time. Liberals think that they have needed no recourse to the "extraordinary constitution" and the emergency executive action it offers because they conceive of parliament as already possessing the power to suspend rights (LL 70–71). But Schmitt argues that this kind of thinking and the practice that results threaten the very reason-to-be of the Rechtsstaat. This logic allows legal-parliamentarians to render themselves superfluous: "The legislative state with its statutory priority and legislative-reservation knows just one lawgiver, namely, its legislature, the parliament. The legislative state tolerates no competing extraordinary legislative power. According to this system, the 'measures' of the office empowered for extraordinary action are not contrary to law, but they also do not have the force of law. These measures need not and cannot have the force of law, because the suspension of the basic rights is provided for and, through this suspension, the limitations of the legislative state, which had made a statute and the force of law necessary, collapse." (LL 76). The freedom-preserving form of the statute—that it is formulated and applied by separate institutions—is violated by such parliamentary action, which thereby revokes the moral supremacy of the institution of parliament. Later in the text, Schmitt refers to those who would maintain this view of parliamentary lawmaking as "representatives of 'Rechtsstaat' thinking" (LL 86), with the important term itself presented in quotation marks because the adherents of such a view have themselves, with their facilitation of the Sozialstaat, violated the precepts of the nineteenth-century Rechtsstaat model (LL 80).

THE PERMANENT PRESIDENT Schmitt suggests that only the President can properly redirect and realize this transformation of law from Rechtsstaat statute to Sozialstaat measure or decree that parliamentary government has been pursuing "in Germany through ten-year-long governmental practice" (LL 76). Thus Schmitt reveals that he is not only addressing a concrete situation but settling old scores as well: in other words, you liberals who deposed the Kaiser and turned the Reichstag against the wealthy will now get what you deserve. Seitzer's translation allows these rhetorical and polemical aspects of the text to show through in all their fighting force: "The ordinary legislature can intrude on the fundamental rights only on the basis of the statutory reservation. However, it cannot set them aside. The extraordinary lawgiver, by contrast, can do both and, leaving aside all other factors, thereby surpasses the ordinary legislature and is superior to it in a novel way" (LL 77).

But if Schmitt consistently invokes emergency circumstances, can he be charged with promoting a permanent presidential-decree state? After all, he begins discussing the emergency powers of the President in terms of a classical dictatorship, according to whose criteria an emergency actor may not change or terminate a prior constitutional situation but only restore it. The potentially perpetual and abrogating quality of the executive action that Schmitt describes purportedly does not violate this standard because he presents it as maintaining consistency with a constitutional a priori: the initial democratic will or spirit of the document.[38] That this a priori status is admittedly not determinate institutionally but rather is an amorphous pre-institutional will is not a problem for Schmitt in *Legality and Legitimacy*. It certainly would have been problematic for proponents of the republican Roman model from which the term "dictatorship" is derived.[39] In Schmitt's attempt to pass off a constitutionally abrogating emergency dictatorship as a constitutionally preserving one, we witness the transformation of dictatorship from a temporary and task-specific constitutional practice to the modern political phenomenon best represented by the example of a military junta.[40]

The bond that Schmitt forges between a preconstitutional democratic will and its institutional manifestation in the plebiscitarily elected President allows Schmitt to justify emergency action that might endure far beyond the immediate circumstances—especially action that might otherwise be proscribed by the fetid and foreign-influenced formal restrictions associated with strict legality. Schmitt reiterates that since parliamentary practice has been conducted in a manner where statutes have become ephemeral, decrees will be more permanent now that the popular will has been reunited with its institutional embodiment that issues such decrees (LL 80–81).

Schmitt does not insist that every constitution manifests this tension between a hidden, extraordinary lawgiver who has been papered over with artificial and stifling parchment restrictions placed there by invading foreign powers or weak-willed legalists. The French constitution of 1875, for instance, organically embodies what is merely a facade in the Weimar Constitution. Schmitt ridicules the French for having a constitution that inheres within it *no* extraordinary lawmaker, but he concedes that at least it is consistent in its liberal-parliamentary character, even if it exists without a fundamental will (LL 88).[41]

THE NEW DEMOCRACY: RULE BY OR OVER THE PEOPLE? In this spirit, Schmitt is at pains to avoid appearing as a constitutional dogmatist: equating a democratic will with presidential substance is not the only way to configure a constitutional regime. He insists that a parliamentary institution might serve as a sufficient source of unity if it were not, as it has been in Weimar, the amalgam of compromises "of thoroughly heterogeneous power organizations" and "the showplace of a pluralist system" (LL 90) that "no longer has the dignity of an assembly" (LL 92). Schmitt insists that when parliamentary elections were the "selection" of notables, the "elevation of an elite," the institution might have possessed such dignity (LL 92). In other words, when liberalism was still sufficiently aristocratic, before it was commandeered by the mass-democratically, redistribution-obsessed forces of 1848, it was an appropriate foundation of a constitutional regime.

But these parties that have supplanted liberal elites must now be prevented from (and Schmitt's text implies perhaps punished for) dishonoring the German state by the heroic part of the constitution. Schmitt exults at the thought that the venal power-seeking parties are now "run[ning] up against the system of a plebiscitary-democratic legitimacy [that has been] set against the parliamentary legislative state's system of legality" (LL 92). But he emphasizes that the President is not merely taking up tasks that parliament can no long conduct. Rather, in acting faithfully with an unverifiable preconstitutional will, the President conducts a qualitatively different kind of politics, one in which public reason associated with parliament is supplanted by popular will identified by the president: "The meaning of the plebiscitary expression of will is . . . *not norm establishment,* but *decision through one will,* as the word 'referendum,' or popular decision, aptly expresses" (LL 92, emphasis added).

Again, lest one think that this signifies the empowerment of the people, Schmitt describes what democratic practice amounts to under this scenario: "The people can only respond yes or no. They cannot advise, deliberate, or discuss. They cannot govern or administer. They also cannot set norms, but can only sanction norms by consenting to a draft set of norms laid before them. Above all, they also cannot pose a question, but can only answer with yes or no to a question placed before them" (LL 93). This acclamatory model of democracy conjures up the image of hostages, bound and gagged, relegated to mere head-nodding or -shaking when their captor proposes a meal. Like Odysseus's sailors or Caligari's zombie, the demos has no real will apart from its master's direction or manipulation.[42]

The issue of elite manipulation is the clearest indication that Schmitt has exploited Weber's reduction of legal legitimacy to "belief" in the law's validity. The people's belief that law is valid may stand independent of the particular procedure of formulating or applying the law. There is no reason why the people cannot believe that law is valid, and hence legitimate, because elites say that it is, or because the latter narrow the means by which people validate the law so as to render the process meaningless. According to this shrinking of rationality and procedure, plebiscites can be as rational a method of validating the law as parliamentary practices. Schmitt duly notes earlier in the work that Weber associated legal validity with political legitimacy in contemporary regimes (LL 16–17). But here Schmitt draws on Weber's lack of confidence in that assertion to merge legal validity with charismatic authority instead of logical or procedural rationality: "[P]lebiscitary legitimacy is the single type of state justification that may be generally acknowledged today as valid" (LL 93). Schmitt goes so far as to admit the "authoritarian" quality of this assertion, but insists nevertheless that "plebiscitary legitimacy is the single last remaining accepted system of justification" (LL 93). If government is going to be legitimate in contemporary circumstances —circumstances of mass democracy, pluralist interests, and complex bureaucratic governance—authority must be justified plebiscitarily.

Yet Schmitt proposes as the only limit on the authority of plebiscites the faith in its administrators to ask the appropriate question, and do so at "the right moment" (LL 94). The constitutional guidelines and restrictions of the Rechtsstaat are replaced by "confidence" that the extraordinary lawgiver "will pose the correct question in the proper way and not misuse the great power that lies in the posing of the question" (LL 94). Weber's relegating to "belief" the substance of legal legitimacy has the effect of collapsing law into charisma: "belief" can be easily equated with the faith generated by the charisma of a person who "embodies" the popular will. Schmitt tries to show that plebiscites are self-limiting and actually demonstrate a leader's dependence on the people rather than their power over or manipulation of the latter: "the appeal to the people will always lead to some loss of independence, and even the famous example of the Napoleonic plebiscites shows how precarious and reversible such legitimating devices are" (LL 94). But the tyrannical rule of the first Napoleon, at least, was not, as we know, terminated by plebiscite, but rather through the force of opposing armies. This does not promote confidence in plebiscitary-presidential democracy as a stable regime type fully accountable and responsive to the general populace.

THE INHERENT VULNERABILITY OF CONSTITUTIONAL DEMOCRACY? In conclusion, I would reiterate that a major problem with the "inherent weakness" thesis of legal or constitutional democracy, for which Weimar consistently serves as the model, is that it ignores the extralegal intimidation and thuggery—tolerated and often encouraged by Schmitt's associates—against Social Democrats and Communists that more directly contributed to the "formally legal" victory of the Nazis. Just as the historical facts of the demise of the Republic cannot be captured by the story that the Nazis gained power through formal legal means, so *Legality and Legitimacy* cannot be understood as a neutral, purely analytical diagnosis of the Weimar Republic that lacks a substantive agenda of its own. This would put the work in a bizarrely awkward position, given its author's criticisms of value-neutrality as one of the main problems plaguing the Republic. More specifically, I have suggested that the substantive-value agenda of the work does not conform with a temporary suspension of the liberal-legal parliamentary components of the constitution so that the democratic-plebiscitary presidential components might reinstitute them once the crisis had passed. On the contrary, *Legality and Legitimacy* is a blueprint for the permanent supersession of the former by the latter, a work whose intention may not be "Nazi" in 1932, but certainly is fascist. It should be recalled that in 1932 the NSDAP did not yet have a monopoly on fascist political alternatives in Germany or in Europe, a fact to which the policy proposals and practices of Mussolini, Papen, and, perhaps, Schleicher attest.

In this sense, *Legality and Legitimacy* is the historical document that bears witness to a dubious historical "truth" contrived in Germany by natural law jurists and brought to America by figures like Leo Strauss after World War II: that the greatest danger to stability in modern societies is popular government too easily enabled by legality, and not, say, the subversion of legal democracy by conservative elites.[43] The latter is closer to the truth of Weimar's collapse, as Schmitt's subsequent career certainly illustrates, the narratives of natural law theorists and Strauss notwithstanding. Schmitt was correct when he declared in *Legality and Legitimacy* that truth would have its "revenge" (LL 98). The content of that truth, however, was not necessarily the weaknesses of constitutional democracy but rather the proclivity of authoritarian elites to exploit those weaknesses in potentially devastating ways.

LEGALITY

AND LEGITIMACY

INTRODUCTION

———

The Legislative State System of Legality Compared to Other State Types (Jurisdiction, Governmental, and Administrative States)

If at the outset of this essay about "legality" and "legitimacy" the current domestic political condition of Germany is characterized in terms of public and constitutional law[1] as the collapse of the parliamentary legislative state,[2] then that is meant only as a brief, specialized scholarly formula that summarizes developments.[3] Optimistic or pessimistic suppositions and prognoses are not of interest here; various crises–whether of the biological, medical, or economic variety, postwar crises, crises of confidence, those involving health, puberty, weight loss, or what have you, will also not be considered. To correctly understand the entire problematic of today's legality concept and of the parliamentary legislative state, as well as of prewar legal positivism,[4] it is necessary to define the concepts of public and constitutional law one has in mind regarding the connections between present-day domestic political circumstances and the state.

By "legislative state," I mean a particular type of political system that is distinctive in that norms intended to be just are the highest and decisive expression of the community will. These norms, therefore, must exhibit certain qualities, and all other public functions, affairs, and substantive areas must be subordinated to them. What in Continental European states since the nineteenth century one understood as the *Rechtsstaat*[5] was, in reality, only a legislative state, specifically, the parliamentary legislative state. The superior and central position of the parliament was based on the fact that as parliament, [1932/8] the lawmaking body, one established norms with the entire dignity of the lawmaker, of the "*législateur.*"

A legislative state is a state type governed by impersonal,

that is, general and preestablished, norms that are meant to be lasting and that [1958/264] have a definable, determinable content, a state type in which the law and legal application, lawmaker and officials responsible for legal application, are separated from one another. "Laws govern," not men, authorities, or nonelected governments. More precisely: laws do not rule; they are valid only as norms. There is no ruling and mere power at all anymore. Whoever exercises power and government acts "on the basis of law" or "in the name of the law." He does nothing other than what a valid norm permits jurisdictionally. Laws establish a legislative organ; however, this lawmaking body does not govern directly, nor does it execute laws itself. It merely establishes valid norms, in whose name officials bound by statute to enforce the law exercise state power. The organizational realization of the legislative state always leads to the separation of law and legal application, the legislative and the executive. That is not merely a theoretical separation, and not merely a psychologically grounded precaution against the human lust for power; it is the directly necessary, constructive, fundamental principle of the legislative state, in which not men and persons rule, but rather where norms are valid. The final, actual meaning of the fundamental "principle of legality" of all state life lies ultimately in the fact that there is no longer any government or obedience in general because only impersonal, valid norms are being applied. In the general legality of all state exercise of power lies the justification of one such state type. A closed system of legality grounds the claim to obedience and justifies the suspension of every right of resistance. In this regard, the specific manifestation of the law is the statute, while legality is the particular justification of state coercion.

There are other systems, in which the decisive political will emerges in other forms and procedures. There are [1932/9] jurisdiction states, in which the deciding judge in the legal dispute has the last word, rather than the norm-setting lawmaker. And, once again, there are other political forms, governmental or administrative states, that correspond to the specific manner, in which the final decision is expressed concretely, and through which the final authority, the "dernier ressort," appears. The typical expression of the jurisdiction state is the decision in the concrete case, in which the correct law, justice, and reason reveal themselves directly [1958/265] without having to be mediated by preestablished, general norms, and which, as a result, do not exhaust themselves in the normativism of mere legality. The typical expression of the legislative state is the predetermined, enduring, general norm, substantively definable and determinable. In the course of the application of such a norm, the judicial decision shows how all state life generally should be comprehended from a closed system of legality made possible by the subsumption of particular factual circumstances in concrete cases. The jurisdiction state seems to be a "Rechtsstaat" insofar as in it the judge directly generates legal doctrine and also applies this law to the norm-setting legislature and its law. At the other end of the spectrum from the legislative state stands the governmental state, which finds its characteristic expression in the exalted personal will and authoritative command of a ruling head of state. And yet there is still another conceivable state type, the administrative state, in which command and will do not appear authoritarian and personal, and which, nevertheless, does not seek the mere application of higher norms, but rather only objective directives. In the administrative state, men do not rule, nor are norms valid as something higher. Instead, the famous formula "things administer themselves" holds true. Even if that may be a utopia, an administrative state is also conceivable, whose specific expression is the administrative decree that is determined only in accordance with circumstances, in reference to the concrete situation, and motivated entirely by considerations of factual-practical purposefulness.[6]

Historically, of course, linkages and mixtures continuously appear, because legislation, as well as adjudication, government, [1932/10] and administration, is part of every political system. In every state, there is not only obedience and command, but also the establishment of statutory norms and administration through internal directives. Relying on Richard Thoma (Anschütz and Thoma 1930–32, 2:127), one can also discover, in every individual state action, an element of legislation as well as of administration and even of judicial decision.[7] Specifically, all of these elements and manifestations of state action are reunited in the sovereign. The sovereign is highest legislator, judge, and commander simultaneously. He is also the final source of legality and the ultimate foundation of legitimacy. In weak states, a legitimate government would gladly make use of the positive resonance from the legality of the [1958/266] lawmaking body's decisions. An administrative state, for example, will use the judiciary in order to sanction its political measures. Nevertheless, it also remains for the most part self-evidently clear where the focal point of the deciding will lies, which of the different possibilities is central for the normal, average life, and which type of highest will emerges definitively or decisively at the key moment and determines the system type. A suspension, a combination, or confusion of the highest court, government, legislature, or administration is also certainly possible. In transitional, intermediary periods, there is perhaps even a fortuitous balance of several types of mutually dependent, highest powers.

The distinction of the legislative state, with its closed system of legality, from the types of legitimacy, such as jurisdiction, governmental, and administrative states, themselves all different from one another, seems to be more fruitful for knowledge of the contemporary state than distinctions developed in previous contexts, such as the antithesis of state and society, authority and freedom, Rechtsstaat and dictatorship, etc. Also, the traditional triad of monarchy, aristocracy, and democracy with their variants will not be used here. It is not that the Aristotelian teaching is not modern and has been superseded. Today, however, the normative fiction of a closed [1932/11] system of legality emerges in a striking and undeniable opposition to the legitimacy of an instance of will that is actually present and in conformity with law. This is currently the decisive contradiction, rather than that between the legitimacy of monarchy, aristocracy, oligarchy, or democracy, which mostly only obscures and confuses [the situation]. Moreover, our state form is undergoing a transformation, and the "turn toward the total state" characteristic of the moment (instead of, a hundred years ago, toward "freedom") seems typical today of the turn toward the administrative state.[8] By its nature, the total state is an administrative state, even if it makes use of the judiciary, and, indeed, the full gamut of legal forms, such as criminal and civil law, civil service regulations, and administrative or constitutional adjudication—whether as an instrument or as a corrective. That in particular an "economic state" cannot possibly also work as a legislative state and must become an administrative state is already almost universally known today.[9] To what extent the core of every state lies in administration is another question. Both Plato's *Republic* and Aristotle's *Politics* are, as Lorenz von Stein said, "teachings about stateless societies and, therefore, those without administrations."[10] Max Weber considers an "administrative cadre" a defining feature of political association generally.[11] The close connection between state and administration enters our historical consciousness most clearly in the sixteenth and seventeenth centuries, when the evolution of political systems occurs; associations, in the form of "states," differentiated themselves from the legal communities of the medieval "state of legal guarantees," in Fritz Kern's apt expression, through their well-functioning, bureaucratic apparatus. Otherwise, the parliamentary legislative state, with its separation of statute law and legal application, presupposes for statutory application an executive that operates in conformity with law, but which, despite its subordination to law, is still independent and distinguishable [from other organs]. At issue here is the specific system of justification in which the state administrative apparatus stands, and in the seventeenth and eighteenth centuries that was the dynastic legitimacy of the absolute princes.

In times of stable views of justice and consolidated property holdings, the jurisdiction state predominates, and a judiciary [1932/12] separated from the state reaches final decisions as guardian and guarantor of the law, which is not merely distinct from the state, but is also prior to and superior to the state. In such a system, one can hardly still speak of the "state" because there is a mere nonpolitical community in place of a political unity, at least according to the fiction. During periods of great change or even transformation, a governmental, administrative, or, depending on the type and duration of the change, even a parliamentary legislative state appears, whose norms seem best able to facilitate adaptation of law to changing living conditions and encourage a connection between progress and legal certainty. So the different state types are appropriate for various domestic political tendencies. In general, one can say that a consistently administered jurisdiction state, with its highest activity in court decisions, is the proper means of conserving the social *status quo* and of acquired rights, corresponding to the often demonstrated conservative tendency of each and every instance of adjudication. The corrupt forms [1958/268] of these regimes in an Aristotelian sense, the type of state that makes its *ratio essendi* the guarantee of acquired rights, would be best characterized by the following saying: "Everything is sinecure, but no longer secure." The governmental and the administrative state both adapt themselves more readily to use as instruments of radical change, whether revolutionary or reactionary, and as comprehensive, systematically planned formations intended to last for the long term. The legislative state is the typical vehicle of a reformist-revisionist era armed with a party program, which attempts to bring about "progress" through the appropriate statutes passed through legal parliamentary channels.

The ethos of the jurisdiction state is that the judge renders judgment directly in the name of law and justice without mediation of norms of justice from other, nonjudicial, political powers. That is a simple principle and is illuminating so long as law and justice have unambiguous content, without intervening norms, and are not merely tools of the powerful and of propertied interests. The governmental state does not have so much an [1932/13] ethos as a great pathos. Its principle became most visible in the government of the absolute princes of the seventeenth and eighteenth centuries, particularly in the catalogue of representative emblems of the princes, who clothed their personal realm with words like *majestas, splendor, excellentia, eminenta, honor*, and *glory*. It is the great pathos of *glory* and *honor* that the Prussian administrative state of Friedrich Wilhelm I and Frederick the Great could not deny itself. Already in the seventeenth century, the republican-democratic *vertu* opposed the governmental state's principle as a polemical counterconcept against *honor*, seeking to disqualify the representative quality of *honor* and to expose representation itself as mere "theater," while republican-democratic *vertu* set the homogeneous people's democratic and self-identical presence against the representation of the prince and his court. At the same time, however, one also made use of the specific ethos of the properly norm-setting legislative state, with its just law, its wise and incorruptible *législateur*, and its always good and just *volonté générale*. The administrative state can call on factual necessity, the condition of things, the force of circumstances, the necessity of the moment, and other non-normative, situation-specific justifications. Correspondingly, the administrative state finds its existential justification in the purposefulness, [1958/269] the usefulness, and, in contrast to the conformity to norms of the normatively grounded legislative state, the directly concrete, factual appropriateness of its administrative measures, orders, and commands. Both the governmental and the administrative states perceive a distinctive quality in concrete commands, which are directly executable or easily obeyed, and they make an end of the advocate's pleas accompanying the jurisdiction state as well as of the parliamentary legislative state's tendency toward endless discussion, recognizing already in decisionism the immediately executable directive as a legal value in itself.[12] In this regard, it still holds true: "The best thing in the world is a command."

Rudolf Smend ([1928] 1994, 115) argues that liberalism, along with the parliamentarism based on it, has no unique pathos, no "claim to value," and, therefore, no "legitimating power peculiar to itself." Liberalism "also does not need to make any [1932/14] effort at all to develop a corresponding legitimization for itself."[13] But one must not overlook the fact that the parliamentary legislative state, with its ideal, closed, and gapless system of legality of all state action, developed a thoroughly distinctive system of justification. "Legality" here has the meaning and purpose of making superfluous and negating the legitimacy of either the monarch or the people's plebiscitarian will as well as of every authority and governing power, whether in a form that provides its own foundation or one claiming to be something higher. If in this system words like "legitimacy" and "authority" are still generally used, then they are only an expression of legality and derived from it. Max Weber's principles of sociology should be understood in the same way: "legality can be valid like legitimacy," or "the most widely prominent form of legitimacy today is the belief in legality."[14] Here both legitimacy and legality are traceable to a single legitimacy concept, whereas legality is in direct opposition to legitimacy. I accept, therefore, Otto Kirchheimer's formulation in an essay about legality and legitimacy that the legitimacy of parliamentary democracy "resides only in its legality," and today "obviously legal restrictions are equated with legitimacy."[15] Linguistic usage today has certainly already proceeded so far that it perceives the legal as something "merely formal" and in opposition to the legitimate. [1958/270] Without a sense of contradiction, for example, one can today consider a dissolution of the Reichstag "strictly legal," even though it is, in fact, a coup d'état, and, vice versa, a parliamentary dissolution might substantively conform to the spirit of the constitution, and yet not be legal.[16] Such antitheses document the breakdown of a system of legality, which ends in a formalism and functionalism without substance or reference points. Such a result is only explicable in reference to the forsaking of the essential presuppositions and the specific pathos of the legalistic concept of law. These changes give rise to the illusion that one can open legal channels [1932/15] and the legal process to all conceivable aspirations, goals, and movements, even the most radical and revolutionary, enabling them to achieve their aim without violence or disruption through a legal process that establishes order while at the same time it functions in a completely "value-neutral" way.

The distinctive rationalism of the system of legality is obviously recast into its opposite. This process essentially characterizes the current situation of the parliamentary legislative state. Subsequent chapters will provide complete, detailed explanations of it. With regard to the concept of legality, one must keep in mind, both historically and conceptually, that it is a product and a problem of the parliamentary legislative state and its specific type of normativism. The concept of legality inherits the situation established by princely absolutism: specifically, the elimination of every right to resistance and the "grand right" to unconditional obedience. But the concept of legality provides the parliamentary legislative state the dignity of legality, which it creates through general, preestablished norms. The jurisdiction state and the administrative state remain in the closest possible direct connection with the actual concrete situation, and, consequently, they have a certain concrete presence. The governmental state has all the qualities of representation in the person of its chief executive or in the dignity of its directive body. The legislative state, by contrast, is placed in an altogether different sphere by virtue of its dominant principle of the general, preestablished norm, and its essential distinction between law and legal application, legislative and executive. It suffers, though, from a certain abstractness. But the legislative state seems to be something higher and ideal so long as the belief in the rationality and ideality of its normativism is still vibrant in times and in peoples that remain able to cultivate a (typically Cartesian) belief in the *idées générales*. [1958/271] This is also the case as long as the legislative state can call on a several-thousand-year-old distinction and realize an ancient ethos, above all, that of the νόμος [*nomos*] against the mere θεσμός [*thesmos*]; the *ratio* against the mere *voluntas*; intelligence against the blind will without a basis in norms; the idea of the law backed by justified norms against the administrative measure and command, both based on mere practicality and dependent on changing conditions; reasonable rationalism against pragmatism and emotionalism; idealism and just law against utilitarianism; [1932/16] validity and moral command against coercion and the force of circumstances. From the perspective of the legislative state, the representative, governmental state, with its *gloire* and its *honneur*, appears to be a mere power state and immoral; the administrative state, a dictatorship unbounded by norms and without spirit; the medieval jurisdiction state, a vehicle of feudal and estate privileges hostile to progress. The legislative state can make reference to the fact that the affective and legitimating formulation, in "the name of the law," is not transferable, least of all to the measures of the administrative state. There is no "equality before the measure," as there is "equality before the law." I can also not apply law, impose sentences, or generally act authoritatively in the name of practicality, of "factual necessity," or in the name of the force of circumstances instead of in the name of the law. It would be obviously grotesque if one announced court decisions in the "name of a measure," instead of that of the king, of the people, or of the law, or if one would swear an oath to measures or affirm "loyalty to administrative directives."

The state's civil service and the armed forces, when they are being considered only as a technical apparatus in the hands of the government, are by themselves neither a distinct source of law nor a ground of legitimacy. The civil service and armed forces cannot alone support the administrative state, which naturally requires a bureaucratic apparatus. In contrast to the different state forms and types, the "bureaucracy" often exhibits the neutrality of a mere technical instrument, which with certain reservations, such as regard for the "acquired rights of officials," can serve various, even contradictory, political directions. Yes, indeed, "the civil servant must also be versatile," states Rudolf Smend ([1928] 1994, 31). In a supposedly "value-neutral" category of Max Weber's sociology, the term "bureaucracy" above all has the meaning [1958/272] of permitting the bureaucracy to appear as the technical-rational, value-neutral machinery of an official apparatus principally interested in the bureaucracy's smooth operation. This interpretation certainly stands in a thoroughly polemical relation to the situation of the prewar German state and brings the German professional civil service as something [1932/17] "nonpolitical-technical" into an unfair opposition to parliament, which Max Weber famously held to be a means of selecting political leaders and forming elites.[17] The French expression *bureaucratie* involves something truly instrumental. The parliamentarism of the French Republic obliterated the idea that the army and civil service themselves have legality and legitimacy or could develop them on their own, and it discredited fundamentally both the connection with the dynastic legitimacy of a royal house as well as the Bonapartist linkage with plebiscitary-democratic legitimacy. In Germany, the civil service of the nineteenth century participated in a large number of constitutional monarchies. Absent until today, consequently, has been a direct organizational connection with the entirety of national unity and with the parliamentary representation of the whole German people in the Reichstag. The distinctive property of the constitutional monarchy enabled the civil service to support simultaneously the foundations of monarchical legitimacy as well as the legality of the legislative state. One must not overlook what Hans Gerber recently showed at a meeting of the teachers of public law in Halle during 1931 (Gerber 1932). Specifically, without the firmly guaranteed position of the civil service, this type of "Rechtsstaat," that is, the legislative state, would not have been conceivable. Gerber's correct observation, I believe, expresses the historical fact that the professional civil service can also be more than a mere "apparatus," which functions under the control of any given system. More accurately, elements of a genuine elite in the sociological sense of the word, an elite that is capable of producing authority and legitimacy, could be borne through a professional cadre that creates stability and is entrusted with the guarantee of the public interest. Such an elite would have qualities like incorruptibility, separation from the world of striving for money and profit, education, sense of duty and loyalty, plus certain obviously diminishing tendencies toward cooptation. If these three necessary conditions—stability, quality, and self-recruitment—are the marks of a state-reinforcing political elite, then one may view the German professional civil service of the nineteenth century [1932/18] as an elite-like factor [1958/273] in German state life, only that precisely the decisive quality of every political elite—the ability and willingness to risk the political— is not evident.[18]

Once the dynastic legitimacy of the constitutional monarchy disappeared, the German army, which after the disarmament and demilitarization of the German people is no longer an army in the traditional sense, and the national civil service, especially the newly created financial bureaucracy, found the possibility of a new basis in the plebiscitary legitimacy of the German President elected by the entire German people.[19] Because it lacked this foundation, the civil service of the individual German states is occupied to a great extent by the forces of the pluralist *Parteienstaat*.[20] The area of legislative competence of the German states, and with it the space for the parliamentary legislative state, is not significant enough to make possible an independent system of legality for these states. That the different German Land governments have varying interpretations of "public security, order, and hostility to the state" is bound up with the fact that a share in the political premium on the legal possession of power, discussed below (p. 35 [1932]), fell to different powers today. Considered under the concept of legality and legitimacy, the German professional civil service today is no longer a unified whole with its own distinctive political significance. Nonetheless, given the absence of another authority, the individual parts of the German civil service could become a focal point of the strong need for and tendency toward an authoritarian state, and the civil service on its own could attempt to "produce order" in an administrative state. A large chunk of a governing administrative state has already developed in the practice of legally binding emergency decrees in accordance with Article 48, 2, which has been in use for over two years.[21] What this development in the parliamentary legislative state means will be explained further below (part 2, chapter 5). Of interest here is that when it is transformed into the empty functionalism of momentary majority decisions, the normative legality of a parliamentary legislative state can be linked with the impersonal functionalism of bureaucratic, [1932/19] regulatory necessities. In this peculiar, though practical, alliance of legality and technical functionalism, the bureaucracy in the long run remains the superior partner and transforms the law of the [1958/274] parliamentary legislative state into the measures of the administrative state.

The word "Rechtsstaat" should not be used here. Both the legislative state and the jurisdiction state could present themselves, *eo ipso*, as a Rechtsstaat. But this is also true of any governmental and administrative states when they actually rely on themselves to develop law, in order to replace unjust old law through proper new law and, most importantly, to create the normal situation, without which every system of norms is a deception. The term "Rechtsstaat" can mean as many different things as the word "law" itself and, moreover, just as many different things as the organizations connoted by the term "state." There is a feudal, an estate-based, a bourgeois, a national, a social, and further a natural-law, a rational-law, and a historical-legal form of Rechtsstaat. It is conceivable that propagandists and advocates of all types could claim the word for their own purposes, in order to denounce the opponent as the enemy of the Rechtsstaat. The following saying applies to their Rechtsstaat and concept of law: "Law should above all be what I and my friends value." For state and constitutional theory, it comes down to this. With the help of the distinction among the legislative, jurisdiction, governmental, and administrative states, one ascertains specific characteristics, through which the concrete distinctiveness of the system of legality and its current position can be better and more clearly recognized.

PART I

The System of Legality of

the Parliamentary Legislative State

CHAPTER 1

—

The Legislative State

and the Concept of Law

The nineteenth-century constitutional monarchy was a legislative state. It was to a great extent a parliamentary legislative state precisely in the decisive point, specifically, its concept of law. Only a decision receiving the consent of the representative assembly, or legislature, was a valid law in the formal sense. Such formal concepts of constitutional law are essentially political concepts. For this reason, it was the decisive triumph of the legislature that law appeared essentially in the form of statutes and that positive law was in essence statutory law, but that by definition a valid statute required a decision of the legislature.[1] Indeed, one adhered firmly to the view that under statute was understood "every legal norm" and also that customary [1958/275] law was valid as positive law. But, of course, customary law was valid only as simple law and could be eliminated or circumvented by the wave of the lawmaker's hand, and, in this regard, the legislature may act more swiftly than customary law. Moreover, in certain, especially important areas of legal life, such as criminal law, but also in constitutional and in administrative law, the permissibility of customary law is still very controversial. Practically speaking, the recognition of customary law is always a certain restrictive reservation working to the disadvantage of the lawmaker. Consequently, the acceptability of customary law is denied where one fears it could damage the trust in the legislator so central to the legislative state. One must not forget that the German theory of customary law came to fruition in the Historical School of Law before 1848, so its actual polemical-political significance was determined through the opposition against the legislative right of the absolutist Monarchs [1932/21].[2] Regarding the effects on the organization of the state, the recognition of customary law always means a limitation on the parliamentary lawmaker to the benefit of other organs, especially, of course, the judiciary. The same holds true for all constructions of some "conceptual necessity," that is to say, that which is also substantively compelling for the lawmaker. A good example of this is Fr. Eisele's 1885 essay, to which G. Husserl has thoughtfully brought attention again. Another example is provided by the current opinion of the Reichsgericht on the question of the essential character of the civil servant.[3] According to the decision, the transfer of authoritarian state grants of authority without a formal post should itself justify the properties of the civil servant by virtue of the "inner essence of the matter," because the opposing assumption would be "nonsense" and the lawmaker cannot institute "something that is legally impossible and not executable."[4] In the essay just mentioned (p. 278), Eisele expressed what is at issue here: "It is a question of the boundaries of legislative power." Such boundaries can be derived from logical or reflective necessities just as well as from customary law.

Apart from such limitations, which are very controversial in their concrete application, the images of legal science and legal practice were [1958/276] (and still certainly are) mastered by a series of simple equivalencies. Law = statute; statute = the state regulation that comes about with the participation of the representative assembly. Practically speaking, that is what was meant by law when one demanded the "rule of law" and the "principle of the legality of all state action" as the defining characteristic of the Rechtsstaat. In the final analysis, everything that in the course of the nineteenth century would develop into a still efficacious system and inventory of concepts, formulas, and postulates pertaining to the Rechtsstaat rested on this congruence of law and statute. The state is law in statutory form; law in statutory form is the state. Obedience will be granted only to the statute; only through the law in statutory form is the right to resistance eliminated. There is only legality, not [1932/22] authority or commands from above. Under the heading "The Rule of Law" in a classic chapter of his work on administrative law, Otto Mayer wrote: "The highest type of state will is that which is expressed in the name of the law" (1924, 64). According to Otto Mayer, three features characterize such a legislative state: the statute's power to create law that is objective (in contrast to the internal administrative order and instructions to subordinate organs and officials); the primacy of the statute (namely, primacy over all other conceivable types of state activity); and the legislative reservation clause, more specifically, the monopoly to interfere in constitutionally guaranteed fundamental and liberty rights, which the statutory regulation has in contrast to all other types of state activity. In other words, the lawmaker, and the legislative process under its guidance, is the final guardian of all law, ultimate guarantor of the existing order, conclusive source of all legality, and the last security and protection against injustice. Misuse of the legislative power and of the lawmaking process must remain out of consideration in practical terms, because otherwise a differently constituted state form, an entirely different structure and organization, would become immediately necessary. The preexisting and presumed congruence and harmony of law and statute, justice and legality, substance and process dominated every detail of the legal thinking of the legislative state. Only through the acceptance of these pairings was it possible to subordinate oneself to the rule of law precisely in the name of freedom, remove the right to resistance from the catalogue of liberty rights, and grant to the statute the previously noted unconditional priority. In regard to the priority of the statute, one saw in the subordination of the judge to the statute a guarantee of judicial [1958/277] independence, found in the legality of the administration the most important protection against misuse of state power, and set all of the constitutionally guaranteed fundamental rights undoubtedly at the disposal of the legislature, which can interfere in these rights at its discretion by virtue of the "legislative reservation" clause.

The lawmaker in the legislative state is obviously always only the one, simple legislature. As has already been emphasized, every congruence of [1932/23] different types of lawmakers and of mutually relativizing concepts of law destroys the legislative state itself. In the legislative state with a closed system of legality, there cannot be numerous "sources of the law," as under Roman public law, for example: *leges, Plebiszite, Senatusconsulte; constitutiones principum*, magistratische *Edicte, Consulta prudentium*, etc. The lawmaker of a logically consistent legislative state must retain its "monopoly" of legality. However, what should occur when the trust in the lawmaker ceases to be based on the harmony of justice and legislative results was hardly considered in the prewar era, let alone answered. With its complicated restrictions and counterbalances—bicameral legislature, independent, royal government, supported by army and civil service, federal controls and counterweights—the legislative process contains sufficiently strong guarantees of moderation and an adequately secure protection of freedom and property against arbitrariness and misuse of the legal form. In such a state form, a purely formal concept of law, independent of all content, is conceivable and tolerable. Even if one unconditionally, without compromise and presuppositions, views everything that those in responsible positions decide via the legislative process as alone definitive of positive rights, all the typical, fundamental principles and institutions pertaining to the Rechtsstaat, such as, for example, the legal obligation of the independent judge to faithfully enforce statutes, the guarantee against arbitrary punishment contained in the principle "no sentence without statute," or the statutory reservation on fundamental and liberty rights, would still be sensible and tolerable. They would be genuine bonds, effective guarantees, and real reservations, because the unerring, unproblematic, direct confidence in the simple lawmaker and the legislative process does not require any further bonds, guarantees, or reservations. Only because of the unshakable confidence in the [1958/278] legislature and its type of laws can principles remain unexpressed, principles such as "[t]he right of the lawgiver is unlimited; all other rights of state power are limited" (Leuthold 1884), or "[t]he legislature can infringe on property" [1932/24] (Anschütz 1912).

This confidence remains the prerequisite of each and every constitution that organizes the Rechtsstaat in the form of a legislative state. Otherwise, the legislative state would be a rather complicated absolutism; the unconditional claim to obedience would be an open, coercive act of domination; and the honorable renunciation of the right to resistance would be an irresponsible act of stupidity. When the concept of law is deprived of every substantive relation to reason and justice, while simultaneously the legislative state is retained with its specific concept of legality concentrating all the majesty and dignity of the state on the statute, then any type of administrative directive, each command and measure, every order to any officer or soldier, and all detailed instructions to a judge, by virtue of the "rule of law," can be made legal and given the form of law through a decision of parliament or by the other organs participating in the legislative process. The "purely formal" reduces itself then to an empty term and to the slogan "statute," giving up the connection with the Rechtsstaat. All the dignity and majesty of the statute depends exclusively and directly, more specifically with directly positive-legal meaning and effect, on this trust in the justice and reason of the legislature itself and in all the organs participating in the legislative process. All legal guarantees and insurance, every protection against misuse, are placed in the person of the all-powerful lawmaker or in the distinctiveness of the lawmaking process. If that is not to be completely senseless and pure arbitrariness, it must be dominated entirely by the presupposition of the already noted trust, which first leads to the congruence of justice and formal law. By no means is this system of legality without presuppositions. An unconditional equivalence of law with the results of any particular formal process, therefore, would only be blind subordination to the pure decision of the offices entrusted with lawmaking, in other words, a decision detached from every substantive relation to law and justice, and, consequently, an unconditional renunciation of any resistance. It would be *sic volo sic jubeo* in its most naive form and only conceivable [1958/279] psychologically on the basis [1932/25] of the remnant of some superstition or as residues of an earlier, substantively richer, religious-like belief in the statutory form. One can term that "positivism," just as one can designate uncritically every type of decisionism as positivism. Only this term no longer deceives one that the former, unconditional formalism is a purely politically motivated claim to subordination, with an equally politically motivated denial of every right to resistance.

Prewar German state theory always recognized a substantive concept of law alongside a formal one. "One cannot get by in theory and practice without the substantive concept of law," according to Anschütz (1901, 33), "and the Prussian Constitution cannot be understood or explained without it."[5] On this basis, the objectively determined characteristics of law are also acknowledged. Law in the substantive sense is a legal norm or legal principle, a determination of what should be right for everyone. One retained the view that a formal statute normally contains a substantive legal principle and is distinguishable from any command. Also, the dominant understanding of the need for a sanction to make a command into a legal rule in the form of a statute shows that the distinction of norm and command, of statute and measure, was still current. "Every statute is comprised of two different parts, the one containing the rule itself, the other the legal command, or the order of obedience" (Laband).[6] But one did not conclusively render this connection between legal norm and statute into a public law definition of the statute that clearly distinguishes, for example, the statute as a general, lasting rule from a sheer command or mere measure. Alongside this concept enters a second, entirely different concept of the statute, which, however, was also termed "law in the substantive sense" (specifically, therefore, because the concept was not "formal"): namely, the statute as an "interference in the freedom and property of the citizen." This circumstance is only explicable in reference to the situation of the nineteenth century and rests on the opposition of state and society, government and representative assembly, bureaucrats (subordinated to a "specified power [1932/26] relationship") and the free state citizen, finally on the general distinction pertaining to the bourgeois Rechtsstaat between the free (in principle unlimited) private sphere and the preexisting, statutory [1958/280] (hence, in principle limited and definable) grant of state power. A further distinction stemming from this is that between the statute or, more precisely, a decree with the force of law as an "interference with the freedom and property of the state citizen" and the administrative decree as an act that does not intrude on this sphere of freedom, but rather only applies "inside the organs of administrative authority" (Anschütz).

Of course, defining statutes as involving "interference with freedom and property" had only a political meaning in a polemical sense directed against the authoritarian state executive, more specifically, against the royal government and its army and bureaucracy. That one compared the two entirely disparate criteria of a statute (substantive right and interference!), both "substantive," with a "formal" criterion was not elegant in abstract-logical terms, but it was readily understandable given the concrete domestic political situation of the nineteenth century. By contrast, it had to confuse the concepts of a legislative state that current thinking, despite both its "substantive" concepts of law, ascribed to the formal lawmaking process the capacity to take advantage of the form of the statute for any intended purpose, though the resulting statute was no longer a law in the substantive sense and, therefore, had nothing more to do with one or the other substantive, conceptual definitions. In this way, the entire dignity of the Rechtsstaat, which was derived from the first substantive concept of law, law = legal norm, and which radiated out to include the formal legislative procedure, was cut off from its origin and from its source, particularly from its objective connection with the law. At the same time, the idea of protection and security residing in the second concept of the statute (interference with freedom and property) was surrendered to the lawmaker, specifically in favor of a formal, purely political concept of statute detached from every relation to law and justice. The statute no longer needs to be, according to its purpose, a general (in the sense of like handled as like), lasting regulation with a [1932/27] definable and certain content. The lawmaker creates what he wants in the lawmaking process; that process is always "law," and it always creates "right." Through this change, the way was open to an absolutely "neutral," value- and quality-free, formal-functional concept of legality without content. While in administrative law, one still strictly retained the general character of the decree (in contrast to the administrative directive) and considered the generality requirement in this context conceivable and even [1958/281] necessary; and though also in this context otherwise definite characteristics of the norm were acknowledged, such as determinable content, proportionality, equality, one dealt with everything in regard to the statute in public law, where it had far greater practical significance, as a pointless theoretical game lacking firm boundaries.

As long as the domestic situation was normal and peaceful, and while the confidence in the functioning of the organs constituting the legislature was unshaken, theoretical ambiguity was certainly not an issue. When the dualism of state and society was set aside at the same time as the dualistic structure of the constitutional monarchy, the state's will and the people's will became identical, as one would expect under democratic logic, designating every expression of the people's will as "statute" and giving it the entire dignity and majesty due this concept by virtue of its connection with law and justice. In a democracy, law is the momentary will of the people present at that time, that is to say, in practical terms, the will of a transient majority of the voting citizenry; *lex est, quod populus jubet.* The distinction between norm and command, intellect and will, *ratio* and *voluntas*, which supports the parliamentary legislative state with its distinction between statute and statutory application, is here again subsumed under a "formal" concept of law and threatens the structure of the parliamentary system of legality. Nevertheless, that is tolerable for other reasons in a logically consistent democracy. For, according to democratic presuppositions, the homogeneous people have all the characteristics that a guarantee of the justice and reasonableness of the people's expressed will cannot renounce. No democracy exists without the presupposition [1932/28] that the people are good and, consequently, that their will is sufficient. *Il suffit qu'il veut.* In the parliamentary democracy, the will of parliament is identified with that of the people. Here, parliament's simple majority decision can be both just and law, as long as it is presupposed that the majority decision contains in itself the previously noted qualities of the people's will. Also in this regard, a "formal" concept of law is conceivable and acceptable, though not unconditionally formal. It is, instead, entirely connected with the confidence in the congruence between the parliamentary majority and the will of the homogeneous people. In regard to the French constitutional law of 1875 and the French parliamentary democracy, an [1958/282] exceptional author of French public law, Carré de Malberg (1931), could therefore recently explain that all objective traits of the concept of law, such as its general character or the permanence of the rule, are to be rejected because the will of the parliament is directly that of the sovereign people, the *volonté générale* itself. That is the characteristic formula of parliamentary democracy. Today, in practical terms, this formula is directed most of all against the judicial review of statutes because such control of legislative jurisdiction would infuse the parliamentary legislative state with elements of a jurisdictional state [*jurisdiktionellen Staates*], which, as a foreign body, endangers this state type's clear system of legality and renders problematical parliament's central position as the source of legality.[7]

If the assumptions underlying the legislative state of the parliamentary-democratic variety are no longer tenable, then closing one's eyes to the concrete constitutional situation and clinging to an absolute, "value-neutral," functionalist and formal concept of law, in order to save the system of legality, is not far off. The "law," then, is only the present decision of the momentary parliamentary majority. As noted, that is conceivable and tolerable given the unstated, presupposed confidence in the capacity of parliament, both parliamentarians and of parliament generally, to guarantee right and reason through a process distinguished by discussion and publicity. Already at this point, however, another necessity [1932/29] must be stressed, the unavoidability of which is for the most part insufficiently acknowledged: the written constitution of the parliamentary legislative state must ultimately limit itself to organizational and procedural rules. That corresponds to the neutrality of a system, in relatively liberal as well as absolutist-functional terms, whose process and method should stand open and be accessible to different opinions, directions, movements, and goals. Moreover, it must be self-evident that the written constitution of every legislative state will not preempt the legislature that the constitution establishes, while the constitution itself plays the role of legislature through its own substantive legal rules. The legislative state acknowledges only a single, ordinary legislature, which must hold the monopoly on the creation of substantive law. Indeed, the legislative state of the nineteenth-century German [1958/283] constitutional monarchy recognized a threefold concept of law. For the formal concept of law, however, the consent of the popular assembly was alone essential and conceptually definitive. Moreover, both the struggle for the independent royal right to issue decrees with the force of law as well as the recognition of the royal sanction of parliamentary passage of statutes showed that a legislative state of the parliamentary-democratic variety had not yet come about. But even the supporters of the independent royal decree power did not dare designate the King's legal decrees as law in the formal sense. The clear and illuminating axiom that a legislative state may have only one concept of law, only one lawmaker, and only one legislative process was to that extent at least formally preserved, and the system of legality of this type of state allowed itself to operate without self-destructive, internal contradictions.

CHAPTER 2

Legality and the Equal Chance

for Achieving Political Power

Article 68 of the Weimar Constitution establishes the parliamentary legislative state: Reich statutes are passed by the Reichstag. Comprehending law and statute without relation to any content as the present conclusion of the transitory parliamentary majority corresponds to a purely functional manner of thinking. In this way, law, statute, and legality become "neutral" procedural mechanisms and voting procedures that are indifferent toward content of any sort and accessible to any substantive claim. Indeed, the parliamentary legislative state's concept of law inherently has a wide-ranging neutrality regarding the most varied content. But this concept of law must contain certain qualities, such as normative generality, substantive definiteness, and permanence, if it is to support the legislative state at all. Above all, it may not be "neutral" toward itself and its own presuppositions. If the parliamentary body is made into a mere function of general majority elections; and if its majority decision constitutes law, but without regard to the qualities of its members [1958/284] and in disregard of any substantive requirement of law; then all guarantees of justice and reasonableness, along with the concept of law and legality itself, end in an internally consistent functionalist view without substance and content that is rooted in arithmetic understandings of the majority.[1] Fifty-one percent produces the majority in parliament; 51 percent of the votes in parliament produces law and legality; 51 percent also demonstrates the confidence of parliament and produces the parliamentary government.

[1932/31] The method of will formation through simple majority vote is sensible and acceptable when an essential similarity among the entire people can be assumed. For in this case, there is no voting down of the minority. Rather, the vote should only permit a latent and presupposed agreement and consensus to become evident. As noted, since every democracy rests on the presupposition of the indivisibly similar, entire, unified people, for them there is, then, in fact and in essence, no minority and still less a number of firm, permanent minorities. The process of determining the majority comes into play, not because finding what is true and proper has been renounced on account of relativism or agnosticism—that would be, in view of the momentous political decisions at issue here, a suicidal renunciation and is possible, as Hans Kelsen (1928, 77) concedes, "only in relatively peaceful times," thus only when it does not matter.[2] One must assume that, by virtue of being a part of the same people, all those similarly situated would in essence will the same thing. If the assumption of an indivisible, national commonality is no longer tenable, then the abstract, empty functionalism of pure mathematical majority determinations is the opposite of neutrality and objectivity. It is only the quantitatively larger or smaller, forced subordination of the defeated and, therefore, suppressed minority. The democratic identity of governing and governed, those commanding and those obeying, stops. The majority commands, and the minority must obey. Arithmetic calculability also stops, because one can only reasonably produce a sum from that which is very similar. One can [1958/285] designate the functionalism of shifting majorities lacking both content and presuppositions only as "dynamism," although the lack of stasis and of substance actually still does not yet need anything dynamic. But when one perfects this substantively indifferent and neutral process even more and takes it to the absurdity of only a mathematical-statistical majority determination—a substantive principle of justice will nevertheless always still have [1932/32] to be presupposed, if one wishes to keep the entire system of legality from collapsing immediately: the principle that there is an unconditional equal chance for all conceivable opinions, tendencies, and movements to achieve a majority. Without this principle, majority calculus would be a grotesque game, not merely because of its indifference toward every substantive result. The concept of legality derived from this principle would also be a shameless mockery of all justice. But, with this system, the principle would also already come to an end after the first majority is achieved, because that majority would immediately establish itself as the permanent legal power. Preserving the availability of the principle of equal chance cannot be read out of the parliamentary legislative state. It remains the principle of justice and the existentially necessary maxim of self-preservation. Also, the thoroughly settled functionalism of purely mathematical majorities cannot renounce this indispensable presupposition and foundation of its legality.

That state power is legal should, above all, eliminate and negate every right to resistance as law. But the ancient problem of "resistance against the tyrant" remains, that is, resistance against injustice and misuse of state power, and the functionalistic-formalistic hollowing out of the parliamentary legislative state is not able to resolve it. This leads only to a concept of legality that is substantively noncommittal, neutral in a way that undermines its own validity, and dismissive of all substantive justice. The emptiness of mere majority calculus deprives legality of all persuasive power. Its neutrality, first of all, is neutrality toward the difference between justice and injustice. The possibility of injustice, the possibility of the "tyrant," is eliminated from the world only through a formal sleight of hand, namely, only by no longer calling injustice injustice and tyrant tyrant, much as one eliminates war from the world by terming it "peaceful measures accompanied by battles of greater or lesser scope" and designating [1958/286] that a "purely juristic definition of war." By "conceptual necessity," then, legal power simply can no longer do injustice. The old teaching of a right to resistance distinguishes among two types of "tyrants": he who [1932/33] arrives at the seat of power in a legal manner, but then exercises and abuses power badly and tyrannically, that is, the *tyrannus ab exercitio*; further, the *tyrannus absque titulo*, who achieves power without legal title and is indifferent as to whether it exercises power well or badly. Under the substantive neutrality or under the utter substantive emptiness of a functional concept of legality, there can generally no longer be the first sort of tyrant, in particular, the illegal use of legal power. However, the "tyrant without legal title" could also never occur, if the majority attained lawful title to the legal possession of power. Only he who exercises state or state-like power without the 51 percent majority on their side is illegal and a "tyrant." Whoever has this majority would no longer do injustice, but rather everything he does is transformed into justice and legality. With such consequences, the principle of a functional concept of law without content carries itself *ad absurdum*.

The claim to legality renders every rebellion and counter-measure an injustice and a legal violation or "illegality." If legality and illegality can be arbitrarily at the disposal of the majority, then the majority can, above all, declare their domestic competitors illegal, that is, *hors-la-loi*, thereby excluding them from the democratic homogeneity of the people. Whoever controls 51 percent would be able legally to render the remaining 49 percent illegal. The majority would be permitted to use legal means to close the door to legality, through which they themselves entered, and to treat partisan opponents like common criminals, who are then perhaps reduced to kicking their boots against the locked door. With this troubling possibility in view, one attempts today to ensure a certain protection mostly through the introduction of threshold requirements and qualifications of the voting majority, demanding for selected issues a two-thirds and similar majorities. On the one hand, one gives protections against 51 percent majorities under the misleading slogan of "minority guarantees," but then, on the other hand, one adheres to the empty functionalism of a mere arithmetic majority and minority calculations. The following chapter will show that the introduction of such numerically [1958/287] qualified [1932/34] majority calculus also devalues and destroys democracy as well as the parliamentary legislative state and its concept of legality. Indeed, it is already evident that this mathematical functionalism of the transitory majority calculus continually undermines itself when the principle of the equal chance of achieving a majority is not strictly observed. The parliamentary legislative state, which today rests on the rule of temporary majorities, can deliver the monopoly of the legal exercise of power to the majority parties and can demand that the minorities renounce the right to resistance only so long as the equal chance of achieving a majority really remains open and this assumption of its principle of justice is somehow still believable. Most of what has been presented to justify majority rule is traceable to this principle, especially what the single available monograph (Starosolskyj

1916, 63–64) on the subject has to say about the indispensable "exchange in the personal composition of the majority" or the necessary "indeterminacy" of its rule.

In his famous book about the theory of the estate-based right to resistance, Kurt Wolzendorff (1915) grounded and justified the elimination of the right to resistance in reference to the introduction of an ordered system of courts or of dispute resolution. Much more important, however, for the parliamentary legislative state than the establishment of a system of legal protections or the preservation of a chance for a trial before established courts is the maintenance of the equal chance to achieve the majority, which means political power. For when a party controlling 51 percent of the lawmaking body can legally set definitive statutes for the judiciary, then it also dictates to the judiciary the content of the judges' decision for civil law, labor law, criminal law, civil service law, and all other types of legal disputes, because judges are obligated to enforce statutes. Moreover, the party with 51 percent control of the legislature forms the legal government, which has at hand all the means of state power involved in legal application. Thus the equal chance at a judicial solution for the nondominant party transforms itself into the [1932/35] opposite of such a chance. Whoever has the majority makes the valid statutes. Moreover, those in the majority themselves enforce the statutes they make. They have a monopoly over the validity of statutes and their execution as well as over the production and sanction of legality. Most important, [1958/288] however, is that the monopoly over the enforcement of valid statutes confers on those in the majority the legal possession of state means of power and with it, a political power that extends far beyond that over the mere validity of norms. The ruling party can make use of the advantage, which comes along with the mere possession of the legal means of power in a state type dominated by this form of legality. The majority is now suddenly no longer a party; it is the state itself. In the state, as Otto Mayer once said, "that which is without limits breaks through" the norms, in which the legislative state and statutory application bind themselves, however narrow and limited these sets of norms may be. Therefore, the mere possession of state power produces an additional political surplus apart from the power that is merely normative and legal, a supralegal premium on the lawful possession of legal power and on the achievement of a majority that lies beyond any normative consideration.

This political premium is relatively calculable in peaceful and normal times; in abnormal times, it is entirely incalculable and unpredictable. It always has a threefold character. It emerges, first, from the concrete interpretation and use of undetermined and evaluative concepts, such as "public security and order," "danger," "emergency," "necessary measures," "hostility to the state and constitution," "peaceful disposition," "life and death issues," etc. Such concepts, without which no state type could survive, are distinctive in that they are bound directly to the momentary situation, that they receive their specific content initially through concrete application, and, most of all, that their concrete application and execution are alone decisive in all difficult and politically important times. Second, the legal holder of state power has the presumption of legality on his side in hard cases, which, of course, with such indeterminate concepts one always encounters in difficult political circumstances. Finally, third, even in cases of doubtful legality, [1932/36] the directives of the legal holder of state power are directly executable in the immediate instance, even when opportunities for legal challenges and judicial protections are provided. In a race between the executive and the judiciary, the judiciary will mostly arrive too late, even if one provides it the power of issuing measures and rulings for use in political cases that are valid only temporarily, under certain conditions, and in a single instance, and that, therefore, are themselves not unquestionable instruments. Consequently, the judicial chance signifies, in fact, a necessary corrective and a protection that one should not dismiss, but it cannot be politically [1958/289] decisive and cannot alone support this type of legality's principle of justice, the preservation of the equal chance. Added to the current German legal consciousness, sharpened through many foreign experiences, is the fact that judicial procedures for resolving political conflicts have generally lost value and standing. In none of the life-and-death questions of German foreign policy, as things stand today, could one still impudently insist on the opportunity to win an international law case affirming Germany's death penalty.

Everything thus hinges on the principle of an equal chance to win domestic political power. If principle is no longer defended, then one gives up on the parliamentary legislative state itself, its justice and legality. In this regard, however, are good will and the best intentions of much use? Every critical moment endangers the principle of the equal chance because it reveals the inevitable opposition between the premium on the legal possession of power and the preservation of the availability of the equal chance for achievement of domestic political power. On the one hand, the equal chance is already eliminated through the mere supposition of the legality of every expression of state authority. On the other hand, no legal state power can do without this supposition. On the one hand, part of the essential content of the principle of equal chance is that its concrete interpretation and use is not one-sided, but rather that it is taken up by all parties under full legal equality. On the other hand, a concept like "equal chance" itself is again one of the indeterminate concepts tied directly to a specific situation, whose interpretation and proper use is necessarily a matter of legal power, therefore, of the present ruling party. On its own initiative, the ruling party determines what possibilities [1932/37] for action it permits domestic opponents. In this way, the ruling party decides when the illegality of competitors commences. Obviously, that is no longer equal competition and no longer an equal chance.

The principle of equal chance is of such sensitivity that any serious doubt about the loyalty of all participants already renders the principle's application impossible. For it is self-evident that one can hold open an equal chance only for those whom one is certain would do the same. Any other use of such a principle [1958/290] would not only be suicide in practical terms, but also an offense against the principle itself. Due to this necessity, the party in legal possession of power, by virtue of its hold on the means of state power, must itself determine and judge every concrete and politically important application and use of the concept of legality and illegality. That is its inalienable right. However, it is just as much an inalienable right of the minority seeking to gain possession of the state means of power, on the basis of its claim to an equal chance with full legal equality, to render judgment itself over not merely its own concrete legality or illegality, but also over that of the opposing party in control of the means of state power. So the principle of equal chance does not contain in its own inner assumptions an answer to the question that arises at critical moments and is the only decisive question in practical terms: in a case of conflict, who removes doubts and resolves differences of opinion? Precisely for the proper use of the previously mentioned indeterminate concepts that are tied to particular situations, such as public order, hostility to the state or the constitution, peaceful or not, but, above all, also legal or illegal attitudes, an essential part of the equal chance is that ruling and non-ruling parties, majority or minority, have unconditional parity. A practical remedy would be to seek a solution in the introduction of an "impartial" third party, who decides the conflict, whether judicially or otherwise. But the system of legality of the parliamentary legislative state would be betrayed. For in contrast to the parties to the dispute, this third party would be a supraparliamentary, [1932/38] indeed, suprademocratic, higher third, and the political will would no longer come about through the free competition among political parties, which have fundamentally the same chances for power. The problem stemming from the principle of equal chance would not be solved through the principle itself. It would, rather, only be acknowledged that the principle merely leads to irresolvable questions and critical situations. As soon as the assumption so essential for this system of legality collapses, specifically, that of legal disposition held equally on all sides, then there is no longer a remedy. The majority party in legal control of the means of state power must assume that the opposing party, when it achieves power legally, will use legal means in order to ensconce itself in possession of power and to close the door behind it, hence, legally eliminating the principle of legality itself. [1958/291] The minority seeking power maintains that the ruling majority has long done the same. Whether *explicite* or *implicite*, the minority is on its own declaring the existing state power illegal, which no legal power can permit. So at the critical juncture, each denounces the other, with both playing the guardian of legality and the guardian of the constitution. The result is a condition without legality or a constitution.

With every concept of so-called political right, which rests on legal equality and harmonization, one such critical moment can appear. Concepts involving foreign policy and international law, such as security, the danger of war or of an invasion, threat, attack, war guilt, etc., recognize the same sort of dialectic. For example, in the so-called war ban clause of the Kellogg Pact of 1928,[3] several powers expressly made the reservation that every violation of the pact relieves other states of their treaty obligations toward the aggressor. That is not an inappropriate reservation; it is actually self-evident. But one sees immediately that the pact became worthless for the critical case at which it was directed, specifically the case of war, at least so long as the pact is applied with unconditional legal equality, and, for example, so long as an imperialistic [1932/39] great power or group of powers plays the higher third and itself interprets and sanctions the indeterminate concepts of the pact, including especially the concept "war," which is likely to occur in political reality. In domestic political terms, however, an analogous, concrete decision regarding the irresolvable antimony may only be achieved through the party in possession of the legal power. In this way, the party becomes the higher third and, in the same moment, eliminates the principle of its legality, the equal chance. In other words, the advantage of the legal possession of state power decides the case.

The threefold great premium on the legal possession of power is grounded in the ease of judgment, the supposition of legality, and the ability to achieve the immediate execution of one's dictates. Its entire, primary effect eliminates any thought of the equal chance and becomes manifest in the proper use of the extraordinary powers in the state of exception. Moreover, the premium provides the ruling party control not only over the "plunder," or the "spoils," as it is traditionally known, but also over the gross domestic product that is bound up with the taxing and spending power in a quantitative total state. [1958/292] It is enough to suggest this side of the legal possibilities in order to recognize its effect on the legality principle of the parliamentary legislative state. A number of smaller premiums should be added to the large one. For the elections and votes of the next election period, for example, a majority party can alter the election law rules to its advantage and to the disadvantage of its domestic political competitors. The majority party can act like the slim majority of the Prussian legislature in the decision of April 12, 1932, at the end of the election period. With the help of a change in the order of business (§ 20) for the following election period, it intentionally rendered the choice of a Minister President more difficult, in order to take an opportunity away from its opponent and to improve its own chances for the continuation of the legal possession of power despite no longer having a majority. The "caretaker governments," which today in several countries last months, even years, offer an especially illuminating example of the type of premium from holding power that is of interest here. These caretaker governments settle not only all "current business," [1932/40] as the Prussian Constitution prescribes, for example. Rather, one reads simply "all business" instead of "continuing business," first because one relies on the Staatsgerichtshof,[4] which refuses to clarify the distinction (Lammers and Simons 1929, 1:267), but also because it is difficult for one with a disloyal disposition to distinguish between continuing and other business. Also for these reasons, in regard to its powers, but not its limitations, one places the caretaker government completely at the same level as the duly constituted parliamentary cabinet. So a formerly ruling majority without current majority support remains in possession of the means of state power to the extent that the opposing party did not win for itself a clear counter-majority. Obviously, the inner justification then is no longer the majority principle, but still only the factual possession of state power once it has been gained legally. The equal chance is no longer valid, but is still only the triumph of the *beatus possidens*. In the same degree to which such premiums on the possession of power retain a defining political meaning and their ruthless exploitation becomes a self-evident means of partisan power maintenance, the principle of equal chance loses its persuasiveness and, consequently, its foundation in the legality of the parliamentary legislative state. When things really have gone that far, it ultimately comes [1958/293] down to who holds the reins of power at the moment when the entire system of legality is thrown aside and when power is constituted on a new basis.

PART II

The Three Extraordinary

Lawgivers of the Weimar Constitution

CHAPTER 3

———

The Extraordinary Lawgiver

Ratione Materiae: The Second Principal Part of the

Weimar Constitution as a Second Constitution

In the parliamentary legislative state, law is the present decision of the transitory parliamentary majority. In direct democracy, it is the transitory will of the present people's majority. Among the [1932/41] consequences of the democratic majority principle is, first, the transitory character of majorities and, second, the simple, thus 51 percent majority. But there are, indeed, exceptions to the principle of the simple majority in most democratic constitutions. For certain cases a smaller majority is required, while for others a higher quorum is demanded. It is important to determine whether such deviations from the principle of simple majority are related to procedural questions: for example, whether a qualified majority of two-thirds is necessary to exclude the public under Article 29 of the Weimar Constitution; whether for the convening of the Reichstag according to Article 24 only a one-third vote is required; or whether the deviation is for certain substantive decisions, as when a principle of substantive law is introduced. Also, the question of constitutional amendment (Article 76) is essentially different depending on whether under "constitution" is understood organizational and procedural rules or also principles of substantive law. Only cases involving a substantive law norm exhibit an obvious and fundamental deviation from and change in the principle of the simple majority. In these cases, however, it is constantly a matter of making the process of decision more difficult, not easier, by stipulating that passage requires more than 51 percent. In the Second Principal Part of the Weimar Constitution, these substantive law qualifications, when viewed in terms of constitutional history, are introduced in unparalleled scope through empty "anchorings," guarantees, inviolability declarations, securities, and other substantive law entrenchments.[1] This Second Principal Part of the Weimar Constitution [1958/294] bears the inexact, actually misleading title: "Fundamental Rights and Duties of the German People." In truth, set against the First Principal Part organizing the parliamentary legislative state, it is a second, heterogeneous constitution.

The deviation from the principle of the simple majority takes the form of the requirement that statutes with definite substantive law content need a qualified, two-thirds majority under Article 76. If for the sake of clarity we consider here only the Reichstag as the ordinary legislature, and if we leave aside the Reichsrat's right of inquiry, then the [1932/42] "protection" is essentially that instead of 51 percent, now 66.67 percent must consent to the passage of a statute. The mathematical difference extends to 15.67 percent. But through this difference of 15.67 percent, which, in arithmetic terms, is naturally only quantitative, one introduces a consequential qualitative change, even a transformation, in the legality of the parliamentary legislative state. For now the question arises, what is actually the *ratio* of this addition of a further 15.67 percent? On what is the quality and dignity of the additional quantum based, which is, in contrast to the simple lawgiver, capable of constituting a higher type of lawgiver and a more robust legality? That the simple majority is decisive for the question at hand justifies it as a method of will determination and does not violate the assumption of the homogeneity of the democratic people. Obviously, it is different with the requirement of the additional 15.67 percent.

One might perhaps object that only a practical-technical problem is involved here, in particular, the interest in making passage of a statute more difficult. Sixty-six or 67 percent would not be as easy to achieve as 51 percent. Solely at issue then would be the interest in restraint and, perhaps, the thought of a corresponding probability of better, more just decisions. When considered more closely, this explanation, which is in itself thoroughly plausible, says nothing more than that sixty-six is quantitatively more than fifty-one, which is without doubt true, but which does not address the substantive constitutional problem. The question from constitutional theory is directed at something else, namely, at the central value of the legislative state, the lawmaker, the concept of statute, and of legality. If a new type of lawmaker is established through the additional 15 percent, then the point about merely making the process of decision more difficult is in no regard conclusive, when one ignores any special quality [1958/295] of the additional 15 percent and the democratic presupposition of homogeneity is left out of account. If the simple and qualified majority is one and the same identical lawgiver, then it is only a matter of an internal modification, so to speak, in the order of business, so there is also not a contradiction between lower and higher [1932/43] norms. Considered only as quantitative obstacles, threshold requirements can be at most negatively a practical means of limitation. But they contain neither a general positive principle of justice or reason nor a special constitutional perspective. They are not even something especially democratic. In general, it would be a peculiar type of "justice" to declare a majority all the better and more just the more overwhelming it is, and to maintain abstractly that ninety-eight people abusing two persons is by far not so unjust as fifty-one people mistreating forty-nine. At this point, pure mathematics becomes simple inhumanity. Yet it would be in no way especially democratic to say of the passage of a statute that its quality and its significance in terms of justice is judged as such by the numerical size of its majority, and that in view of the preceding and without any regard for content, a decision achieved with 67 percent of the votes is a norm that is sixteen degrees higher in value than one finding only a 51 percent majority. In the cases of interest here, the distinction between simple and higher statutes rests not on the principle of the quorum, but rather on the will of the constitution. Once again, however, according to general democratic principles, these can come about with a simple majority.

The requirement of an additional number of votes beyond that of a simple majority cannot be justified, therefore, by democratic principles and still less by the logic of justice, humanity, and reason, but only by practical-technical considerations of the present situation. Every democracy, even the parliamentary variety, fundamentally rests on a presupposed homogeneity that is thorough and indivisible. As noted, if democracy is to flourish, every vote only has the sense of

bringing about agreement, as a mode of confirming the unanimity that must always be present at a lower level, instead
of an agreement in the form of a majority voting down, dominating, and violating a minority. Since democracy generally
provides no legitimate basis for a lasting and organized division of the people into majority and minority, there is also
not an interest that merits and [1958/296] needs enduring protection from the majority. In reality, this need for protection
can be very great. But [1932/44] one must recognize that with
such protections, democracy is already negated, and it is of
little use to expect a genuine minority protection from a "true"
or higher democracy. As soon as the perspective of the desirability of and the need for such protection of substantively
definite interests and rights intrudes violently and decisively
into the constitution, the democratic principle is not only
modified, but an essentially different type of constitution is
established. In this way, more specifically, either an undemocratic, even antidemocratic mistrust of the majority is being
expressed or certain protected objects, persons, or groups of
persons are taken out of the democracy, exempted from the
bonds of the legal system, and in this way privileged as a more
or less exclusive, special community vis-à-vis the majority.
Thought through consistently to the conclusion, recognizing
the desirability of and the need for the protection of definite
interests or groups threatened by the majority leads to their
complete shielding from the transitory functionalism of parliamentary and democratic voting methods. Logical consistency
requires exemption with *itio in partes* or recognition of the
right to exodus and secession. This is certainly not the intention of the Second Principal Part of the Weimar Constitution. It is only a fragment of another type of constitution,
which opposes the empty value neutrality of the democratic-
parliamentary legislative state's constitution.

   If the object of protection is granted security from the majority because of its special inner value, perhaps actually due
to its sanctity, then the insurance thereby extended, that an
additional 16 percent must be added to a 51 percent majority,
obviously constitutes a half measure and only emergency assistance. For in terms of its character, the additional 16 percent
is not qualified to determine the object of protection itself.
It does not have any properties that distinguish it from the

other 51 percent. They also do not stand in a specific relation, whether objective or personal, to the protected object, which would justify requiring their consent to the interference with the object and to the [1932/45] violation of its secured status. For example, it is not as if in the elimination of the specially guaranteed interests of religious societies some [1958/297] representation is accorded them and their consent must be given, or as if the acquired rights of civil servants declared inviolable in Article 129 cannot be impinged on against the unanimous will of the civil service agents or all members of parliament who are civil servants. Rather, it remains a purely mathematical-quantitative calculation. That means nothing other than that, in the same manner as in the simple arithmetic majority, unconditional homogeneity is also assumed in this qualified majority, because otherwise addition would not at all be possible according to the still valid principles of primitive arithmetic. Under this presupposition of homogeneity, another vote calculation besides that of the simple majority cannot be justified, at least not in reference to objectively defined interests and groups. On the other hand, if the assumption of thorough homogeneity is given up, if it is acknowledged that the mass of state citizens no longer thinks as a unity, but rather in pluralist fashion, divided into a plurality of heterogeneous, organized configurations, then it must also be acknowledged that in regard to such heterogeneous power groupings every arithmetic majority principle loses its meaning.[2] One can only add together sums that are quite similar. Either a single power configuration has the necessary majority, whether simple or qualified, at its disposal. Then, everything it does is without question legal, and there is no more protection for all opposing parties. In this case, the additional 15 or 16 percent means no new justification, because the group of persons constituting this 15 or 16 percent is comparable in an essential sense to the 51 percent of the simple majority. But, on the contrary, it would justify a still stronger need for protection. Faced with a similar two-thirds majority, the mistrust of the simple majority must increase yet further, because the dangerous, stronger majority is obviously much more of a threat than the dangerous simple majority. Or the necessary majority first comes into being through a compromise among heterogeneous party constellations. A statute then is the momentary compromise of heterogeneous power groupings. [1932/46] Then, every type of thoroughgoing vote count is also impermissible, and the intro- duction of a qualified voting majority in place of the simple majority only means that the additional 15 or 16 percent is heterogeneous and retains in a completely disconnected way a key position permitting them to demand unrelated counter- measures. For example, in regard to a conservative-Christian group, on the one hand, and to a culturally radical [1958/298] group, on the other, a middle-class party could make its con- sent or denial of consent to dechristianization and to the secu- larization of the state contingent on the elimination of the mortgage interest tax. It is well known that similar political business is conceivable and possible at all times and under all state forms, and some agreements between cabinet coun- cils of the absolute monarch and his mistresses probably also rested on very heterogeneous motives and perspectives. How- ever, in the formation of simple and even more in qualified majorities of the pluralist party state, these types of "compro- mises" are typical and institutional, so to speak. For the small and midsize parties, the practice of such combinations is quite simply a matter of survival. As J. Popitz (1929, 20) emphatically points out, these parties have an interest in advocating the pos- sibility of a constitutional change through statute because in this way they participate in the constitutional amending ma- jority.[3] But, for the fundamental question of interest here, the deviation from the principle of simple majority becomes a spe- cial problem, first because threshold requirements for will for- mation introduced on substantive grounds must remain in a substantive relation to the matter meriting protection. Under the currently valid regulation, however, that is just not the case. Among such deviations from the democratic principle, precisely this disconnect between the reason for making the process of will formation more difficult, which has a definite object, and the means of rendering the process more difficult, which does not have an object, is the most contradictory. If one does not trust the democratic majority, then depending on changing circumstances perhaps much, though also maybe little, is gained when a few percent more votes are [1932/47] required. By what right could these additional votes restore the lost trust? When for objective reasons certain interests and groups should be protected from the majority, then one must take them out of the process of democratic will formation through the use of special institutions, which are no longer democratic. In other words, one must exempt these interests from and privilege them in the democratic process. But it is not fully consistent to take these interests out of the functionalism of mathematical-statistical methods through purely quantitative threshold requirements and, at the same time, to leave them in. In this way, one abandons the underlying democratic principle of the simple majority, which is based on a presupposed homogeneity, without going [1958/299] over to some new principle. As noted, such a remedy can be seen at most as a practical-technical emergency measure of a still unclarified intermediate stage.

It is not a question here of whether substantive legal guarantees or constitutions like that of the Weimar Constitution's Second Principal Part are reasonable and justified. Undoubtedly, they are. Nonetheless, they constitute a structural contradiction with the value neutrality of the First Principal Part organizing the parliamentary legislative state. And they not only limit the parliamentary legislative state; they also destroy it, first because each such guarantee and entrenchment means above all security from the simple, ordinary, and normal lawgiver, more specifically, the parliamentary majority. What had been the foundation of the parliamentary legislative state, the unconditional trust in the ordinary legislature and its current majority, is undermined through constitutional channels, so to speak. Moreover, the scope of these substantive legal guarantees of the Second Principal Part is extraordinarily wide and indefinite. With the help of the "positivization" and "actualization" of the indefinite concepts, principles, and guidelines contained in the Second Part, the range of their applicability can be extended indefinitely. But, in the connection of interest here, it is especially noteworthy that substantive legal guarantees of this type create confusion in the functionalism of the legislative state, which had been retained, despite everything, and for which law is the present will of the transient majority. The substantive [1932/48] constitutional guarantees should guard directly against the transitory nature of the ordinary legislature, securing a particular matter from an empty, majoritarian functionalism that surrenders up all substantive values to the current majority, while, on the contrary, parliamentary democracy's legislative process should be open to every concern, each opinion, and any aspiration or goal. Now because of the requirement of the higher majority, a new type of the momentary and transitory apparently enters: higher law (constitutional law) is then simply the current will of the transitory two-thirds majority. But this new and "higher" type of the transitory contradicts the first and "lower" type, because it is not considered a form of value neutrality without substance and, hence, is not conceived of in functional terms. Its point of departure is that there are particular substantive values, singled out by the constitution itself, [1958/300] indeed, even sacred institutions and entitlements, such as marriage (Article 119) and exercise of religion (Article 135), which should stand under the protection of the constitution itself, while in its unconditional value neutrality the functionalist form of the momentary in the parliamentary legislative state should also be serviceable for the elimination of just these sacred objects. On the one hand, obviously, this "value emphasis," this "system of meaning" (R. Smend), or whatever one wishes to call the nonfunctional formulations of the Weimar Constitution's Second Principal Part, conceived of as substantive and essential, is in an irreconcilable opposition to the unconditional, neutral functionalism of the organizational First Part. According to the dominant interpretation of Article 76, on the other hand, the Constitution's First Part is even indifferent to itself and its own system of legality. One cannot put marriage, religion, and private property solemnly under the protection of the constitution and in one and the same constitution offer the legal means for their elimination. One cannot simultaneously reject emphatically "godless cultural radicalism" and then give it full "vent" legally by offering it an equal chance. And it is an inadequate, indeed, an immoral excuse, when one declares that the elimination of marriage or of churches is legally quite possible, but that it would hopefully not come to a simple or two-thirds [1932/49] majority, which would abolish marriage or establish an atheistic or a secular state. When the legality of such a possibility is recognized, and it is self-evident for the dominant functionalism of the concept of law and of constitutional law, then all the declarations of the Second Part of the Constitution are actually "hollow," sacred relics. The legal theory and legal practice of such a constitution faces a simple choice: give up either the value neutrality of the organizational portion, which is logically consistent in legal, moral, and political terms, or the substantive "system of meaning" of the Second Part of the Constitution. For the constitution is a unity, and the more immediate as well as the "remote effects" of its axioms are inescapable even for an entirely rudimentary administrative and judicial routine. There is no middle road between the principled value neutrality of the functionalist system of legality and the principled value emphasis of the substantive constitutional guarantees. The functionalism of the weighted majorities would at least be a reasonable "compromise." In regard to the question of neutrality or nonneutrality, whoever intends to remain neutral has already decided in [1958/301] favor of neutrality. Value assertion and value neutrality are mutually exclusive. Compared to a seriously intended value assertion and affirmation, conscientious value neutrality means a denial of values.

The degree to which the fundamental and unconditional value neutrality of the now functional system of legality is self-evident for the received view, which considers itself the prevailing opinion, is best seen in G. Anschütz's commentary on the Weimar Constitution (1932, 404f.). With special emphasis, this leading commentary of a recognized master terms a "new theory" and a "new type of theory" the opinion held by many current public law scholars that there must be some boundary to constitutional amendment according to Article 76. These ever more numerous "new" theorists—H. Triepel, Carl Bilfinger, E. Jacobi, O. Koellreutter, H. Gerber, O. Bühler, R. Thoma, W. Jellinek, K. Loewenstein, and others—differ significantly among themselves in regard to reasoning as well as definitional issues. The first and most important difference may consist in the fact that a few of these [1932/50] authors recognize substantively defined interests or issues as sacrosanct. Others, by contrast, above all R. Thoma and certainly also W. Jellinek, consider as inviolate only individual, internal presuppositions that are conceptually and existentially necessary for the otherwise value-neutral system, such as, for example, a minimum of an objectively determined concept of law, of an equal chance for attaining political power, of free discussion, and of electoral and voting rights. Especially R. Thoma, who seeks to discount Carl Bilfinger's and my interpretation of

Article 76 as "fantasy law" (Anschütz and Thoma 1932, 2:154), says himself that decisions suppressing freedom of conscience or trampling under foot "any of the other principles of freedom and justice" considered sacred in the entire current cultural world—with the exception of fascism and bolshevism— could be unconstitutional despite a majority sufficient for a constitutional amendment. In this regard, the bourgeois-legal system itself, with its concepts of law and freedom, is at least still sacred, and liberal value neutrality is viewed as a value, while fascism and bolshevism are openly termed the political enemy. With Anschütz, however, the value neutrality of a still only functional system of legality is taken to the extreme of absolute neutrality toward itself and offers the legal means for the elimination of legality per se. Hence, value neutrality here is pushed to the point of system suicide.[4] Anything [1958/302] is legal, without presuppositions or conditions, that is passed by way of simple statutes or those amending the constitution, more specifically, that really means "everything without regard to content and political significance," as Anschütz himself says.

When this form of value neutrality is the dominant and "traditional" theory, there are no unconstitutional goals. Any goal, however revolutionary or reactionary, disruptive, hostile to the state or to Germany, or even godless, is permitted and may not be robbed of the chance to be obtained via legal means. Any limitation of or restraint on this opportunity would be unconstitutional. I would like to stress in regard to the many consultants' reports and court judgments about the legality or illegality of National Socialist organizations, about the civil service law and labor law evaluation of the membership in such organizations, about the "peacefulness" of their gatherings, etc., that for National Socialists, [1932/51] Communists, the godless, whatever, the decisive answer to such questions should be taken from this fundamental interpretation of the system of legality and, especially, of Article 76.[5] More specifically, they should be given in terms of objective legal scholarship, and may in no way be taken from individual, isolated constitutional articles, for example, Article 118 (freedom of opinion) or Article 130 (political attitudes of civil servants, or, indeed, from individual provisions of occasional statutes or emergency decrees. In my treatise *Der Hüter der Verfassung*

(1931, 113), this view has already been elaborated on in the discussion of the word "neutrality" and its many meanings:

This dominant interpretation of Article 76 deprives the Weimar Constitution of its political substance and its foundation, making it into a neutral amendment procedure that is indifferent toward every content. More importantly, this amendment procedure is even neutral toward the currently existing state form. Under these circumstances, justice requires that all parties be given the unconditional equal chance to produce the majorities that are necessary, with the help of the valid procedure for changing the constitution, to achieve their desired goal—soviet republic, national socialist Reich, economic-democracy state of labor unions, corporativist state organized by professions, monarchy of the traditional form, some type of aristocracy—and bring about another constitution. Every privileging of the existing state form or, indeed, of the current governmental parties, whether it is through subsidies for propaganda, discrimination in the use of radio broadcasters, office papers, application of film censorship, disadvantaging of party political activity, or of party membership for officials in the sense that the current party of government only permits membership in its own party or those parties that are not too far from the governmental parties politically, prohibitions of meetings directed at extremist parties, the differentiation of legal and revolutionary parties according to their programs, all these are crude and enraging constitutional violations in the sense of the reigning interpretation of Article 76, when this interpretation is thought through consistently to its conclusion.

In the dominant "traditional" theory, no parties, aspirations, organizations, and associations can be illegal because of their goals or the content of their goals. To this extent, [1932/52] Häntzschel (1932) is right in comparison with O. Koellreutter (1932, 32), who wants to base illegality on the revolutionary goal. From the standpoint of value neutrality of the functional system of legality of the Constitution's First Part, logic is fully on Häntzschel's side. When the current majority party or party coalition intends to declare the opposition party and its organizations illegal as such, it can only do so by misusing its legal power. With the help of an attribution procedure, which is very interesting in terms of legal history, punishable actions of individual members of an organization are ascribed to the organization as such. Then, on the basis of collective responsibility, one party, association, organization, etc., is similarly considered illegal, which, once again—especially in terms of criminal law, civil service law, and labor law—has a reciprocal effect on every individual member of the organization, indeed, has such an effect on "activities" of individual officials or state citizens. Such suppression of party opponents belongs to the above noted (p. 35f. [1932]) political premium on the legal possession of power. But it is one of the partly avoidable, partly unavoidable causes of the collapse of the entire legal system itself.

The Weimar Constitution is literally divided between the value neutrality of its First Principal Part and the excessive value commitments of the Second. The difficulty becomes yet greater and irresolvable, because in the Second Principal Part substantive goals are set out next to the genuinely "positive" and "effective" value entrenchments, which are not yet positive and valid, but which, nevertheless, should be capable of being rendered positive and efficacious (through legislation, administration, and legal practice). [1958/304] As elsewhere in this constitution, two elements stand uneasily alongside one another. Only later will it be clear who succeeds in taking full advantage of the legal possibilities, but especially in exploiting the political premium from the legal possession of power to use the Weimar Constitution as an instrument and means to their party goals. When the Weimar Constitution gave up the functionalism of the present and transitory simple majority to such a degree [1932/53], it is certainly conceivable psychologically that a deeply engrained, formal-functional legal theory and practice was able to see the Weimar Constitution's Second Principal Part not as a second, differently constituted constitution. But, with a certain inevitability, this legal theory and practice took flight into a new level of this functionalism, held on to the now substanceless functionalism of the legislative state also in regard to the content-rich guarantees of the substantive system of meaning in the Constitution's Second Part, and simply attempted to save the entire image of the "omnipotence of the lawmaker" now all the more decisively with the notion of the omnipotence of the constitutionally amending legislature. Considered more closely, however, it is evident that logically and practically, it is completely impossible to carry over the functionalism of the simple majority to one such qualified majority. The threshold requirements, more specifically, direct themselves precisely against the transient and the momentary quality of the simple majority. In regard to the constitutional law guarantees that are under consideration here, it is a matter of protecting substantively determined interests and claims and, to their benefit, rejecting functionalism and its value neutrality generally, not of introducing the new type of functionalism of the two-thirds majority. Even if for reasons of practical necessity the possibility of interference in interests guaranteed and declared "inviolable" must be kept open, it is not meant as if the lawmaker amending the constitution in an analogous manner should now function normally for the inviolable interests as the legally established legislature, that is, the simple parliamentary majority. Violating interests that the constitution itself declares inviolable can never be a normal, constitutionally granted competence. Also, in the parliamentary legislative state, one may certainly not speak of "temporary two-third majorities" as one speaks of a "current simple majority." A current, simple [1958/305] majority must *always* be present, if this system of legality is to function at all, whereas a two-thirds majority is thought to be available only as an exception, because otherwise no increase in difficulty lies in the qualification of the majority. There can, indeed, be a parliamentary legislative state as a type that works with a simple parliamentary majority, [1932/54] but not a constitutional legislative state as a type that works with a two-thirds majority.

Even an abstract-arithmetic examination shows that the parliamentary legislative state's system of legality only becomes entangled in contradictions with the introduction of such substantive constitutional guarantees and abandons the functional perspective of momentary presence. According to Article 76, a two-thirds majority, sufficient for amending the constitution and present at a particular moment, can pass substantive legal norms with the authority of constitutional law and, through it, limit the area of authority of the ordinary legislature, that is, the simple majority. But by abandoning the principle of the simple majority in this way and requiring stronger majorities, the functional principle of the transitory is also simultaneously destroyed. Under these conditions, specifically, the present two-thirds majority can create lasting effects and obligations, even for itself and beyond its momentary presence, that are unreasonable and unjust under any conceivable perspective. In an undemocratic, even antidemocratic way, a two-thirds majority can place limitations on the will of the people itself, even when it no longer has control over a majority. If the total number of representatives is 600, then 400 votes can decide on a substantive legal prescription with the effect of a constitutional law, such as issuing an alcohol prohibition, for example. If later the number of the prohibitionists falls back under 301, hence still under the simple majority, so that the former two-thirds majority, according to its present number of votes, could no longer have issued the alcohol prohibition even as a simple law, the alcohol prohibition, nevertheless, remains as a lasting, retroactive premium on an earlier, one-time achieved, two-thirds majority, when on the opposing side over 300 votes demand its elimination. Under these circumstances, it is of no use to these 300 votes that they do not have a simple majority, as long as they do not themselves achieve control of 400 votes, while it does the prohibitionists no harm that they no longer have even a simple [1958/306] majority. The number of prohibitionists may sink as low as 201, with 399 opposing votes poised against them. The content of [1932/55] the will of the 201 now compels the will of the 399, only because, under the violation of the functional perspective of the present and momentary, a type of premium on an earlier, once qualified majority is being introduced, a premium that, considered democratically, is senseless, even immoral.

The introduction of norms that are more difficult to change contains a direct invitation to exploit such premiums and to extend inappropriately the duration of the current majority's hold on power. Such efforts come noticeably into view when the substantive constitutional guarantee secures constitutionally a factual or legal position created through simple statute or, indeed, through mere administrative act. Through the appointment of officials, for example, the party in power via a simple majority can occupy the personnel of state administration and of the judicial apparatus. This extension of power can be secured even against the subsequent majority due to the constitutional guarantee of the acquired rights of civil servants under Article 129. As shown above, such temporal extension of legal power beyond the duration of its fleeting presence is also possible with a simple, momentary majority for the intermediary period of indecisive majorities. But, here, it is a matter of a present, temporary majority being bound by a no longer present, prior majority because the constitutional solidification has the consequence of discrediting and destroying the majority principle. The introduction of qualified majorities contradicts the principle of the parliamentary legislative state, which, finally, permits itself to be taken so far that its last, though formally fully consistent, consequence is the legal elimination of the principle of legality itself. The two-thirds majority amending the constitution could use the moment of its majority to decide with constitutional force that certain interests and persons are in the future protected against 100 percent of all votes, and that specific norms are not subject to change through any type of majority or even unanimity. For an abstract, formal form of thought, that is legal, quite in [1932/56] order, and forever placed beyond the possibility of legal revision. [1958/307]

The fact that, with its guarantees, the Second Principal Part of the Weimar Constitution contains a counterconstitution in the first instance stems from the contradiction between the value commitments and value neutrality of the constitutional system. At the same time, however, the principal contradiction is a directly constructive, organizational one, namely, that of a jurisdiction state vis-à-vis the parliamentary legislative state. A constitution that to a great extent places priority on substantive constitutional laws over simple statutes not only changes the principle of the current will of the majority and the legality principle that rests on it; such a constitution changes the organizational structure of such a legislative state from the ground up. In a legislative state as a state form dominated by general, predetermined, thus lasting norms, law and legal application, lawmaking and officials responsible for legal application, must be distinguished from one another and remain separate, and this "separation of powers" determines the organizational construction of the state. Law in a legislative state must typically be a simple statute and a generally normal process of state life. Fortunately, under proper circumstances, one cannot say the same of a constitutional amendment. As noted, passing a constitutional law that is a higher type of statute is an extraordinary procedure. Consequently, in such a legislative state, the constitutional lawgiver cannot simply step into the function of the ordinary legislature, when the latter's position is shaken through the assertion of the higher norm. The distinction of higher law and simple statute has unavoidable organizational effects, regardless of whether these effects are anticipated and regulated in the constitution itself or whether they occur as more or less unintended consequences in legal and administrative practice. Where in a larger radius a particular substantive law complex stands opposite the substantive law set by the simple legislature, as configurations of a lower and higher form, respectively, and this distinction rests precisely on the mistrust toward the simple, that is, the [1932/57] ordinary legislature, the configuration of higher norms has need of concrete, organizational institutions in order to be protected from the ordinary legislature. For no norm, neither a higher nor a lower one, interprets and applies, protects or guards itself; nothing that is normatively valid enforces itself; and if one does not intend to trade in metaphors and allegories, there [1958/308] is also no hierarchy of norms, but rather only a hierarchy of concrete persons and organs.

Organizationally, the legislative state is characterized by the fact that it places the norm, on the one side, and norm execution distinct from the norm, on the other. In this way, the distinctive system of legality should arise, of which one can say with some justification that in it neither persons nor officials, nor even lawmaking bodies, command, but only the norms that these bodies issue are valid. This is conceivable under entirely situation-specific presuppositions. But it is no longer conceivable, at least not as a legislative state, when a qualitative difference is incorporated into the singly definitive concept of norm, therefore, when for substantive reasons there is a definite differentiation of higher and lower legality. If it is not to succumb to a meaningless and abstract functionalism, the legislative state must, indeed, retain certain qualities of its concept of law, but these qualities may not be of a substantive law variety. To this degree, it is neutral in terms of content. However, not only is the lower norm as norm degraded through the previously mentioned, substantively grounded differentiation internal to substantive legal norms; the juxtaposition of law, on the one side, legal application, on the other, and the essential organizational construction of the parliamentary legislative state that rests on this separation, are all put into question. Moreover, those responsible for legal application face cases involving the application of higher as well as of lower norms, and it is possible that, in the internal procedures of offices applying the law, the higher norm will be validated by those at a [1932/58] lower position in the overall hierarchy. When no specific institutions form to protect the higher against the lower law, and, consequently, the organizational boundaries of the parliamentary legislative state are openly ruptured, then it becomes a matter for the organs applying the law in the judiciary, government, and administration to define in the course of their official duties the limitations of ordinary law, to which they are "subordinated," by reference to a higher law. One readily sees that everything here depends on the type and scope, the number and the structure, the definiteness or indeterminacy, of the previously noted higher norms. And with larger numbers and with the more general content [1958/309] of these higher norms, the subordinate legislation's realm of validity is not only quantitatively limited and hemmed in, but also to the same degree the power of the executive and judicial offices responsible for legal application grows in regard to the ordinary legislature. How, then, the executive and judiciary conduct themselves in relation to one another, whether the one makes use of the other or subordinates it, or whether a contradiction also occurs here, is another question in and of itself. In regard to the ordinary legislature, perhaps it then subjects itself to the higher legality realized through legal application in the judiciary, the government, or the administration; that is, the legislature rescinds its statute, passes another, and, in this way, recognizes the higher organs as the new guardians of the constitution. But perhaps the ordinary legislature finds support in one part of the apparatus of legal application, for example, the government against the judiciary or the judiciary against the government, and insists on its standpoint. In the first case, the state transforms itself from a legislative state into a partly jurisdiction state or partly governmental or administrative state, depending on which office makes use of the higher type of legality. In the other case, there develops a series of freestanding, independent power configurations that adhere firmly to their position in an unordered proximity to one another, so long as the pressing need for or the violent force of a unifying decision does not bring this type of mixed state form to an end. In any case, through the fissure of the system of legality into higher and lower forms, although apparently only a [1932/59] quantitative, arithmetic differentiation of the voting majorities is present, the legislative state is shaken deep into its organizational foundations. Divisions, restraints, and counterbalances internal to the legislative process, such as the bicameral system and other complications, do not eliminate the legislative state, so long as one still insists on the qualitative, unified value of statutes that come into being in this way. On the contrary, the distinction between substantive statutes of higher and lower form forces the lawgiver out of the position of central setter of norms, through which the state first becomes a legislative state. This distinction slices like a knife into the comprehensive organizational construction of the legislative state and reshapes it through the fact that, in the course of applying and enforcing the higher legality, agencies and organizations unavoidably arise that are superior to the ordinary legislature. [1958/310]

All the concepts peculiar to the legislative state, such as the rule of law, omnipotence, priority of the statute, and legislative reservation, always have the simple legislature in mind.[6] These concepts also count on a constitution with no substantive law regulations of significant scope, but rather one that contains a fundamental rights section that guarantees the bourgeois sphere of civil and political freedom in general and, as such, stands opposed to an organizational part regulating the process of state will formation. The priority of the statute is the precedence of the statute itself over its application, while the statutory reservation is a potentially broad legislative restriction on a general liberty right. The priority of the constitutionally amending statute, by contrast, is a precedence of one type of statute over another. It is a priority that divides the sphere of the statute into a higher, superior type of legality and a lower, inferior one. The reservation of a statute amending the constitution favors special interests and protected objects with particular content. By lending statutes constitutional status, the statutory reservation solidifies substantive law and the acquired rights of particular groups. Substantive constitutional law, therefore, deviates from all the principles of the parliamentary [1932/60] legislative state, just as it does from the democratic constitution. It is qualitatively different from simple, properly concluded statutes, and it is also evident here that it is not possible to carry over concepts and formulas from the nineteenth-century legislative state, developed for simple statutes, and apply them to the statute in the form of a constitutional amendment without changing the state fundamentally.

In terms of state and constitutional theory, one comes to the conclusion that next to the well-known distinction between states with and those without written constitutions, another distinction comes into play, which is not less "definitive": specifically, that between states with a constitution limited to organizational-procedural regulations and general liberty rights, on the one hand, and those with constitutions containing extensive entrenchments and guarantees in the form of substantive law, on the other. In truth, these are states with two different constitutions or constitutional components, which contradict one another in principle, both structurally and organizationally. Actually, it should be self-evident that the type of state form is determined by its variety of basic and fundamental rights, and that the general liberty rights, both civil and political, of the bourgeois Rechtsstaat with its legislative-reservation [1958/311] clauses permitting restrictions on rights in the form of simple, properly passed statutes constitutes another type of state form, which also stands under the "reservation" that certain types of statutes can amend the constitution. General liberty rights define the social structure of an individualistic order, the maintenance and preservation of which the organizational regulation of the "state" should serve. In this way, they are genuine fundamental principles and, as one said of the principles of 1789, the "foundation of the entire public order" (la base du droit public). These fundamental principles contain a supralegal dignity, which raises them above every regulation of an organizational and constitutional type facilitating their preservation as well as over any individual regulations of a substantive law variety. As an outstanding French public law specialist, Maurice Hauriou (1923, 297), puts it, these principles have a "superlégalité constitutionnelle" that raises them not only above routine, simple statutes, but also over the laws of the written constitution [1932/61] and rules out their elimination through statutes amending the constitution.

I agree with Hauriou that every constitution recognizes such fundamental "principles," that these principles belong to what Carl Bilfinger terms the "constitutional system," which is, in principle, unalterable. We are also in agreement that it is not the intent of the constitutional provisions concerning revision of the constitution to open a procedure for the elimination of the system of order that should be constituted through the constitution. When a constitution envisions the possibility of constitutional revisions, the constitution does not intend to provide, for example, a legal method for the elimination of its own legality, still less the legitimate means to the destruction of its legitimacy. But even apart from the already discussed (p. 49 [1932]) question of the boundaries of a constitutional amendment, one should not fail to recognize the difference between general, bourgeois liberty rights and special guarantees of a substantive law nature. The Second Principal Part of the Weimar Constitution contains an assortment of different types of higher legality, the complete heterogeneity of which has until now hardly been recognized and even less well thought through. It also contains part of a counter-constitution. As a result, there are two different "principles" and "systems" here. Contemporary German public law must come to terms with this contradiction, and yet it wants to remain on the neutral middle road of a value-free functionalism. Consequently, the remarkable result occurs that the [1958/312] fundamental principles of general freedom and property, both pertaining to the Rechtsstaat, have only the 51 percent "lower" legality, whereas the rights of religious societies and officials (in successful cases, even the rights of unions), by contrast, have the "higher" 67 percent legality. Moreover, there is the further consequence for the entire state structure that the institutions and power elements of a governmental, administrative, or jurisdiction state directed against the legislative state become unavoidable.

CHAPTER 4

———

The Extraordinary Lawgiver

Ratione Supremitatis: Actual Meaning—Plebiscitary

Legitimacy instead of Legislative State Legality

The first occasion in the Weimar Constitution for calling into question the parliamentary legislative state lies in the introduction of substantive constitutional guarantees. Through these provisions, substantive principles in the form of values that are set and secured encounter the value neutrality and openness of the legislative state's system of legality, and the legislature is split into an extraordinary higher lawmaker and simple lower one. In the resulting rupture of the parliamentary legislative state, elements of a jurisdiction state intrude. Principally through judicial examination of the substantive legality of ordinary statutes, though in other ways as well, these jurisdiction state elements are constantly at work to ensure that the fissure perpetually widens and deepens. Thus introducing an extraordinary lawmaker at the same time means a change in the originally conceived state type, which is determined by the dominant position of the legislature. But the Weimar Constitution contains still another, second relativization and problematization of the ordinary legislature and its system of legality. The constitution introduces a legislative process in the form of direct, plebiscitary democracy. There are the four cases of referendum (Article 73, 1; 73, 2; 74, 3; 76, 2) built into the parliamentary legislative process, in which the people voting directly on a question appears as the last, conflict-resolution organ at the conclusion of the parliamentary legislative process.[1] In addition, an autonomous, [1958/313] directly democratic, popular legislative procedure is introduced through Article 73, 3, which runs parallel to and competitively with the ordinary parliamentary legislative process, and in which a statute comes about through a referendum in response to an initiative. The substantive guarantees of the Second Principal Part of the Weimar Constitution constitute an extraordinary, superior lawmaker next to an [1932/63] ordinary, subordinate one, more specifically, for the protection of certain objects and interests on the basis of their content, hence *ratione materiae*; in the referendum, by contrast, the people appear as extraordinary lawmaker in opposition to and certainly also superior to the parliament. And their extraordinariness as well as their superior status produces *ratione supremitatis* from their characteristic as sovereign.

In a logically consistent essay, Erwin Jacobi (1929, 233–77) shows that in a democratic state form, the expression of the people's will through a direct vote is superior to every indirect form of expression, thus even parliamentary decisions, and a statute that consequently comes about through a referendum cannot be eliminated or amended through the passage of a statute by the Reichstag. That is fully consistent in terms of the principles of a democratic state form. At this point, it can remain undiscussed whether the will expressed in the general popular vote itself is in every case already the sovereign, specifically, the direct sovereign, or whether this will stands only, as Jacobi once said, "in the general vicinity of the sovereign." Next to the instances of the extraordinary, plebiscitary decision, the Weimar Constitution preserves the overall organization of the parliamentary legislative state, whose system of legality has a different internal logic than plebiscitary democracy. In its Second Principal Part, the Weimar Constitution contains not only a second constitution standing in opposition to the First Principal Part, but also inside the First Part, concerning the organizing of the legislative state, two different systems of parliamentary legality and plebiscitary legitimacy stand side by side. On these grounds, there is no compelling reason to grant higher legal status to "laws" resulting from a referendum than to statutes stemming from an act of parliament. In my opinion, this result would only be certain and beyond question if the constitution had put the plebiscitary system of direct democracy unequivocally in place of the [1958/314] parliamentary legislative state and its system of legality. The constitution undoubtedly did not intend this. While the constitution only [1932/64] organized a "constitutional democracy," it sought to remain true to the idea of a parliamentary legislative state, which was valid simply on the basis of a 100-year tradition as the constitutional state. On the other hand, the constitution certainly accorded lawmaking status to the people deciding in plebiscitary directness. However, the regulation remained stuck in a contradictory ambiguity and incompleteness, not only because a parliamentary decision is integrated even into the people's actual legislative procedure of Article 73, 3, through which again parliament retains the possibility of channeling the plebiscitary lawmaking procedure into the parliamentary process. But, above all, because the different "referenda," all designated by the same term, differ from one another according to the legislative procedure in which they appear. In one instance, a referendum folds itself into the parliamentary legislative state's system of legality, and, in another, it has the distinctive, specific value of a plebiscitary expression of the people's will. The four cases of referenda that decide conflicts, in which the referendum appears at the conclusion of the parliamentary lawmaking procedure (Article 73, 1; 73, 2; 74, 3; 76, 2), are incorporated into this process. Here, the directly voting people are put to use as an organ of the parliamentary lawmaking procedure, and it was already said above that diverse organs (government, first and second chamber, king, and others) can participate in the legislative process without the foundations of the parliamentary legislative state system being disturbed as a result.

Even here, given the democratic foundation, it is not the same whether the king or the people oppose the "popular assembly." According to the well-known argument, especially Rousseau's version, that the representative must fall silent when the represented themselves speak, the democratic consequence is that the popular assembly must always recede into the background, if opposed by the people it represents. But that is an argument of the direct, plebiscitary, nonrepresentative democracy. Certainly, when the representation of parliament collapses and no longer finds supporters, the plebiscitary process is always stronger. The result, [1932/65] however, differs from the juristic consequence that E. Jacobi drew. As remains to be shown below, the quality of parliament itself is changed [1958/315] through these plebiscitary elements. Parliament is transformed into a mere intermediary phase of the plebiscitary system. But the constitutionally provided legislative process and the system of legality that rests on it are not directly changed. On the contrary, one can firmly believe that the plebiscitary decision is a "statutory conclusion" in the sense of the system of legality. Obviously, then, the plebiscitary decision stands alongside parliament's statutory one as of equal, not superior, value. It is already clear from the text of the written constitution that there is a great difference between the referendum of the parliamentary legislative state and one in response to an initiative under the popular legislative procedure. In the first case, the system of the parliamentary legislative state is only modified. A different type of legislature is not established through the organization of a new variety of legislative process specific to this other lawmaker. With the popular legislative procedure under Article 73, 3, by contrast, just such a new legislative process is introduced. One type of referendum belongs to the system of the parliamentary legislative state, whereas in the other "the people" emerge as the exclusive, definitive figure of a democratic-plebiscitary system. The latter, in fact, has plebiscitary legitimacy, instead of the legality of the legislative state. These referenda are expressions of two entirely different state types. Just as one rightly puts the institutions of direct democracy, as an unavoidable consequence of democratic thinking, in a position superior to the so-called indirect democracy of the parliamentary state, so, on the other hand, the parliamentary legislative state's system of legality remains a remarkable formation, both conceptually and organizationally, which is in no way derived from democracy and the will of the people at a given time. The legislative state culminating in the establishment of norms appears essentially and appropriately "purer" in the guise of the parliamentary legislative state than in the forms of [1932/66] direct democracy, which give expression to *voluntas*, not *ratio*, demanding legitimacy and not legality. To the same degree, the logical consistency of a system built on the idea of representation is different than that of the plebiscitary-democratic sovereign people, which is directly present [1958/316] and thus not represented.

If the statute in the parliamentary legislative state forgoes any quality of the law, and yet is still understood only as the momentary decision of the present parliamentary majority; and if in the democratic state the current will of the present popular majority decides, with the constitution incorporating both the parliamentary and popular majorities; then two not necessarily congruent types of transitoriness stand independently alongside one another. From the standpoint of functional thinking that leads to the recognition of momentary presence, the logically consistent result seems to lie with the popular vote. For the parliament is elected for four years, or, as noted, not from moment to moment, and, as a result, its transitory character is constantly present only in the context of a wide-ranging suppression[2] of the transitory, namely, in the course of a multiyear election period. Accordingly, even the logical consistency of functional thinking would arrive at the result put forth by Erwin Jacobi: that the referendum is always a higher form of decision. Nevertheless, the current result of the temporary popular vote is present and momentary in a higher degree than the current will of a more established assembly that is constituted for a longer duration. While the extraordinary lawmaker of the Weimar Constitution's Second Principal Part introduced by the *ratione materiae* specifically limits, on constitutional grounds, the functionalism of the transitory parliamentary majority of the parliamentary legislative state, the majoritarian functionalism is further increased and driven to the logical extreme through the simultaneous introduction of a second, once again differently constituted, extraordinary lawmaker, specifically, the people deciding through plebiscites. Rationally considered, it is quite clear that there is a contradiction here.

The contradiction becomes especially evident in the fact that the double-sided manner of calculating the voting results and [1932/67] the majority numbers proceed parallel to one another without any relation between them. For a statute amending the constitution, one needs a two-thirds, rather than a simple, parliamentary majority. One does not dare demand the same sort of qualified majority of the directly present people during a referendum; the contradiction with the democratic principle of the simple majority here would be all too striking. In this way, Article 76 is satisfied, for it demands only the consent of a simple majority of those entitled to vote in a referendum in response to a people's initiative to amend the constitution. By contrast, for a referendum proposing to set aside a decision of the Reichstag, Article 75 only requires the participation of the majority of those entitled to vote in the referendum, thus a [1958/317] mere quorum or a minimum number needed to reach a decision. Despite the jurisdictional legitimization through the Electoral Review Commission in the Reichstag,[3] the current practice of Article 75 refers this determination (in my opinion incorrectly) to a referendum in response to an initiative. Today, consequently, it is the case that the participants in a referendum are only those who vote "yes." If that is the majority of those entitled to vote, then a referendum with "yes" occurs, which always simultaneously satisfies even the requirements of a referendum amending the constitution under Article 76. Whoever is successful generally in bringing about a referendum, readily and *eo ipso*, has also brought about a referendum amending the constitution. If one's point of departure is that the people are entirely and fully represented in parliament according to the theoretical foundation of the representative system and, moreover, that the constitution attempts to orchestrate the most exact possible arithmetic congruence between a people's majority and a parliamentary majority, then one must ask why the consent of a two-thirds majority is required for a constitutional amendment in parliament, while a simple majority is sufficient for a referendum through an initiative for the same purpose. The logic of the voting calculus is often peculiar, but anchored *implicite* here is a remarkable no confidence declaration against the parliamentary legislative state. Whoever [1932/68] trusts the parliamentary legislator, because he considers parliament an elite, or because he believes in the discussion and openness characteristic of the parliamentary legislative process, must find in parliament the stronger guarantee of reasonableness and justice. Nevertheless, one provides threshold requirements and limitations for parliament, though not for the direct expressions of the people's will itself, about which one has known since ancient times that the people cannot discuss and deliberate. Of the legislative assembly, whose entire purpose as "législateur" rests on the reason and moderation that is assumed to reside in it, one demands a two-thirds majority decision; in regard to the people, which bursts onto the scene in its complete, though incommunicative, directness and emotionality, one is satisfied with a simple majority. As plausible as [1958/318] arithmetic and "technical" considerations for the most part are as long as one utilizes them in abstract purity without an object, the majority calculus of the constitution and its "technology" of political will formation also becomes confusing and contradictory once one considers them in the concrete connection of a system of legality.

In this regard, therefore, the Weimar Constitution also contains two different types of logical consistency. From plebiscitary-democratic considerations, the Weimar Constitution has situated the people in the popular democratic legislative process as an extraordinary legislator next to the parliament as the ordinary legislator and has added some plebiscitary-democratic legitimacy to the system of the legislative state, which is founded entirely on the basis of legality. In view of the unsystematic incompleteness with which that occurred, one cannot discern with rational arguments of legal scholarship which of the two systems is the superior one. The question is, can two different legal systems exist side by side? In any case, one will not be able to say that through a haphazard intervention that explodes the constitution's systematic framework (not only of the fifth section, "Federal Lawmaking," but also that of Article 73 itself due to the inclusion of [1932/69] paragraph 3 with its disintegrative effects), the Weimar Constitution intended to eliminate, intentionally and according to a systematic plan, the parliamentary legislative system, proclaimed with such emphasis and decisiveness in Article 68. On the other hand, the plebiscitary-democratic system of legitimacy inexorably develops its own inner logic. It will be shown below which practical effects will result from this unsystematic pairing of parliamentary and plebiscitary lawmaking. From the written constitution itself, one can only theoretically glean the image that Walter Jellinek (1927, 46) presented very graphically when speaking of a "race between both sovereigns." He adds that in this race, the Reichstag will always win, though it is doubtful that the Reichstag could dare to take up battle with the people. In this formulation, measured with model objectivity, the question at issue found an unprepossessing, though, nevertheless, apt expression: when it is merely a matter of a single race, one may not only ask who has the best prospects [1958/319] of overtaking the other. Instead, one must also keep in mind a thoroughly momentous consequence for the legal system of the constitution itself. For the duality of both types of legislation and legislature is a duality of two divergent systems of justification: the system of legality of the parliamentary legislative state and that of plebiscitary-democratic legitimacy. In both types of races, there is not only a competition of organs, but also a struggle between two forms of law. In this struggle, as in every such race, the current possessor of momentary power, the present parliamentary majority, has a great head start. Yet, as will still be shown, that is not decisive for the final result and does not restore the pure parliamentary legislative state.

CHAPTER 5

The Extraordinary Lawgiver

Ratione Necessitatis: Actual Meaning—

The Administrative State Measure Displaces

the Parliamentary Legislative State Statute

[1932/70] The practice of the President and the Reich government, though contrary to the wording of the Weimar Constitution, brought about an additional, third extraordinary lawmaker in German state life in the last decade: specifically, the President's decree powers under Article 48. It did so under the toleration of the Reichstag, with the acceptance of state theorists, and with the sanction of court doctrine. Currently, it is unanimously recognized that a right to issue decrees with the force of law, even of Reich statutes, is also among the extraordinary powers the German Constitution confers on the President under Article 48. And until the issuance of the enforcement legislation envisioned in Article 48, 5, the constitution supplies the provisional condition established by Article 48, 2, with positive legal content.[1] Two fundamental decisions of the Staatsgerichtshof of December 5, 1931,[2] along with numerous decisions of the Reichsgericht as well as all other high courts, have accorded this practice under Article 48, 2, a legitimating sanction in the jurisdiction state sense.[3] Whoever wishes to judge such a summary legislative process with [1958/320] the concepts of the traditional legislative state and with the slogans of the struggle against the monarchical government's independent right to issue decrees must be wary of high-profile "constitutional violations." But even a jurist who is independent of the party dogma of the nineteenth-century opposition will find it remarkable that an extraordinary lawmaker is introduced here without an express textual basis in the constitution, an extraordinary lawmaker who competes with the ordinary national legislature and who establishes rights that are not only *praeter*, but also *contra legem*, that is, who creates right in opposition to the ordinary legislature of the parliamentary legislative state. For the extraordinary lawmaker's "measures," everything is valid that, according to the theory and practice completely accepted today, the parliamentary [1932/71] legislative state has developed and achieved for its law, including the rule of law as well as the priority of the statute and the statutory or legislative reservation. In the nineteenth century, one had to bitterly battle the independent royal right to issue decrees with the force of law, because the recognition of an independent lawmaking procedure that ran parallel to the legislative process, and yet was separated from it, would have destroyed the parliamentary legislative state itself. Under the Weimar Constitution, by contrast, which in Article 68 pointedly proclaims the parliamentary legislative state— "Reich statutes are concluded by the Reichstag"—the President's authority to make law under Article 48 had been recognized in Germany precisely by such authors, who, in contrast to others, considered themselves the actual guardians and defenders of concepts pertaining to the Rechtsstaat. The same authors also rejected dismissively the elementary distinction between statute and measure, labeling it an "overly intellectual" insight. In fact, all sides emphatically stress that "the constitution"—by which, however, is mostly meant only the individual constitutional legal provisions—must remain "inviolable" apart from seven fundamental rights enumerated in Article 48 itself (Articles 114, 115, 117, 118, 123, 124, and 153), which can be suspended. Otherwise, despite the "inviolability of the constitution," one seems to find nothing remarkable in the fact that the extraordinary lawmaker, who creates law, enters into the constitution's system of legality without the Rechtsstaat-like quality of his orders being considered in any way different from the statute of the ordinary national legislature. [1958/321]

Here, we would have the third extraordinary lawmaker of the Weimar Constitution, that of Article 48, 2. This third lawmaker is extraordinary not in the sense of *ratione materiae*, as is the constitutional legislature, which has control over substantive constitutional norms; the third one is extraordinary also not in the sense of *ratione supremitatis*, as are the people, who decide directly; but rather, the third one is extraordinary, if I may say so, in the sense of *ratione temporis ac situationis*. In the third extraordinary lawmaker, the simple truth of legal scholarship becomes evident through all the normative fictions and obscurities: that norms are [1932/72] valid only for normal situations, and the presupposed normalcy of the situation is a positive-legal component of its "validity." However, the lawmaker under normal circumstances is something different than the special commissioner of the abnormal situation who reestablishes normalcy ("security and order"). When one considers the special commissioner a "lawmaker" and his measures "statutes," there is still, in fact, an important difference despite such blurring of conceptual boundaries. Precisely that conflation of "legislative measures" with "statutes" induces the destruction of the system of legality of the parliamentary legislative state.

In contradistinction to both of the other extraordinary lawmakers, that of Article 48, 2, in no way takes the place of the ordinary parliamentary legislature, but, on the contrary, he is apparently even subordinated to parliament. According to Article 48, 3, the measures of the third extraordinary lawmaker are subject to suspension on the demand of the Reichstag. These measures, therefore, must be "tolerated" by the Reichstag. Considered more closely, this actually reveals the very clear superiority of the third extraordinary lawmaker in the abnormal situation, which prompts his introduction. Because the Reichstag can demand that every measure be set aside, the superiority of the third extraordinary lawmaker cannot be openly made effective against the ordinary legislature. For the question at issue here, that concerning the system of legality, the superiority of a special commissioner permitted to make "laws" lies less in the fact that this type of extraordinary lawmaker naturally has a head start in a race between both lawmakers in extraordinary situations. The head start is certainly very large. By his own discretion, the extraordinary lawmaker determines the presupposition of his extraordinary powers (danger for public security and order) and the content of the "necessary" measures. Accordingly, in the shortest possible time, he can also reissue measures [1958/322], the elimination of which the Reichstag demanded. The Reichstag's suspension order has no retroactive effect, so the extraordinary lawmaker can create accomplished facts in opposition to the ordinary legislature. Indeed, especially consequential measures, for example, armed [1932/73] intervention and executions, can, in fact, no longer be "set aside." All of these are the practically important and significant grounds of a great factual superiority. But they still do not necessarily affect the parliamentary legislative state's system of legality so fundamentally, as is the case in other instances of interest here concerning the superiority of the third extraordinary lawmaker.

If we consider him more closely, it is evident first of all that the third extraordinary lawmaker is superior to the Reichstag, that is, to the ordinary, national legislature in regard to the scope and content of its recognized legislative power. While the ordinary legislature of the parliamentary legislative state is only permitted to pass statutes and, according to the nature of the legislative state, is separated from the apparatus for applying law, the extraordinary lawmaker of Article 48 is able to confer on every individual measure he issues the character of a statute, with the entire priority that the statute unquestionably has in the parliamentary legislative state. Certainly according to a formal concept of law, the ordinary legislature could also pass any given administrative measure as a "statute." But these cases are rare, with such "individual statutes" running into many traditional obstacles associated with the Rechtsstaat and with federalism in the Reich, obstacles that overwhelm the absolutist theory of the "omnipotent lawmaker." In the case of the "dictator," by contrast, it emerges that he is actually a special commissioner and not "législateur." The practice that was only a groundless theory in parliament becomes self-evident in the dictator, and the legislative power becomes a weapon useful for completing his mission. Instead of issuing a general decree, therefore, the dictator can issue an individual order, even immediately and directly, such as, for example, prohibiting an assembly or declaring an organization illegal and disbanding it. In this way, he renders practically meaningless the entire system of legal protections that was built up with great artistry to counter the orders of the executive. With its organizational separation of law and legal application, the parliamentary legislative state [1958/323] forms all its protective institutions that are linked to and distinctive of the Rechtsstaat with a view to defending against [1932/74] the executive. But for the extraordinary law-maker of Article 48, the distinction between statute and statutory application, legislative and executive, is neither legally nor factually an obstacle. The extraordinary lawmaker combines both in his person. Also, action that would otherwise only be an act of legal application has "legislative" character when he so determines. As the lawmaker of Article 48, he can directly issue an order that would "in itself" constitute a police ruling that could be understood as stemming from legal norms governing police action, thereby evading the administrative law instruments established to provide legal recourse against the police.[4] The presidential decree for the Security of State Authority of April 13, 1932, contains an application of such a possibility, which immediately dissolved, by name, the Storm Troopers (SA) and Security Department (SS), etc., of the National Socialist German Workers Party,[5] while the second decree for the Security of State Authority of May 3, 1932, speaks generally of "political associations, which are militarily organized or act as such," and envisions opportunities for legal petitions.[6] The President is free to intervene in the entire system of existing statutory norms and use it for his own purposes. He can also issue general norms and order on his own authority new special institutions and create extraordinary enforcement organs for their application and execution. In other words, he unites in himself lawmaking and legal execution and can enforce directly the norms he establishes, which the ordinary legislature of the parliamentary legislative state cannot do, so long as it respects the separation of powers with its distinction between law and legal application so essential for the legislative state.

Besides the power to issue extraordinary measures, Article 48, 2, 2, grants this exceptional lawmaker the unusual authority to set aside seven fundamental rights. The suspension of fundamental rights is not, as one might presume, a formal procedure. As G. Anschütz (1912, 227) states, it is entirely "deformalized." According to the interpretation of the Reichsgericht,[7] [1932/75] a suspension of fundamental rights must in no way be [1958/324] explicit or preemptive. In the formulaic references to Article 48, 2, there is already a sufficient and legally effective announcement of the intention to set aside the previously mentioned fundamental rights. This means that these fundamental rights, among which in particular are personal freedom (Article 114) and property (Article 153), or the core of the bourgeois Rechtsstaat, are simply not available to the extraordinary lawmaker of Article 48. If one remembers that prewar German state theory considered it necessary to have a definition of law that designated statutory law as an "intrusion into freedom and property," and that the prewar state theory viewed this "substantive concept of law" with the corresponding "legislative-reservation" as something essential and indispensable to the constitutional state, then one must recognize that the prewar parliamentary legislative state is changed from the ground up, if there is an extraordinary lawgiver for whom these basic rights do not apply. According to the fundamental principles of the parliamentary legislative state, only the ordinary legislature through a statute can intrude in the previously noted basic rights, which are only at the disposal of the legislature by virtue of the legislative-reservation clause. When the constitution provides for the suspension of basic rights in the case of an exception, it intends to preserve for the organ that is not precisely a legislature the obstacles and restrictions inhering in the fundamental rights and their legislative reservation clause. Consequently, that this organ is not a legislature must be presupposed, as is already entirely self-evident, because otherwise the basic rights would already have been delivered over to it through the general legislative-reservation clause. If the parliamentary legislative state typically permits a "state of exception" with the suspension of basic rights, its intention is not to render the special commissioner equivalent with the legislature or the special commissioner's decrees equivalent with statutes, but to create the freedom to issue measures that are necessary and effective. This setting aside of basic rights can only have the sense that a protection of [1932/76] freedom and property, contained in the recognition of basic rights, should be suspended. And what does this legal protection consist of in the legislative state system? In regard to Rechtsstaat-based protection, the unified trial procedures and complaint possibilities characteristic of Germany today were inconceivable in the year 1848, because the entire edifice of contemporary [1958/325] administrative law adjudication was still unknown. But legal protection in the legislative state lies essentially in the legislative-reservation clause, the protective power of which, once again, requires trust in the legislature as an indispensable foundation, more precisely, confidence in the legislature of the parliamentary legislative state, or the parliament that decides on the basis of a simple majority. The unproblematic congruence and harmony of law and statute is also in this regard the existential question for the parliamentary legislative state. For a definite period during the state of exception, certain basic rights, the legislative-reservation clause and, with it, the legislative state, indeed, the cornerstone of the constitution itself, freedom and property, can be suspended simultaneously. Through these actions, however, a new extraordinary lawmaker should not be introduced into the organization of a legislative state. The legislative state with its statutory priority and legislative-reservation knows just one lawmaker, namely, its legislature, the parliament. The legislative state tolerates no competing extraordinary legislative power. According to this system, the "measures" of the office empowered for extraordinary action are not contrary to law, but they also do not have the force of law. These measures need not and cannot have the force of law, because the suspension of the basic rights is provided for and, through this suspension, the limitations of the legislative state, which had made a statute and the force of law necessary, collapse.

If these "measures" now become decrees with the force of law, as has occurred in Germany through ten-year-long governmental practice, sanctioned through the approval of court doctrine and recognized by constitutional law experts, then a new, heterogeneous way of thought forces its way into the constitution's system of legality. The new [1932/77] extraordinary lawmaker of Article 48 can now have power over freedom and property, both by way of measures and via decrees with the force of law. In particular, on the basis of a remarkable double foundation, the extraordinary lawmaker under Article 48 has authority over the substance of the bourgeois Rechtsstaat with its civil and political rights: first, through his equivalence to the ordinary legislature, by virtue of which the extraordinary lawmaker can fulfill the requirements of the statutory reservation for intrusions into the freedom and property of citizens; second, moreover, thanks to the explicit power to suspend basic rights, the basic rights are no longer an obstacle to his measures. The ordinary legislature can intrude on the basic rights only on the basis of the statutory reservation. However, it cannot [1958/326] set them aside. The extraordinary lawmaker, by contrast, can do both and, apart from everything else, thereby already surpasses the ordinary legislature and is superior to it in a novel way.

The practice of the extraordinary powers of Article 48, 2, however, has led to a still more wide-ranging legislative power for the extraordinary lawmaker. In contemporary Germany, the typical, simple, and plausible interpretation of Article 48 takes as its point of departure the view that the President is certainly equivalent to the simple legislature; yet the President can do nothing that is reserved to the Reich legislature, which alone has the power to alter the constitution. Meanwhile, decrees on the basis of Article 48, 2, are issued with the approval of state theory and court practice, especially with the recognition of the Staatsgerichtshof. Such decrees interfere with the legislative jurisdiction of the Länder governments and, consequently, should undoubtedly not have come about by way of a simple Reich statute. The clearest example in this regard is the President's Credit Union Decree of August 5, 1931,[8] which was issued on the basis of Article 48, 2. At the same time, the Reich statute of March 21, 1925, concerning the same subject, the acceptance of foreign loans by localities, and specifically taking account of the legislative jurisdiction of the Länder governments, was issued as a Reich statute amending the constitution according to Article 76.[9] [1932/78] In its decision of December 5, 1931, the Staatsgerichtshof relied on the interpretation that the President is empowered to issue decrees with the force of law even in areas under the legislative jurisdiction of the Länder.[10] The Staatsgerichtshof even recognizes that the President can ignore Article 5 and, according to Article 48, 2, can empower the Land government to create Land law deviating from its [Land] constitutional provisions. The justification given here relies on the arguments of Poetzsch-Heffter and R. Grau and runs essentially that Article 48 contains an "independent grant of jurisdiction" under the Weimar Constitution. This means nothing other than that the ordinary, organizational provisions of the Weimar Constitution cannot resist the extraordinary powers of Article 48. Therefore, they are not "inviolable." Similarly, for the essential organizational provision of Article 87, [1958/327] according to which grants of credit may be extended "only by Reich statute," the Reich government firmly holds the position that a decree under Article 48 can in any case substitute for a Reich statute of this kind that grants credit.[11]

The organizational provisions of the Weimar Constitution are not merely impinged on through this interpretation, which is supported by the prevailing reading in legal theory and practice. They are, rather, essentially changed. That is true both for the just-mentioned provisions about the jurisdictional division between the Reich and Land levels and for Article 5 of the Weimar Constitution, which is fundamental for the law of federalism, as well as for the central principle by which the constitution attempts to constitute the parliamentary legislative state: "Reich statutes are concluded by the Reichstag" (Article 68). All these organizational provisions are now [1932/79] no longer (according to G. Anschütz's coinage) "dictator-proof," because one finds in Article 48, 2, an extraordinary lawmaker equivalent to the simple legislature. In this case, one should at least acknowledge that an organizational minimum must remain inviolable both for the federation and for the preservation of the Land governments, if the entire constitution is not to be overturned by Article 48. In any case, a theory that permits a decree power extending beyond even the scope of the national legislative authority in the form of decrees with the force of Reich laws may no longer designate itself as "the theory of inviolability," in order to discredit E. Jacobi's and my own interpretation of Article 48, 2, as "infringing the constitution." According to our theory, even apart from the seven suspendible fundamental rights articles, not every single constitutional law provision forms an obstacle to the actions of the dictator under Article 48. Just as in my lecture on the emergency decree of December 1, 1930 (1931, 17) and in my book *Der Hüter der Verfassung* (1931, 121), I would like to stress that I still adhere to the previously mentioned interpretation of Article 48, 2. [1958/328] The connection between the President's decree power and the disparate jumble of clauses under the misleading title "Basic Rights and Duties of Germans" in the Second Principal Part still provides for something altogether different than the authority to issue genuine statutes. It is only because of the developments of the last decade that the President's decree powers now include the authority to issue decrees with the force of law. This result is today accepted and recognized as the fulfillment of the provisional measure contained in Article 48, 2, which remains positive law until the issuance of the enforcement legislation called for in Section 5. This provisional measure also justifies the President's decrees regarding the granting of credit, which have the force of law in regard to finance. Max E. F. Kühnemann (1931, 745) attempted to demonstrate that these decrees are unconstitutional in writings, whose insight and profundity are no doubt very significant, but whose weakness lies in the fact that the arguments are dominated by the concepts and presuppositions of the public law of the constitutional monarchy [1932/80] and that they interpret the finance law provisions of the constitution without regard for the entire framework of the remaining constitutional provisions and concepts. The Weimar Constitution has an essentially different constitutional system than the traditional constitutional type of 1848. In particular, it has a concept of law that has not only changed considerably and is no longer unified, but is now also problematical. The resulting great difficulties justify neither Kühnemann's facile retention of nineteenth-century ideas about finance law nor the self-contradictions in which the prevailing theory is stuck when it declares essential provisions of the organizational part of the constitution not "dictator-proof" but the non-suspendible "fundamental rights" as non-inviolable.

For the foundations of the parliamentary legislative state and its system of legality as a whole, it is thoroughly trivial when the substantive principles of the Constitution's Second Principal Part are designated all the more emphatically and solemnly as holy, non-infringeable, and "dictator-proof." This is even the case when in line with the changes in the organizational part of the constitution, instead of those brought about through the "independent jurisdiction provision" of Article 48, the constitutional provisions are not only "infringed," but fully changed. From what should each of the diverse individual provisions of the Second Part of the Constitution derive such power and [1958/329] dignity, when fundamental provisions of the First Part, in particular the source of legality itself, are no longer "dictator-proof?" When the "independent grant of jurisdiction" of Article 48 has the force of constitutional law to eliminate other jurisdictions and the rights of the Länder, which are defined and secured by constitutional law, then the principle of "inviolability" of every single constitutional provision is abandoned. If one acknowledges the necessity and appropriateness of the interpretation put forth by the Reich government and approved by the Reichsgericht, then it is difficult to remain committed to the doctrine of the inviolability of every single provision concerning the rights of civil servants or of religious societies vis-à-vis measures issued under Article 48. Because for a constitution with the content [1932/81] and structure of the Weimar Constitution, that which is law for the Land governments must at least be justified for the religious societies and for civil servants. If fundamental organizational and jurisdictional provisions are not "dictator-proof," every single substantive constitutional guarantee can itself only then be "dictator-proof" when the substantive law guarantees are intended as genuine exemptions and privileges, and the Second Principal Part already contains a second constitution, a counterconstitution. Then, however, the conclusion for the boundaries of constitutional amendment according to Article 76 must be drawn, from which the dominant opinion still diverges considerably.

That the dominant interpretation of Article 48, 2, has entangled itself in irresolvable contradictions has become obvious today. Consequently, Poetzsch-Heffter (1932, 770) rightly demands that one engage the organizational framework, in which the "dictatorial powers" stand constitutionally, better and more systematically than previously. In this regard, however, one must above all keep in mind the previously (in part 2, chapter 3) outlined diversity of the Second as opposed to the First Principal Part of the Constitution. Self-contradictions in the theory and practice of Article 48, 2, that meanwhile have become obvious are, finally, only a result and an application of the previously noted deviation from the principles of the parliamentary legislative state. These self-contradictions also mistake to what degree the Second Part of the Constitution inaugurates another, new constitution. The logical inconsistency regarding the principles of the parliamentary legislative state that lies in the introduction of substantive guarantees becomes [1958/330] especially visible through the contradictions, in which each interpretation of Article 48, 2, not conscious of this connection must entangle itself. The drafting history of Article 48, in particular the development of the previously enumerated seven suspendible basic rights, clearly confirms this. For this enumeration, which first appeared in the governmental draft of February 17, 1919 (cf. Triepel 1922, pp. 8/12 and 20/23), and extends back to the negotiations in the Committee of State Representatives of February 5–8, 1919,[12] counted on a fundamental rights section of twelve Articles, in which [1932/82] all remaining seven basic rights articles other than a couple of practically insignificant general principles (equality before the law, freedom of conscience, artistic freedom and scholarship, minorities) are declared suspendible. In other words, so far as it contains current law or came into consideration in practical terms at all for prevailing opinion, the entire fundamental rights section should be suspendible. In the course of the later drafting history, the enumeration of rights remained unchanged apart from the adaptation of the numbers, while the basic rights section expanded in rapid fashion and became the Second Principal Part of the Constitution without anyone being made aware of the effects that this expansion could have on the previously mentioned, still unchanged seven basic rights articles in the context of a state of exception. During the haste of the summer of 1919, the portion of a second newly configured constitution that arose with the new basic rights section was brought into an organic connection or agreement neither with the organizational system of the parliamentary legislative state nor with the regulation of the state of exception, which was considered provisional until the issuance of enforcement legislation. In view of the desperate situation in which the Weimar Constitution had to be drafted and edited, it would be unreasonable to denounce its creators for such discrepancies. On the other hand, one should also certainly not be permitted to close oneself off from the experiences that an eventful decade of constitutional development meanwhile brought about. Today, therefore, knowledge of the previously mentioned contradictions should no longer elude one.

Basically, the parliamentary legislative state does not recognize substantive guarantees, because it trusts unconditionally the parliament as the ordinary legislature. However, if one mistrusts [1958/331] the ordinary legislature, then one can place the dictator, whom one also mistrusts, in a position equivalent to the former. In this case, it is only seemingly plausible, but in reality senseless and destructive of the system, when the trust taken from the simple legislature is automatically passed on to the legislature with the power to revise the constitution. At least, it is [1932/83] not possible to distinguish among substantive constitutional provisions that are or are not "dictator-proof." By contrast, it would be in itself conceivable and in no way an intrinsic logical contradiction to declare all substantive guarantees of the Second Principal Part sacred and inviolable. Only that would be a different state form than a parliamentary legislative state, which, indeed, the Weimar Constitution is still considered. Above all, moreover, one may not rip out just the bourgeois Rechtsstaat cornerstone of the Second Principal Part, the protection of freedom and property, and deliver it over to the dictator, when as in the case of Article 48 one declares just these basic rights suspendible, while other provisions, for example, those regarding religious societies and civil servants, remain off limits and inviolable. Fundamental organizational provisions, the federal guarantees of the Länder, the traditional consent powers of the Reichsrat, the true "sacred relics" of the bourgeois Rechtsstaat, freedom and property, even the legislative monopoly of parliament, which is essential to the parliamentary legislative state, are not dictator-proof, but certainly the privileged status of civil servants to their personal papers and the preservation of the theological faculties are beyond question! And this right, therefore, would in no way be appropriate because one intends to exempt matters that are politically unimportant and for this reason uninteresting for the dictator under the perhaps reasonable perspective of *minima non curat dictator*. But, on the contrary, because one intended to secure higher interests in need of protection and the substantive guarantees of the Second Principal Part as a qualitative higher type of law, these were removed from the system of legality of the normal parliamentary legislative state.

In terms of constitutional theory, the actual basis of confusion in both public and constitutional law lies in the degeneration of the concept of law. There can be no legislative state without an accepted, distinct concept of law. Most importantly, such a [1958/332] state must insist that law and [1932/84] statute, statute and justice, stand in a meaningful relation to one another, and, consequently, that the legislature's norm creation, undertaken on the basis of its legislative powers, is something other and higher than a mere measure. In a legislative state, whose entire system of legality rests on the priority of such statutory sets of norms, it is not possible to issue a measure as a statute and a statute as a measure. The judge cannot speak in the name of the measure, instead of in the name of the law. "When the judiciary can no longer recognize what a statute is, it runs the risk of surrendering itself to dependence on non-statutes," Ernst Fraenkel (1931, 336) very aptly points out. Article 48, 2, empowers the President to issue "measures" or, as it was put in the 1919 drafts, "orders." The current interpretation declares it self-evident that there may even be "legislative measures." In this regard, a logical deception escapes notice, which is not without symptomatic significance. "Legislative measures" are only measures of the legislature, orders passed by the legislature, but not administrative directives, which another besides the legislature issues. The precise question is whether another organ besides the ordinary legislature may issue decrees with the force of law, and this question can in no way be answered with the help of the formulation "legislative measures."

In other cases, the character and distinctiveness of the "measure" in the theory and practice of German legal life is certainly still known even today and does not constitute theoretical hairsplitting at all. For example, it may count as self-evident that a court judgment is not a "measure" and, vice versa, that under "decree" is not understood a court judgment. Even an author like R. Grau (1932, 279 n. 15), who remains entirely unable to understand the distinction between statute and measure, and who with a brief remark would like to derisively dismiss the distinction as a foolish idea, hastens to add: "Of course, certain state acts must be separated out from the realm of the measure according [1932/85] to their functional qualification, namely, those which are made by the independent judicial authority." Even in reference to the contrast between punishment and a mere coercive measure, a discriminating [1958/333] legal consciousness is still vibrant. Thus the Prussian Cameral Court emphasizes that the coercive instruments of police officials (according to Section 9 of the Prussian Police Administrative Statute of June 1, 1931) should be a deterrent, not retribution, because retribution as the "punitive response" (compensation) is independent of the presence or absence of the risk of disorderly circumstances, that is, from concrete factual conditions.[13] Court sentences and punishments can, therefore, still be distinguished from measures. It is all the more noticeable that the fundamental distinction between *statute* and measure, which bears a legislative state's entire system of legality, is no longer respected. Karl Loewenstein (1931/32, 139f.) terms the Danat Bank decree of July 13, 1931, issued on the basis of Article 48,[14] "at least doubtful," because it treated the bank individually; the prohibition of arrests, state-enforced judgments, and bankruptcy filings as applied against the bank is declared an "unprecedented case in the history of the German Rechtsstaat" and, in this way, causes violations of Article 105 (statutory remedy) and of Article 109 (equality before the law), which do not actually belong to the suspendible fundamental rights of Article 48, 2. What is characteristic of a measure, the consideration of just the singular circumstances of a case, is used in this way to determine constitutional violations, because the action of the "dictator" is understood tacitly as self-evident "statutory law" and brought under the equality clause of Article 109 expressing only the comprehensive, general character of the Rechtsstaat statute. The President should just be empowered to issue measures. If another extraordinary legislative power is granted the President, this additional authority does not eliminate or limit his power to issue measures. But one would legally bar the President from issuing measures, if one treated them as "statutes" [1932/86] requiring equality before the law. In this way, the disregard of an elementary distinction perverts a clear constitutional provision, transforming it into its opposite. Perhaps the fact that one still distinguishes today a measure only from judicial-administrative acts, but not from legislative acts, is a definite symptom that illuminates the current constitutional consciousness of the jurisdiction and the administrative states, while the specific [1958/334] distinctions of the parliamentary legislative state have become uninteresting and unintelligible.

Also, it is not the fault of the dictator that, in the ten-year-long practice and custom of issuing measures, another full right to issue decrees with the force of law has emerged. First, in regard to the emergency decrees between 1930 and 1931, which are based on a multiyear practice, a distinguishing feature of the substantive concept of law, duration, is to be honored where possible. Now, the representatives of "Rechtsstaat" thinking stress emphatically that the orders of the President according to Article 48 are only valid in a single case. Such directives are not permitted to endure. Among the many doubts and objections that have gathered against the ten-year-old decree practice, this reference to the "provisional character" of measures under Article 48 appears central and to be the most persuasive (cf. the confirmation in Schmitt 1932, 162, and in Anschütz 1912, 280). In the aforementioned opinion of December 5, 1931,[15] even the Staatsgerichtshof stresses that presidential decrees "may not be issued conclusively and in perpetuity." But still absent, unfortunately, is the knowledge that the prohibition of "duration" is derived less from the formulaic terms of Article 48, 2, than from the essence of the measure in contrast to the statute, and, according to the idea of the Rechtsstaat (that means, here, legislative state), duration is a recognizable characteristic of the statute. The distinction of statute and measure is mostly rejected with the justification [1932/87] that it is indeterminate and that it is difficult to draw its boundaries. That is an argument of convenience, which from the difficulty of setting boundaries draws a (logically considered nonsensical) conclusion about the absence of a boundary. But this conclusion about the lack of boundaries is adhered to without any logical consistency at all. Following the just-cited principle that certain decrees under Article 48 are impermissible "for any duration," the Staatsgerichtshof continues that a regulation "for an indefinite time of predictably longer duration" is permissible. It distinguishes, therefore, between "any duration" and "indefinite duration," and this distinction may probably still be more indefinite and more difficult to set boundaries for than the distinction between statute and measure. [1958/335]

The current practice has its ultimate basis in the fact that, in the reality of state life, the legislature itself has long abandoned the inner distinction between statute and measure. There are rarely today any parliamentary majorities that still seriously believe that their statutory decisions will be valid "in perpetuity." The situation is so incalculable and so abnormal that the statutory norm is losing its former character and becoming a mere measure. When under the influence of this reality the legislature itself and, with it, the public law theory[16] of the parliamentary legislative state declares all measures of the legislature to be statutes and, in the legislature, statute and measure are no longer distinguished, then it is logically consistent that the reverse holds true. The fact that the dictator is empowered to issue measures also entails extraordinary legislative right. The legislature can put forth measures, and the dictator empowered to issue measures can also pass statutes. In practice, however, the nondistinction of statute and measure will probably develop at the level of the measure. The "dictator" better conforms to the essence of the administrative state, which manifests itself in the practice of measures, than a parliament that is separated from the executive and whose competence consists in producing general, preestablished, and enduring norms.

CONCLUSION

Three extraordinary lawmakers—*ratione materiae, ratione supremitatis,* and *ratione necessitatis*—appeared in the Weimar Constitution and endanger the parliamentary legislative state's logically consistent system of legality, to which, despite everything, the constitution intends to adhere. At this point, the further complications that stem from the resulting effects of the federal element of the constitution should remain entirely out of account.[1] One can surmise that, in such a position, the ordinary parliamentary legislature may not have withstood the attack of three extraordinary rivals. Indeed, this supposition would be theoretically incorrect, so long as it remains enmeshed in considerations of constitutional structure. For where it is a matter of a fundamental political decision on the constitution, which involves the complete state form, the system the constitution decidedly adopts as a principle of construction is always superior, so long as another system just as fundamental and logically consistent [1958/336] is not being established. The parliamentarism of the French Republic, for example, succeeded in making harmless and safe the approach to plebiscitary legitimacy contained in the possibility of the dissolution of parliament under the constitutional law of 1875. The complete "secularization" of the French state corresponds to a logically consistent, liberal value neutrality in confessional and religious matters. For the foreseeable future, a control of parliament through the exercise of a substantive form of judicial review or other methods of the jurisdiction state will not come into consideration in practical terms for the French Republic. Certainly, these French constitutional laws of 1875 limit themselves to organizational provisions and do not recognize the extraordinary lawmakers of the Weimar Constitution.[2]

Despite this, the parliamentary system of legality could have remained victorious even under this constitution. For the deviations [1932/89] from the parliamentary legislative state's fundamental precepts and structural principles that lie in the introduction of the previously mentioned three extraordinary lawmakers are in themselves unclear and, in the constitution itself, not thought through to the end. They contain institutional experiments and approaches that are meant rather as correctives to certain deficiencies of the parliamentary system, which, as such, save this system, but should not be taken as establishing a new type of state, whether or not it is now a jurisdiction, governmental, or administrative state. The previously mentioned deviations immediately lose a great deal of their practical significance when the parliament reasserts its power with a decisive, unified will. Even a simple majority has the means, through its statutes and the government dependent on its confidence, to become legal master of competition in the jurisdiction state without great difficulty. The substantive constitutional guarantees allow themselves to be divided into parts that, due to their unpolitical form, are uninteresting to the present majority, and into others that, because of their political significance, could be subjected to the power of the current majority. The parliament also has multiple possibilities to make the second extraordinary lawmaker and its competitor, the plebiscitary legislative process, practically meaningless. That has actually happened with great success in recent years. Because of the previously (p. 67 [1932]) discussed interpretation of Article 75, sanctioned by the Electoral Review Commission and already considered "conclusive" by G. Anschütz (1912, 400), [1958, 337] one demanded the participation of the majority of voters even during a referendum in response to an initiative. In this way, one effectively eliminated the secret ballot and a democratic calculation of the voting results and rendered the holding of such a referendum almost impossible. It is of the greatest interest that precisely in opposition to this plebiscitary lawgiver, and also on account of the government, one recalls a substantive concept of law and a principle of the separation of powers, through which one excluded measures, government acts, among other things, from this legislative process.[3] Finally, the third [1932/90] extraordinary lawmaker, the dictator of Article 48, 2, can be legally active only so long as the parliamentary legislature tolerates it, that is, the parliament makes no use of its right to demand that measures be rescinded and also does not cast a no-confidence vote in the Reich government that must countersign it. Several applications of Article 48, 2, especially the practice of emergency decrees of recent years, appear as an appropriately used, summary legislative procedure, which is grounded on the tacit grant of authority from parliament. In all three cases, of course, conflicts are conceivable, and yet the constitutional division of power is such that, with a firm and recognizable will, the majority in the Reichstag as the legal victor can easily hold the field.

Nonetheless, the parliamentary legislative state's system of legality is not restored in this way. The current will of the present parliamentary majority has long since only been based on a compromise of thoroughly heterogeneous power organizations, and the parliament has become the showplace of a pluralist system. The pluralist splintering becomes quite evident even during the attempts to create a type of substitute for parliament in the form of advisory bodies, committees, and the like, such as, for example, the President's so-called Economic Advisory Board of October 1931.[4] A logically executed pluralism needs a type of justification other than the legality of the parliamentary legislative state. The bearers of the pluralist system, in other words, firmly anchored power organizations that encompass their members totally in respect to their worldview and their economic and other perspectives, transform all jurisdictions, those of the state generally, the federal system, the localities [1958/338], the system of social welfare law, and others, into points in their power constellations. These organizations form the defining state will, and, for what matters here above all, issues of life and death for them, they cannot allow themselves to be voted down or to be subsumed in a majority through alliances and compromises with other partners of the pluralist system. For the sake of themselves and their political existence, they cannot renounce influencing definitively the concept of the constitution and its interpretation, so long as they exist politically as such. [1932/91] If they become caught up in the logic of a system of legality that is a threat to their type of existence, they must either give up their political existence or make good on a right to resistance in some form. As noted, however, the elimination of every right to resistance is the actual function of the legality concept, and, once again, this is essential to the parliamentary legislative state in a specific way. The powers of the pluralistic Parteienstaat have, in fact, little interest in logical consistency. They gladly remain in the twilight of an intermediary state, which permits them to emerge first as "state," then as "solely social power" and "mere party," all the while enjoying the advantages of influence on state will without the responsibility and the risk of the political, in this way playing *à deux mains*. With this will to inconsistency, the parliamentary system of legality is in no way saved. Certainly, such an intermediary condition invalidates the parliamentary legislative state and its concept of legality.

The same is true of a further, unavoidable consequence of pluralist systems, the denial of the principle of the equal chance. All parties that are not partners of the pluralist system will be denied an equal chance. The result is the same, whether one considers the right, left, or center the guilty party, and whether one has a single party that one can denounce for "initiating" the elimination of the prerequisite of legality. It is also an open question, whether a return to the "pure" condition of "unadulterated," that is, homogeneous, parliamentary majorities would restore the system of legality or whether it would not be more reasonable to expect the worst misuse of the previously discussed power premium and the greatest danger for the system of legality precisely from homogeneous, simple, or, indeed, constitutionally amending majorities. For in this way, the essential presupposition of the legality concept in the pluralist Parteienstaat [1958/339] collapses. A new type of constitutional form corresponding to a developed pluralist system has as of yet not become evident. Neither the actual power of the pluralist organizations nor the reigning constitutional theory of the time have brought about specific formations. [1932/92] Till now, moreover, everything runs in the grooves and operates with the formulas of the traditional system of justification. The parties seek the legality of the momentary possession of power, most importantly to exploit the political premiums and the surplus of powers it offers, but they run up against the system of a plebiscitary-democratic *legitimacy*, set against the parliamentary legislative state's system of legality in the same degree to which they undermine the system of legality of the parliamentary legislative state.

Not only does the President, who serves as the counterbalance to parliament, find support in the legitimacy of the popular, plebiscitary election. The parliament itself also no longer has the dignity of an assembly characterized by specific qualities and that issues statutes in the specific sense of the word. It no longer has the distinctive, independent meaning it should have as the source of legality in a legislative state based on legality. For the election has become a plebiscitary procedure. For a long time now, it has not been a selection in the sense of the presentation and elevation of an elite and the founding of an independent representation. Exhibiting the same plebiscitarian effect, the dissolution of parliament has become a normal procedure with the sense of an "appeal to the people," therefore, once again having a plebiscitary meaning and function. The present parliament with its transient majority is still then only a plebiscitary shifting of gears. Solely for "social-technical" reasons, parliament attains a derivative status in a system of plebiscitary procedures. In view of the President's practice of emergency decree, the German state appears in its present, concrete constitutional reality as a combination of administrative and jurisdiction states, which finds its type of final justification in the foundation and in the context of plebiscitary-democratic legitimacy. The meaning of the plebiscitary expression of will is, however, not norm establishment, but decision through one will, as the word "referendum," or popular decision, aptly expresses. It also lies in the nature of things that plebiscites can only be held momentarily and intermittently; the oft-cited "daily plebiscite," the [1958/340] *plébiscite de tous les jours,* [1932/93] is in reality hardly possible to organize. The people can only respond yes or no. They cannot advise, deliberate, or discuss. They cannot govern or administer. They also cannot set norms, but can only sanction norms by consenting to a draft set of norms laid before them. Above all, they also cannot pose a question, but can only answer with yes or no to a question placed before them. If the people are presented a series of party lists, instead of an answerable question, lists that, once again, are produced in the deeply obscure shadows of party committee rooms; and if the government avoids posing a decisive question through parliamentary dissolutions; then the "election" process itself becomes pointless. In terms of its significance, the process is no longer an election, but rather a plebiscite. However, because of the lack of an answerable question, or in the best case only through a fortunate accident, it does not even become an actual plebiscite expressing a yes or a no.

And, nevertheless, plebiscitary legitimacy is the single type of state justification that may be generally acknowledged as valid today. It is also probable that this can explain a large part of the tendencies toward the "authoritarian state" that are without doubt present today. These tendencies may not simply be brushed aside as reactionary or restaurational yearnings. Of much greater significance is the realization that the cause of the contemporary "total state," more precisely the total politicization of all human existence, is to be sought in democracy, and that, as Heinz O. Ziegler (1932) explains, the total state needs a stable authority in order to move ahead with the necessary depoliticizations and to reestablish free spheres and living spaces from within itself. Seen in terms of constitutional theory, however, the strongest impulse behind the previously noted tendencies toward *auctoritas* lies in the situation itself and stems directly from the fact that plebiscitary legitimacy is at present the single last remaining accepted system of justification. Due to their dependence on the posing of a question, all plebiscitary methods presuppose a government that not only attends to business but also has the [1932/94] authority to properly undertake the plebiscitary questioning at the right moment. The question can only be posed from above; the answer only comes from below. Here, again, the formula of the great constitutional designer, Sieyès, holds true: authority [1958/341] from above, confidence from below.[5] Plebiscitary legitimacy requires a government or some other authoritarian organ in which one can have confidence that it will pose the correct question in the proper way and not misuse the great power that lies in the posing of the question. That is a very significant and rare type of authority. It can derive from different sources: from the effect and the impression of a great political success; perhaps from the authoritarian residue of a predemocratic time; or from the admiration of a quasi-democratic elite—of which the presently organized parties are at most only a surrogate or a caricature. Even a government that seeks support in the forces of the army or in the civil service, instead of relying on parliamentary legality or on the plebiscitary legitimacy of an elected president, needs the plebiscitary legitimacy as a sanction, because there is simply no

other type available today. But the government must also resolve to initiate the posing of the plebiscitary question, and
that with the full risk of failure. It is only seemingly more
certain to exploit the type of superiority that the government
gains through the "failure" of all others besides itself, so long
as the government avoids posing a clear question. That is possible for a time. The mantle of plebiscitary legitimacy is broad
and richly textured and can clothe and conceal much. But for
those seeking support, the appeal to the people will always lead
to some loss of independence, and even the famous example
of the Napoleonic plebiscites shows how precarious and reversible such legitimating devices are. It would generally be a
dangerous error to consider the instrument of the plebiscitary
legitimacy as not as harmful as other methods and to hope that
a weak hand or a diminished will could find here an especially
easy application and a welcome supplement.

In its totality, certainly, the momentary, intermediate state is
characterized by the striving for extensions and supplements.
[1932/95] In unclear transition periods, every government will
avoid posing a plebiscitary question that can be answered conclusively with a yes or no, despite the plebiscitary methods of
parliamentary dissolution. The President's dissolution decree
of June 4, 1932, offers as its justification that the Reichstag "no
longer corresponds to the political will of the German people
according to the results of elections to the German Länder parliaments in recent months."[6] [1958/342] The plebiscitary justification is bound up here with the avoidance of a plebiscitary
question, and the "election" following such a dissolution can
offer no answer conclusive enough to contain a secure political
decision. The entire process is neither a genuine election nor a
true plebiscite, and, depending on its results, it only serves the
government or united parties as a supplement to legitimacy
that is absent. But even the civil service supporting the administrative state understandably searches for such extensions.
The civil service is bound up with traditional forms of legitimacy, whether it is dynastic or democratic-plebiscitary, both
of which are not suited to the new tasks of the state in transition toward totality, in other words, the state that is becoming
an economic state, welfare state, and much else. In this way,
the civil service state is also delegated authority (as, according
to Roman public law, the office that had the *jus cum patribus*

agendi itself received the *auctoritas* of the state) and finds opportunities for this partly in the President, partly through the doctrine of the highest courts, especially the Staatsgerichtshof and the Reichsgericht. But it is self-evident that the courts can only fulfill this function so long as their authority lasts and is not yet used up in deciding questions of political power through the judicial process.[7]

In the end, under the characteristic conditions of such a Parteienstaat, the organizational bearers of the pluralist system can generally only survive on supplements, since they produce no inner authority of their own.[8] Although the constitution demands a government with the confidence of parliament, these pillars of the pluralist system ultimately give the government neither a confidence nor a [1932/96] no-confidence vote. Rather, they find a series of in-between formulations, such as "approving" or "tolerating," as an expression of their intermediary condition between state and party. While they grant no enabling act, they also do not demand the suspension of the decrees issued under Article 48. Even in this regard, they prefer the above-noted intermediary condition. A pluralist Parteienstaat becomes "total" out of weakness, not out of strength and power. The state intervenes in every area of life, because it must fulfill the claims of all interested parties. It must especially become involved in the area of the economy, which, until now, was free of state interference, even if it forgoes any leadership in and political influence on the economy. "A state that in the economic-technical age willingly refuses to appropriately acknowledge and guide economic and technical [1958/343] development must declare itself neutral in regard to political questions and decisions, thereby giving up its claim to rule." Nonetheless, even if it were still quite weak, no state would ever renounce its claim to rule under conditions of the denial and elimination of every right to resistance, so long as it is at all prepared to act as a state. On the contrary, it could even confirm what B. Constant said, that the weak and the mediocre use the power they inherit more desperately and dangerously than a genuine power, even when this power lets its passion get the better of it. Consequently, a weak state also searches indiscriminately for legalizations, legitimations, and sanctions, making use of them as it finds them. In a state form that is quantitatively "total" according to the scope and

92   Conclusion

substantive area of its interventions, and yet simultaneously is a highly fragmented pluralist Parteienstaat,[9] there are clumps of power subject to political influence, in fact, power centers that are relatively lasting as well as ephemeral, all of which stand under the same compulsion: to exploit the moment of their power, to get a head start on the domestic opponent, and to consider every type of justification as a weapon in domestic political struggle. Legality and legitimacy then become tactical instruments that each can use for momentary advantage, throwing them to the side when such instruments are directed against oneself, and that one constantly seeks to knock from the hand of the other. Neither parliamentary legality nor [1932/97] plebiscitary legitimacy, nor some other conceivable system of justification, can overcome such a degradation to a technical-functional tool. Even the constitution itself breaks up into its contradictory components and interpretive possibilities such that no normative fiction of a "unity" can prevent warring factions from making use of that part of the constitution and constitutional text that they believe is best suited for knocking the opposing party to the ground in the name of the constitution. Legality, legitimacy, and constitution would then contribute only to the sharpening, not the prevention, of civil strife.

In such a position and with such methods, residual authority exhausts itself just as quickly as legality and legitimacy, and a reshaping of the constitution is generally perceived as necessary. Even the lowest type of *status quo* interests then will [1958/344] harmonize in the call for "reforms." It would be unfortunate to the highest degree, if in such hands the unavoidable reshaping would also become a tactical instrument of compromise and the great possibility of reform would be squandered with some organizational displacement. To this end, what is required is a clearer consciousness of the fundamental constructive connections that distinguish a constitution from some product of the partisan legislative machine. Above all, one must clearly emphasize the first and most important question that confronts every serious plan for a reshaping of the German constitutional system. It concerns the fundamental alternative: recognition of the substantive characteristics and capacities of the German people or retention and extension of functionalist value neutrality, with the fiction of an indiscriminate equal chance for all contents, goals, and drives.

A constitution that would not dare to reach a decision on this question; one that forgoes imposing a substantive order, but chooses instead to give warring factions, intellectual circles, and political programs the illusion of gaining satisfaction legally, of achieving their party goals and eliminating their enemies, both by legal means; such a constitution is no longer even possible today as a dilatory formal compromise; and, as a practical matter, it would end by destroying its own [1932/98] legality and legitimacy. It will necessarily fail at the critical moment when a constitution must prove itself. As shown above, it belongs among the defects of the Weimar Constitution that even here it attempted a combination through which, finally, the First and Second Principal Parts stand opposite one another as two different constitutions with distinct types of logical consistency, spirit, and foundation. As this constitution now stands, it is full of contradictions. But what lay shadowy and unclear in the intention of Friedrich Naumann, mocked by the raucous laughter of an unimaginative prewar positivism as he proposed his draft of the fundamental rights, had, indeed, a closer relation to the essence of a German constitution than does the value neutrality of a functionalistic majority system.[10] Now, if in the knowledge that the Weimar Constitution is two constitutions, one chooses between them, then the decision must fall for the principle of the second constitution and its attempt to establish a substantive order. The core of the Second Principal Part of the Weimar Constitution [1958/345] deserves to be liberated from self-contradictions and compromise deficiencies and to be developed according to its inner logical consistency. Achieve this goal and the idea of a German constitutional work is saved. Otherwise, it will meet a quick end along with the fictions of neutral majority functionalism that is pitted against value and truth. Then, the truth will have its revenge.

AFTERWORD (1958)

———

1. The crisis then [1932] already involved the concept of the constitution itself. The essay was a despairing attempt to safeguard the last hope of the Weimar Constitution, the presidential system, from a form of jurisprudence that refused to pose the question of the friend and enemy of the constitution. This attempt provides the essay with its intensity in a constitutional history sense. The essay encountered bitter resistance, specifically to its core thesis: that the legality of a party can only be denied when the authority to make constitutional amendments is limited. Precisely this thesis had been rejected as not juristic by the leading teachers of constitutional law and disqualified by them as political fantasy law.

The procedure by which a party enters through the door of legality, in order to close this door behind it, therefore, the model case of a legal revolution, is recognized there [in *Legality and Legitimacy* (1932)][1] and reaffirmed once and for all. I quoted an almost page-long passage from my 1931 book *Der Hüter der Verfassung*,[2] which was precisely a debate with leading democratic law teachers of the Weimar period. Neither long quotations nor self-quotations are my style. At that time, however, it was a protest and an affirmation. The essay's conclusion[3] is a warning; the last sentence—"Then, the truth will have its revenge"— a true cry of desperation. The cry of desperation faded away then. But it would be unfair and negligent to write a history of the presidential system of the Weimar Constitution without fully understanding this essay and acknowledging its fate.

Why did the cry of desperation have to fade away without effect? "This theory that the authority of initiating constitutional amendments does not include the authority to recast the constitutional structure fundamentally now finds express recognition in Article 79 of the Bonn Basic Law and in numerous Land constitutions. Unfortunately, this expert opinion, so illuminating to us today, found slight approval during the Weimar period. The famous commentator of the Weimar Constitution, Gerhard Anschütz, cavalierly dismissed the opinion that constitutional amendments may not destroy the political substance of a constitution with the remark that this is solely a demand that is only noteworthy politically *de lege ferenda*, but which finds in Weimar constitutional law no foundation" (Schneider 1953, 216).[4] [1958/346]

The then-prevailing legal positivism rested on the belief in the omnipotence of the legislature and on the plausible conclusion that, if the legislature is already all powerful, the legislature empowered to make constitutional changes must be that much more omnipotent. This thoroughly dominant theory was no longer conscious of its own historical and theoretical presuppositions. It did not know that legality was originally an essential piece of occidental rationalism and a form of legitimacy, rather than its absolute opposite. Value neutralization belonged to the general functionalization at work and made democracy into a worldview of fundamental relativism. In terms of legal philosophy, this found expression in the leading textbook of legal philosophy, by Gustav Radbruch, the third edition of which was just announced in this year 1932: "Whoever is capable of *enforcing* law proves thereby that he is called upon to define law. We feel contempt for the priest who preaches against his conviction, but we honor the judge who does not permit himself to stray from his loyalty to statutory law due to his contrary sense of justice."

2. That was, therefore, the highly influential legal theory advocated by a leading jurist, who had been Reich Justice Minister under the Weimar Constitution.[5] In a large book discussion article directed against my essay in the *Vossische Zeitung* on September 11, 1932, an intelligent and learned democratic jurist, Georg Quabbe, even used the word "impishness." But it would nevertheless be unfair to interpret this blindness as only the result of a specialized, positivist narrowing and of a professional isolation, as if it stemmed from a specialization of a scientific enterprise with a division of labor. More specifically, it corresponded to the legislative optimism of the previous era to consider the statute not in the first instance as a means of stabilization, but rather as a means of and path to peaceful reform and progressive development. For the Social Democracy, the strongest partner of the Weimar Coalition, something more was involved, what Otto Kirchheimer in his essay "The Transformation of Political Opposition" called the "delusion of the 51 percent majority, which played one such role in the socialist literature of earlier times and served to transform the social order *uno actu*, as with the magic wand" (1957, 67).

But in regard to this "delusion," as Otto Kirchheimer calls it, one would already have recognized it as such in the year 1932.[6] "The answers that Lenin, Trotsky, and Radek gave Kautsky's essay *Terrorism and Communism* (1919) leave no doubt that, for example, principled reasons against the use of democratic forms do not exist, but rather that this question, as every other, specifically, even that of legality and legitimacy, must be answered according to the conditions of the individual country and is only an element in the strategic and tactical measures of the Communist plan" (Schmitt [1922] 1989, XIV).[7] [1958/347] Nevertheless, the previously mentioned delusion appears to have been very resilient. Its traces are still recognizable in Article 41 of the Constitution of the Land Hesse of December 1, 1946.[8] These traces are no longer discernible in subsequent Länder constitutions of the Federal Republic of Germany.

Legality as one of three typical forms of legitimacy in Max Weber's sense—charismatic, traditional, and rational—presupposes a rational normative framework. "When the concept of law is robbed of every substantive relationship to reason and justice and, simultaneously, the legislative state is retained with its specific concept of legality concentrating all the majesty and dignity of the state in the statute, every order of any given type, every command and every measure, can become legal."[9] Legal positivism, dominant in the year 1932, must acknowledge this logic; it even found the logic self-evident.

3. While the legislative state makes a transition to an administrative state, the *measure* becomes prominent, making necessary a clarification of the relationship of statute and measure. The reference to the pure "value," in contrast to the "merely appropriate," is still then only an evasive maneuver before the actual problem. At the founding meeting of the Association of German Public Law Teachers in 1924, the distinction between statute and measure is first treated extensively in the reports on the dictatorship of the President according to Article 48 of the Weimar Constitution. Both the experiences of the state of war and siege during the First World War and the practice of Article 48 under the Weimar Constitution established the measure as a decree with the force of law and the decree with the force of law as a measure. The typical Rechtsstaat path lay in the legislative authorization. When this failed due to the negative majorities of parliament, Article 48 proved itself an emergency means of saving the constitution from a parliament that no longer was capable of passing the necessary authorizations and, consequently, tolerated the decree practice of Article 48.

The Bonn Basic Law of 1949 seeks to reestablish the classic concept of law. For the limitation of basic rights, it only permits the statute as general norm (Article 19, 1).[10] It also attempts to narrow the legal bridge to measures that lies in legislative delegation to the executive (Article 80).[11] Gerhard Wacke (1957) even declares the authorization for the issuance of a measure unconstitutional. In reality, under the Bonn Basic Law, statutory measures are also unavoidable, and it can still only be a matter of recognizing and ordering the development properly. The Basic Law, indeed, even sanctions "expropriation through statutes" (Article 14),[12] that is, the most important instance of a statutory measure and the strongest and most open intrusion of the measure into the statute.

In a fundamentally important essay, Ernst Forsthoff (1955, 221/36) considers the [1958/348] distinctiveness of statutory measures especially in reference to the fact that statutory measures offer other uses for administrative court supervision than do normal statutes. Kurt Ballerstedt (1957, 368–402) concludes that economic law as a self-enclosed discipline does not need the distinction between law in a substantive sense and statutory measure. Nonetheless, with the help of this distinction, the legal problem connected with state intervention in the economy can be more sharply drawn. The distinction is indispensable for the liberty guarantees in Article 2, 1,[13] and Article 9,[14] Article 12,[15] and Article 14 of the Basic Law.

The distinction between statute and measure even penetrates into the statute and led to the distinction between statute laws and statutory measures. What is evident in this is nothing other than the irresistible development toward the administrative state for the provision of social welfare. Legality is a bureaucracy's mode of operation, and yet the municipal bureaucracy that has to provide for the industrial masses no longer gets by with the concept of law, which stems from the classical separation of state and society. Instead, it adapts legal concepts to the welfare state's level of development.

4. In connection with the exposition on legality and the equal chance,[16] a theory of the three *premiums* on the legal possession of power developed: presumption of lawfulness, provisional enforceability and compliance (*obéissance préalable*), and fulfillment of the general clauses. The theoretical and practical significance of these three premiums is so great that no constitutional theory and no philosophy of law may do without them. It was already noted elsewhere that a substantive evaluation of the legislature's constitutional supervision must retain these three premiums.[17] Even a juristically tenable theory of the right to resistance must take them as their point of departure. Nevertheless, precisely this theory of the normal premiums remained disregarded.

By contrast, another type of premium sparked interest at least in the foreign literature: the election law premiums, which bring about an artificial majority in the midst of a pluralistic splintering of the electorate by conferring additional mandates on a particular share of the electoral votes or mandates. Primary examples are the French electoral law of May 9, 1951, and the Italian electoral law of March 31, 1953, that is, the methods of the so-called *apparentement* (Burdeau 1956, 6:251ff.). Threshold requirements and similar preemptive instruments are a type of negative premium affecting minorities, or *subpremiums*, if, in accordance with the model of the technical term *subprivileges*, I may permit myself this expression. These types of electoral law premiums are symptomatic in the highest degree. But they are somewhat artificial, for they are directed at bringing about a legal majority in the first instance, while the just-named usual premiums on the legal possession of power presuppose this hold on power and are just as typical as they are fundamental for every community, so that they [1958/349] demand notice in constitutional theory terms and are not at all settled with general reflections on legal security.

Alongside the three established and commonplace premiums on the legal possession of power and these previously named, more artificial premiums, there are still other, entirely extraordinary ones. These premiums deserve special emphasis here because they are connected with a thoroughly relevant issue, which, unfortunately, one has hardly become conscious of in a constitutional theory sense. This issue concerns a distinction internal to the constitution, which, on the one hand, is a system of organizational and procedural regulations, but which, on the other hand, can contain a set of substantive law rules. In contrast to the mass of other ordinary substantive laws, these rules of substantive law can gain the rank and dignity of higher law through their reception into the constitution. I believe that it is high time to become conscious of this distinction, before the entire preexisting system of the traditional legislative state alters itself fundamentally. In regard to this extraordinary premium, a party or party coalition exploits the moment of constitution-making (for which, indeed, a simple majority suffices), or even constitutional legislation, in order to bind subsequent simple majorities to certain substantive law prescriptions.[18] Perhaps this tendency lies in the course of pluralist development. In any case, its elaboration would help deepen constitutional theoretical reflection on the contemporary condition of the Rechtsstaat and of the separation of powers. The father of the liberal Rechtsstaat, John Locke, in an oft-quoted expression directed against enabling acts and legislative delegations, pointedly remarked that the legislature is not there to make legislatures, but rather laws. Analogously, one can say that the constitution-maker and even the constitutional legislature are there to make good legislatures and legislative procedures, and not to make laws themselves. Otherwise, it would be consistent to issue the constitution immediately as a type of Corpus Juris with a multiyear plan included as an appendix. As noted, there is certainly a tendency in this direction, and constitutions are becoming ever longer. Indeed, the new Indian Constitution already has 315 articles and eight appendixes. Whoever finds that right and proper should at least know that it is no longer here a matter of the type of constitution on whose foundation past European constitutional law and its theory of the Rechtsstaat and of the separation of powers were formed.

The remarks 1 to 6 provide a survey of the historical development of the relationship of legality and legitimacy.[19] The open letter that the leader of the Center Party, Mr. Prelate Professor Kaas, directed to the Chancellor v. Schleicher on January 26, 1933, shows what a highly influential German party and parliamentary faction leader thought about legality and illegality in the decisive week before January 30, 1933.[20] Kaas speaks there of legal constructions that involve the so-called state emergency and postponement of the election date, and he expressly warns the Reich government about "the basic tendency that Carl Schmitt and his followers have toward the relativization of the entire public law."[21] Whom he actually meant by these followers [1958/350]—whether a few representatives of informed opinion, friends of mine then (Popitz, Ott, and Marck), or whoever else— I have not been able to discover. How he informed himself about my constitutional constructions, I do not know. He certainly did not have the time to read my writings or simply to ask me personally. I myself never engaged in the prattle about state emergencies, because I knew that with it the legality of a constitution would only be surrendered to its enemies, and because I was of the opinion that the legal possibilities, bound up with the premiums of the legal possession of power, were still in no way exhausted. My public law positions stem from my writings, not from rumors or cliques, and also not *ex post* through recollections from subsequent, entirely differently structured situations, which first arose out of the collapse of Weimar legality.

At that time—in the decisive week of January 23 to January 30, 1933—it was clear that the Reichstag had to be dissolved yet again. It was still only a showplace for the maneuvers and demonstrations of negative majorities.[22] The repeated dissolutions did not constitute illegality. The only question was *which* Reich government in the impending electoral campaign had state power in hand and would set the premiums of the legal possession of power to work for itself: the government of Schleicher or, as Kaas demanded, a government resulting from "workable governmental combinations," in other words, a newly appointed Chancellor, therefore, Hitler.[23] The power of a Reich government allied with the Reich Commissar of Prussia was so large as to spark reflection on the power position of the modern state.[24] But in the decisive days before January 30, the Reich government capitulated to a false concept of legality, and the threat of new trials before the Staatsgerichtshof had become an effective legal weapon.[25] According to the open letter of Prelate Kaas of January 26, 1933, the appointment of Hitler as Chancellor had to appear as the correct legal resolution of the crisis.

Both the position and the self-confidence of President Hindenburg were affected most deeply by the newly formed means of struggle, specifically, by the threat of a political trial before the Staatsgerichtshof. Among the tensions of mass democratic methods and in view of the possibility of sudden, radical change, this bearer of a neutral authority, isolated by age and experience, had the effect of an untimely opposition. He stood true to his oath to the constitution, but what this constitution actually was he was not able to know from his own character. Thus, as an upstanding man, he permitted himself to be instructed, and this instruction led in the end to the fact that the object of his oath and of his loyalty was only a screening procedure, only a door that had to open itself to the entry of every enemy as soon as this enemy emerged as a "workable governmental combination" and, in this way, made itself legal.

APPENDIX

———

Selected Articles of
the Weimar Constitution

Article 5 (Reich and Land affairs)

State power is exercised in Reich affairs by the organs of the Reich on the basis of the Reich Constitution, in Land affairs by the organs of the Länder on the basis of the Land Constitution.

Article 24 (Convening of the Reichstag)

The Reichstag assembles every year on the first Wednesday of November at the seat of Government. The President of the Reichstag must convene it earlier, if the Reich President or at least a third of the Reichstag members demand it.

The Reichstag determines the adjournment of the session and the day of the reconvening.

Article 29 (Public sessions)

The Reichstag meets publicly. On the petition of fifty members, the public can be excluded by a two-thirds majority vote.

Article 48 (Measures during the disturbance
of security and order)

1. If a Land does not fulfill its duties according to the Reich Constitution or Reich statutes, the President can compel it to do so with the aid of armed force.

2. If in the German Reich the public security and order are being significantly disturbed or endangered, the President can utilize the necessary measures to restore public security and order, if necessary with the aid of armed force. For this purpose, he may provisionally suspend, in whole or in part, the basic rights established in Articles 114, 115, 117, 118, 123, 124, 153.

3. The President must inform the Reichstag without delay of all the measures instituted according to Section 1 or Section 2 of this Article. The measures must be set aside at the request of the Reichstag.

4. In the case of immediate danger, the Land government can insti-

tute for its territory the type of measures designated in the second section on an interim basis. The measures can be set aside at the demand of the President or the Reichstag.

5. A Reich statute determines the details.

Article 68 (Introduction of proposed statutes)

1. Proposed statutes are introduced by the Reich government or by the membership of the Reichstag.

2. Reich statutes are concluded by the Reichstag.

Article 73 (Referendum and initiative)

1. A statute concluded by the Reichstag is brought to a referendum before its promulgation, if the President so decides within a month [of passage].

2. A statute, whose promulgation is requested by petition of at least a third of the Reichstag, is submitted to a referendum if one-twentieth of those entitled to vote demand it.

3. Additionally, a popular vote should be held if a tenth of those entitled to vote present the demand for the submission of a draft statute. A polished draft statute must be the foundation of the initiative. It must be presented to the Reichstag by the Reich government with its recommendations. The referendum does not take place, if the desired draft statute has been accepted unchanged by the Reichstag.

4. Only the President can institute a referendum on the budget, expenditures, and compensation systems.

5. A Reich statute regulates the procedure during the referendum and during the initiative.

Article 74 (Objection of the Reichsrat)

1. The Reichsrat may object to a statute concluded by the Reichstag.

2. The objection must be introduced by the Reich government within two weeks after the final vote in the Reichstag and must be supplied with reasons within an additional two weeks.

3. In cases of objection, the statute is presented to the Reichstag for an additional vote. If in this way no agreement between the Reichstag and the Reichsrat is reached, then within three months the President can order a referendum over the object of dispute. If the President makes no use of this right, then the statute counts as not having come about. If the Reichstag votes with a two-thirds majority against the objection of the Reichsrat, then the President has to promulgate the statute in the form concluded by the Reichstag or call for a referendum.

Article 75 (Setting aside through a referendum)

A decision of the Reichstag can only be set aside through referendum, when the majority of those entitled to vote take part in it.

Article 76 (Amendment of the Constitution)

1. The Constitution can be changed by way of legislation. However, decisions of the Reichstag on the amendment of the Constitution only come about when two-thirds of the legally determined quorum are present and at least two-thirds of those present vote. Also, decisions of the Reichsrat on the amendment of the Constitution requires a two-thirds majority of votes cast. If a constitutional change is concluded in a referendum through an initiative, then the consent of the majority of those entitled to vote is necessary.

2. In the event that the Reichstag has passed a constitutional change against the objection of the Reichsrat, then the President cannot promulgate this statute, if within three weeks the Reichsrat demands a referendum.

Article 87 (Credits)

Funds in the form of credits may be established only in cases of dire need and, as a rule, only for expenditures for recruitment purposes. Such an establishment as well as assumption of a security service by the Reich may only be pursued on the basis of a Reich statute.

Article 105 (Exceptional courts)

Exceptional courts are not permitted. No one may be removed from the jurisdiction of their lawful judge. The statutory provisions on wartime courts and status courts are not hereby affected. The military honor courts are eliminated.

Article 109 (Principle of equality, equal rights, title, orders)

1. All Germans are equal before the law.

2. Men and women in principle have the same state civil rights and duties.

3. Privileges or disadvantages of birth or of status that are based in public law are to be eliminated. Signs of nobility are valid only as part of the name and may no longer be conferred.

4. Titles may only be conferred, when they designate an office or a profession; academic degrees are not affected.

5. Orders and honorary titles may not be awarded by the state.

6. No German may accept a title or order from a foreign government.

Article 114 (Personal liberty)

1. The freedom of the person is inviolable. An infringement on or deprivation of personal freedom by the public power is only permissible on the basis of statutes.

2. Persons from whom freedom is deprived are to be informed by the next day at the latest by which officials and for what reasons the deprivation of freedom has been ordered; without delay, the opportunity should be given them to present objections against the deprivation of their freedom.

Article 115 (Inviolability of living quarters)

The living quarters of every German is for him a sanctuary and is inviolable. Exceptions are only permitted on the basis of statutes.

Article 117 (Privacy of letters)

The privacy of letters as well as of the mail, telegraphs, and telephone calls are inviolable. Exceptions can be instituted only by Reich statute.

Article 118 (Freedom of opinion, censorship)

1. Every German has the right, within the limitations of the general laws, to freely express his opinion through word, writing, print, image, or in other manner. No work or professional relationship may hinder him in this right, and no one may disadvantage him, if he makes use of this right.

2. Censorship is not permitted. However, exceptions may be established by statute for film. Also, statutory measures are permitted for preventing the display and sale of defamatory and pornographic literature as well as for the protection of youth.

Article 119 (Marriage and family)

1. As the foundation of family life and the preservation and the growth of the nation, marriage stands under the special protection of the Constitution. It rests on the equal rights of both sexes.

2. The purity, health, and social advancement of the family is the duty of the state and of the community. Families with many children have claim to compensating care.

3. Motherhood has claim to the protection and care of the state.

Article 123 (Freedom of assembly)

1. All Germans have the right to assemble peaceably and unarmed without prior notice or special permission.

2. Reich statute may stipulate that open-air assemblies require prior

notification and that they can be prohibited in cases of direct danger to public security.

Article 124 (Freedom of association)

1. All Germans have the right to form associations or societies for purposes that do not run counter to the criminal laws. This right cannot be limited through preventive rules. The same provisions are valid for religious associations and societies.

2. The acquisition of legal capacity is open to every association according to the prescriptions of the civil law. Legal capacity cannot be denied for the reason that the association pursues a political, social-political, or religious aim.

Article 129 (Legal position of the civil servant)

1. The employment of the civil servant is for life, so far as a statute does not provide otherwise. Retirement pay and care for dependents are regulated statutorily. The acquired rights of civil servants are inviolable. Legal redress is available for the monetary claims of the civil servant.

2. Only under statutorily determined presuppositions and forms can civil servants be removed from their office temporarily, placed into retirement for a time or permanently, or transferred to another office with less pay.

3. Against every in-service criminal judgment, a complaint procedure and one for the possibility of reinstatement must be open. In the evidence on the personal characteristics of the civil servant, written documentation of facts unfavorable to him is to be first undertaken, when the civil servant was given the opportunity to express himself in regard to them. The secrecy of his personal documents is guaranteed to the civil servant.

4. The inviolable character of the acquired rights and the holding open of the legal process for monetary claims are also especially guaranteed to the professional soldier. Otherwise, their legal position is regulated by Reich statute.

Article 130 (Civil servants serve the entire society)

1. Civil servants are servants of the entire society, not a party.

2. All civil servants are guaranteed the freedom of their political orientation and the freedom of association.

3. Civil servants receive special civil servant representation according to more specific Reich statutory provisions.

Article 135 (Freedom of belief and conscience)

All inhabitants of the Reich enjoy full freedom of belief and conscience. Undisturbed religious exercise is guaranteed by the Constitution and stands under state protection. The general state statutes remain unaffected.

Article 153 (Property, expropriation)

1. Property is guaranteed by the Constitution. Its content and its limits are derived from statute.

2. An expropriation can be undertaken only for the general good and on a statutory basis. It proceeds against appropriate compensation, so far as a Reich statute does not provide otherwise. Regarding the extent of compensation, the legal process in the ordinary courts remains open in disputed cases, so far as Reich statutes do not determine otherwise. Expropriation by the Reich against Länder, localities, or common-use associations can only proceed against compensation.

3. Property creates obligations. Its use should at the same time serve the general good.

NOTES

———

Abbreviations of Works
Written or Cited by Schmitt

CPD   *The Crisis of Parliamentary Democracy [Die geistesgeschichtliche Lage des heutigen Parlamentarismus].* 2d
ed. 1936. Trans. Ellen Kennedy. Cambridge, Mass.: MIT
Press, 1985.

HV   *Der Hüter der Verfassung* (1931). 3d ed. Berlin: Duncker
und Humblot, 1931.

RGBl   *Reichsgesetzblatt*

RGZ   *Entscheidungen des Reichsgericht in Zivilsachen*

V   *Verfassungslehre* (1928). 7th ed. Berlin: Duncker und
Humblot, 1989.

VRA   *Verfassungsrechtliche Aufsätze aus den Jahren 1924-1954:
Materialien zu einer Verfassungslehre.* 3d ed. Berlin:
Duncker und Humblot, 1985.

John P. McCormick's Introduction

1   *Legalität und Legitimität* (Munich: Duncker und Humblot, 1932).
English renderings conform to Jeffrey Seitzer's translation in this
volume; page references correspond to the 1932 edition, cited
hereafter as LL. Seitzer preserves the 1932 pagination within
brackets throughout the main text.

2   The following collections of primary sources from the period, one
focusing on its legal theorists, the other on the history of the re-
public more generally, are indispensable for the English reader:
Arthur J. Jacobson and Bernhard Schlink, eds., *Weimar: A Juris-
prudence of Crisis,* trans. Belinda Cooper (Berkeley: University of
California Press, 2000); and Martin Jay and Anton Kaes, eds., *The
Weimar Republic Source Book* (Berkeley: University of California
Press, 1994).

3   An attempt to grapple with this fact is my *Carl Schmitt's Critique
of Liberalism: Against Politics as Technology* (Cambridge: Cambridge University Press, 1997).

4   Schmitt's critics were accusing him of undermining the consti-

tution and the Republic even before it collapsed; see Joseph Bendersky, *Carl Schmitt: Theorist for the Reich* (Princeton: Princeton University Press, 1983), 167–71, 178–79. The first in-depth, book-length elaboration of this charge was Hasso Hofmann, *Legitimität gegen Legalität: Der Weg der politischen Philosophie Carl Schmitts* (Berlin: Hermann Luchterhand, 1964). George Schwab offered a rebuttal with *The Challenge of the Exception: An Introduction to the Political Ideas of Carl Schmitt between 1921 and 1936* (Westport, Conn.: Greenwood, 1989).

5   See Heinrich Muth, "Carl Schmitt in der deutschen Innenpolitik des Sommers 1932," *Historische Zeitschrift*, Beiheft 1, Beiträge zur Geschichte der Weimarer Republik (1971), 75–147; Joseph Bendersky, "Carl Schmitt in the Summer of 1932: A Reexamination," *Revue européene des sciences sociales* 16, no. 44 (July 1978): 39–53; and Lutz Berthold, *Carl Schmitt und der Staatsnotstandsplan am Ende der Weimarer Republik* (Munich: Duncker und Humblot, 1999). I rely on these studies for the facts concerning Schmitt's actions during 1932, but I draw my own conclusions about the content of his writings and his possible motivations at the time.

6   Max Weber, *Economy and Society: An Outline of Interpretive Sociology* (1920), ed. Guenther Roth and Claus Wittich, trans. Ephraim Fischoff et al. (Berkeley: University of California Press, 1978), 1:311–38, 2:641–899.

7   See Johannes Winckelmann, *Legitimität und Legalität im Max Webers Herrschaftssoziologie* (Tübingen: J. C. B. Mohr [Paul Siebeck], 1952).

8   See Weber, *Economy and Society*, 2:882–95.

9   See Weber, "Parliament and Government in Reconstructed Germany" (1918), in *Economy and Society*, 2:1381–1469.

10 See Jacob Peter Mayer, *Max Weber and German Politics: A Study in Political Sociology* (London: Faber and Faber, 1944); Wolfgang Mommsen, *Max Weber and German Politics, 1890–1920*, trans Michael S. Steinberg (Chicago: University of Chicago Press, 1984); and, more sympathetically, Karl Loewenstein, *Max Weber's Political Ideas in the Perspectives of Our Time*, trans. Richard and Clara Winston (Amherst, Mass.: University of Massachusetts Press, 1965).

11 See Jürgen Habermas, *The Structural Transformation of the Public Sphere: An Inquiry into a Category of Bourgeois Society*, trans. Thomas Burger with Frederick Lawrence (Cambridge, Mass.: MIT Press, 1989), 48, 54, 80–82, 115, 148–49, 208–11; Habermas, *The Theory of Communicative Action*, vol. 1, *Reason and the Rationalization of Society*, trans. Thomas McCarthy (Boston: Beacon

Press, 1984), 19, 140–41, 190–92, 226, 243–71; Habermas, *The Theory of Communicative Action*, vol. 2, *Lifeworld and System: A Critique of Functionalist Reason*, trans. Thomas McCarthy (Boston: Beacon Press, 1987), 358–73.

12   See Habermas, *Between Facts and Norms: Contributions to a Discourse Theory of Law and Democracy*, trans. William Rehg (Cambridge, Mass.: MIT Press, 1996). In his review of the work, David Dyzenhaus astutely recognizes the importance of the historical and conceptual legacy of Weimar. See Dyzenhaus, "The Legitimacy of Legality: Review of Habermas, *Faktizität und Geltung*," *University of Toronto Law Journal* 46 (1994): 129–80.

13   See Habermas, "Comment on Dieter Grimm's 'Does Europe Need a Constitution?' " trans. I. L. Fraser and J. P. McCormick, *European Law Journal* 1, no. 3 (November 1995): 303–7.

14   See Habermas, *Theory of Communicative Action*, 1:265. His target here is Niklas Luhmann. See Luhmann, *Legitimation durch Verfahren* (1969; reprint, Frankfurt am Main: Suhrkamp, 1997); and Luhmann, *A Sociological Theory of Law*, trans. E. King and M. Albrow (London: Routledge and Kegan Paul, 1985).

15   On the demise of the Republic, see Karl Dietrich Bracher, *Die Auflösung der Weimarer Republik: Eine Studie zum Problem des Machtverfalls in der Demokratie* (Düsseldorf: Droste, 1984); and Gerhard Schulz, *Von Brüning zu Hitler: Der Wandel des politischen Systems in Deutschland* (Berlin: de Gruyter, 1992). See also Eberhard Kolb, *The Weimar Republic*, trans. P. S. Falla (London: Unwin, 1988) and Hans Mommsen *The Rise and Fall of Weimar Democracy*, ed. Larry E. Jones, trans. Elborg Forster (Chapel Hill: University of North Carolina Press, 1998). On Weimar generally see Detlev Peukert, *The Weimar Republic: The Crisis of Classical Modernity*, trans. Richard Deveson (New York: Hill and Wang, 1992); and, in a comparative context, Charles S. Maier, *Recasting Bourgeois Europe: Stabilization in France, Germany, and Italy in the Decade after World War I* (Princeton: Princeton University Press, 1975). I rely on these accounts in the historical summary below.

16   See Diethart Kerbs and Henrick Stahr, *Berlin 1932: Das letzte Jahr der ersten deutschen Republik* (Berlin: Hentrich, 1992).

17   Carl Schmitt, *The Concept of the Political* (1932), trans. George Schwab, with a foreword by Tracy Strong (Chicago: University of Chicago Press, 1996).

18   See Schmitt, "Legalität und gleicher Chance politischer Machtgewinnung," *Deutsches Volkstum* 2 (July 1932): 557–64.

19   See Schmitt, "Der Missbrauch der Legalität," *Tägliche Rundschau*, July 19, 1932.

20 The events leading up to the coup of July 20, the details of the ensuing court case, and the conceptual issues involved are treated extensively by David Dyzenhaus in *Legality and Legitimacy: Carl Schmitt, Hans Kelsen, and Hermann Heller in Weimar* (Oxford: Oxford University Press, 1997), 28–37; and in "Legal Theory in the Collapse of Weimar: Contemporary Lesson?" *American Political Science Review* 91 (1997): 121–34.

21 Ellen Kennedy explores the historical and theoretical ramifications of the crucial but often neglected Schmitt-Popitz relationship in *Constitutional Failure: Carl Schmitt in Weimar* (Durham: Duke University Press, forthcoming).

22 See Thomas Childers, "Proletarization and Collapse: The Elections of 1932," in Childers, *The Nazi Voter: The Social Foundations of Fascism in Germany, 1919–1933* (Chapel Hill: University of North Carolina Press, 1983), 192–261.

23 See his introduction to the edition of the book reprinted in Schmitt, *Verfassungsrechtliche Aufsätze aus den Jahren 1924–1954: Materialien zu einer Verfassungslehre* (Berlin: Duncker und Humblot, 1958), 345–50.

24 See Carl Schmitt, *The Crisis of Parliamentary Democracy* (1923/1926), trans. Ellen Kennedy (Cambridge, Mass.: MIT Press, 1985).

25 For a more progressive, distinctly juridical reinterpretation of the typology of regimes, see Jeremy Waldron, *The Law* (London: Routledge, 1990).

26 See Carl Schmitt, "Die Wendung zum totalen Staat" (1931), in *Positionen und Begriffe im Kampf mit Weimar-Genf-Versailles: 1923–1939* (Hamburg: Hanseatische Verlagsanstalt, 1940), 146–57.

27 This aspect of Schmitt's theoretical strategy is well covered in William E. Scheuerman, *Carl Schmitt: The End of Law* (New York: Rowman and Littlefield, 1999).

28 Weimar was a novel socioeconomic experiment that progressively unraveled; see Mary Nolan, *Visions of Modernity: Fordism and Economic Reform in the Weimar Republic* (Oxford: Oxford University Press, 1994). On industrial policy in the era, see Gary Herrigel, *Industrial Constructions: The Sources of German Industrial Power* (Cambridge: Cambridge University Press, 1996); on social policy, see Young-Sun Hong, *Welfare, Modernity, and the Weimar State, 1919–1933* (Princeton: Princeton University Press, 1998). See also the review of Hong by Michael Geyer in the *Journal of Modern History* 72, no. 3 (September 2000): 832–34. For his part, Schmitt often revealed himself as opposing redistribution on principled, not merely structural, grounds. Note his opposition to the proposed expropriation and general redistribution of princely properties by the Republic; see Schmitt, *Unabhängig-*

keit der Richter, Gleichheit vor dem Gesetz und Gewährleistung des Privateigentums nach der Weimar Verfassung: Ein Rechtsgutachten zu den Gesetzentwürfen über die Vermögensauseinandersetzung mit den früher regierenden Fürstenhäusern (Berlin: Walter de Gruyter, 1926). A plebiscite on the proposal failed in 1926.

29 See Carl Schmitt, *Political Theology: Four Chapters on the Concept of Sovereignty* (1922), trans. George Schwab (Cambridge, Mass.: MIT Press, 1985); and Schmitt, "The Liberal Rule of Law" (1928), in Jacobson and Schlink, *Weimar*, 294–300.

30 Caldwell painstakingly demonstrates how profound a rupture this transition from the nineteenth-century statutory legal model to the twentieth-century parliamentary one was experienced by Weimar jurists, including Schmitt; see Peter C. Caldwell, *Popular Sovereignty and the Crisis of German Constitutional Law: The Theory and Practice of Weimar Constitutionalism* (Durham: Duke University Press, 1997). See also Ulrich K. Preuß, "Die Weimarer Republik—ein Laboratorium für verfassungsrechtliches Denken," in *Metamorphosen des Politischen: Grundfragen der politischen Einheitsbildung seit den zwanziger Jahren*, ed. Andreas Gödel, Dirk van Laak and Ingeborg Villinger (Berlin: Akademie, 1995), 182–96; Bernhard Schlink and Arthur J. Jacobson, "Constitutional Crisis: The German and the American Experience," in Jacobson and Schlink, *Weimar*, 16–18; and Stefan Korioth, "Introduction: The Shattering of Methods in Late Wilhelmine Germany," in Jacobson and Schlink, *Weimar*, 41–50.

31 Weber, "Parliament and Government in Reconstructed Germany."

32 Perhaps with the Reich coup against Prussia in mind, Schmitt is quick to assert that the bureaucracies of the individual *Länder* are not of the same virtuous standing as the Reich bureaucracy. They are territories occupied by the liberal-legally infected parties (LL 17), as opposed to the national administration, that, like the President, reflects a genuine general will.

33 See Bruce Ackerman, *We the People*, vol. 1, *Foundations* (Cambridge, Mass.: Harvard University Press, 1991); Stephen Holmes, *Passions and Constraint: On the Theory of Liberal Democracy* (Chicago: University of Chicago Press, 1995); and Habermas, *Between Facts and Norms.*

34 A recent study of the social bases of parliamentary deadlock in Weimar is Sheri Berman, *The Social Democratic Moment: Ideas and Politics in the Making of Interwar Europe* (Cambridge, Mass.: Harvard University Press, 1998).

35 Compare the passage above with any number in, for instance, Leo

Strauss, *Natural Right and History* (Chicago: University of Chicago Press, 1953), especially chap. 2.

36 On Schmitt's contribution to the elitist model of democracy, see Scheuerman, *Carl Schmitt: The End of Law*, 183–208.

37 Schmitt elaborated his notion of the President as protector of the constitution in a book of that name from the previous year: *Der Hüter der Verfassung* (Tübingen: J. C. B. Mohr [Paul Siebeck], 1931).

38 This invisible will was first discerned and explicated in Schmitt's study of the Weimar Constitution, *Verfassungslehre* (1928; reprint, Berlin: Duncker und Humblot, 1989).

39 As Schmitt well knew; see his *Die Diktatur: Von den Anfängen des modernen Souveränitätsgedankens bis zum proletarischen Klassenkampf* (1922; reprint, Berlin: Duncker und Humblot, 1989).

40 I have attempted to show elsewhere that this transformation is Schmitt's deliberate strategy in the shift from *Die Diktatur* to *Political* Theology, written only months later. See John P. McCormick, "The Dilemmas of Dictatorship: Carl Schmitt and Constitutional Emergency Powers," in *Law as Politics*, ed. David Dyzenhaus (Durham: Duke University Press, 1998), 217–51.

41 On Schmitt's merits as a scholar of comparative constitutionalism, see Jeffrey Seitzer, *Comparative History and Legal Theory: Carl Schmitt in the First German Democracy* (Westport, Conn.: Greenwood, 2001).

42 In this vein, it is not surprising to find the figures of Odysseus and Caligari playing an important part in the Frankfurt School critique of fascist "democracy." See T. W. Adorno and Max Horkheimer, *Dialectic of Enlightenment* (1944) trans. John Cumming (London: Verso, 1997); and Siegfried Kracauer, *From Caligari to Hitler: A Psychological History of German Film* (Princeton: Princeton University Press, 1947).

43 Caldwell shows how postwar natural law jurists blamed the collapse of Weimar on the purported easy formalism and sheer value neutrality of legal positivism rather than on the concrete strategies of conservative lawyers like Schmitt who were pursuing substantive legal agendas. See Peter C. Caldwell, "Legal Positivism and Weimar Democracy," *American Journal of Jurisprudence* 39 (1994): 273–301. More familiar to American audiences are Strauss's charges that the empty nihilism of Weimar democracy undermined the Republic rather than specific tampering with the latter by forces with whom Strauss was likely quite sympathetic. See Leo Strauss, "Autobiographical Preface" (1965) in *Spinoza's Critique of Religion* (1931), trans. Elsa M. Sinclair (New

York: Schocken, 1965), 1–34. This work also contains the English translation of Strauss's 1932 review of Schmitt's *The Concept of the Political* (331–51), a text that Strauss's students claim demonstrates the significant differences between the two thinkers, but that I have suggested emphasizes their profound commonalties. See John P. McCormick, "Fear, Technology, and the State: Carl Schmitt, Leo Strauss, and the Revival of Hobbes in Weimar and National Socialist Germany," *Political Theory* 22, no. 4 (November 1994): 619–52.

Carl Schmitt's Introduction

1 [In the Weimar context, the term *Staatsrecht* refers to the organization and operation of state organs. There is some overlap, therefore, with contemporary constitutional law (*Verfassungsrecht*). However, because Staatsrecht in the Weimar period did not involve constitutional rights, it would be misleading to see it as equivalent to constitutional law, as suggested by Carl Crefield et al, eds., *Rechtswörterbuch* (Munich: C. H. Beck, 2000), 1231. The largely unfamiliar literal rendering "state law" might obscure the limited range of the concept's meaning. I have opted for "public law," though with an important caveat. Germans have a specific term for public law, *öffentliches Recht*, which includes constitutional and state law as well as administrative law (*Verwaltungsrecht*). The reader should keep in mind that unless otherwise indicated, "public law" is a rendering of Staatsrecht, not öffentliches Recht. For a history of Staatsrecht that indicates the range of meaning of the term, see Gerhard Anschütz and Richard Thoma, eds., *Handbuch des Deutschen Staatsrecht* (Tübingen: J. C. B. Mohr [Paul Siebeck], 1930–32), 1:1–95. Trans.]

2 [The paralysis of parliament was a central political problem of the Weimar Republic. From its inception, the Republic was besieged by radical opponents from both the right and left and never enjoyed widespread, wholehearted support. After the early breakdown of the Weimar Coalition that founded the Republic, it was always difficult to build and maintain workable majorities in the national parliament, the Reichstag. This was even the case in the Republic's so-called middle period from 1924 to 1929, when there was a reasonable degree of political stability. But it presented acute problems in the first and second extended crises of the Republic (1918–23 and 1930–33), when the Reich government ruled by presidential emergency decrees under Article 48 and several enabling acts passed by the Reichstag.

Detlev J. K. Peukert, *The Weimar Republic*, trans. Richard Deveson (London: Penguin Books, 1991), is a good short history of
the period. For an overview and analysis of the political history of the Weimar Republic, see Eberhard Kolb, *The Weimar Republic*, trans. P. S. Falla (London: Routledge, 1998). On the role
of economic scarcity and finance problems in the Republic's
governability problems, see Charles Maier, *Recasting Bourgeois
Europe: Stabilization in France, Germany, and Italy in the Decade after World War I* (1975; reprint, Princeton: Princeton University Press, 1988), 483–515; and David Abraham, *The Collapse
of the Weimar Republic: Political Economy and Crisis*, 2d ed.
(New York: Holmes and Meier, 1986). On the role of Schmitt in
the Republic's final crisis, see David Dyzenhaus, *Legality and
Legitimacy: Carl Schmitt, Hans Kelsen, and Hermann Heller in
Weimar* (Oxford: Clarendon Press, 1997), 17–37; and Lutz Berthold, *Carl Schmitt und der Staatsnotstandsplan am Ende der
Weimarer Republik* (Berlin: Duncker und Humblot, 1999). Trans.]

3   [Subsequent notes will discuss in more detail features of German state theory and constitutionalism that are important for
Schmitt's argument. However, a brief sketch of the institutional
changes introduced by the Weimar Constitution is appropriate at
the outset.

The unification of Germany under Bismarck's Reich Constitution in 1871 was achieved by combining elements of the traditional German state and democratic reforms. The new national
parliament, the Reichstag, was elected by universal manhood suffrage. As the lower house of parliament, the Reichstag could introduce legislation, and proposed legislation, including the annual
budget, required its approval. Nonetheless, it did not mark the ad-
vent of a unified, fully democratic German polity, for the true center of authority remained the executive branch, particularly the
plural executive in the upper house of parliament, the Bundesrat.

Composed of delegations of the various state governments, the
Bundesrat voted on proposed statutes, including constitutional
amendments, and supervised the administration of Reich statutes. In fact, the Bundesrat, not the Kaiser, had the veto power
over legislation passed by the Reichstag. The Kaiser, however,
appointed the Chancellor, who chaired the Bundesrat, and the
Chancellor was responsible to the Kaiser, not the Reichstag. With
the consent of the Bundesrat, the Kaiser could declare war; he was
commander of the armed forces and opened and closed the ses-
sions of both houses of parliament.

The rise of mass political parties at the end of the nineteenth
century, particularly the Social Democrats, and the correspond-

ing political decline of the bourgeoisie did not bring about fundamental changes in the system. Because only fourteen votes were required to block a constitutional amendment in the Bundesrat, Prussia was able to prevent any significant change in the system. And, until the Weimar Republic, conservatives controlled the Prussian delegation due to the Prussian three-tiered electoral system weighted heavily in favor of the wealthy, providing conservatives disproportionate political influence in the system overall.

The basic dualistic structure took on a new form with the collapse of the monarchy after World War I. Under the Weimar Constitution, the upper house, now the Reichsrat, had a much less important position. It remained composed of Land delegations, with an undivided Prussia still the largest by far. However, the Prussian provinces were now empowered to select some of the Prussian delegation, reducing the power of the Prussian government, and the Prussian tripartite electoral system was eliminated, lessening the hold of conservatives on the Land government. More importantly, the Reichsrat no longer had a role in adjudicating constitutional disputes among Länder, this role having been shifted to the new Staatsgerichtshof and the existing Reichsgericht. Also, the Reichsrat could only object to Reichstag legislation by exercising a suspensive veto that could be overriden by a two-thirds Reichstag majority or by a referendum. The Reichsrat was reduced to advising the Reich government on proposed legislation and supervising administration that affected Land affairs.

Rather than concentrating all authority in the Reichstag, the Weimar Constitution divided authority between the Reichstag, on the one hand, and the President and the Reich government, on the other. The Reichstag, elected by universal suffrage in a system of proportional representation, had the power of initiative for both ordinary legislation and constitutional amendments, could pass a vote of no confidence in the Reich government, and demand the presence of its ministers to answer questions about the exercise of their lawful authority. The Reichstag could also demand a recall vote for the President, order the suspension of presidential action taken under Article 48, and, by petition of one hundred members, compel the President to appear before the Staatsgerichtshof regarding an alleged violation of law on his part, a power the Reichstag did not have in regard to the Kaiser.

In formal terms, the Reichstag had the authority to enforce its will against the President and the Reich government. The President's powers, however, were considerable and well adapted to use in times of political instability and parliamentary paralysis.

Besides appointing the Chancellor, the President was commander in chief of the armed forces, which, under Article 48, he could use to enforce Reich law against the Länder and keep domestic peace and restore order. The President could also dissolve parliament and call for new elections, though not twice for the same reason. The authority to dissolve parliament at key points proved an effective means of countering parliamentary efforts to control the exercise of presidential emergency powers.

On the German concept of the state, see Rupert Emerson, *State and Sovereignty in Modern Germany* (1928; reprint, Westport, Conn.: Hyperion Press, 1979); and Leonard Krieger, *The German Idea of Freedom: History of a Political Tradition* (Boston: Beacon Press, 1957). Ernst Wolfgang Böckenförde, "Die Bedeutung der Unterscheidung von Staat und Gesellschaft im demokratischen Sozialstaat der Gegenwart," in *Recht, Staat, Freiheit: Studien zur Rechtsphilosophie, Staatstheorie und Verfassungsgeschichte* (Frankfurt am Main: Suhrkamp, 1991), provides a history of the state/society distinction. On the German political system in the Reich and Weimar periods, see Peter C. Caldwell, *Popular Sovereignty and the Crisis of German Constitutional Law: The Theory and Practice of Weimar Constitutionalism* (Durham, N.C.: Duke University Press, 1997), 23, 27, 68, 70. Trans.]

4 [The dominant form of legal theory in the prewar era was "statutory" legal positivism. Shaped in the second half of the nineteenth century by Carl Friedrich von Gerber and Paul Laband and represented in the Weimar period by Gerhard Anschütz and others, statutory legal positivism viewed formal statutes of the duly constituted Reichstag as the sole source of law. Other forms of law, such as customary law, which were given priority in previous eras, were clearly subordinate to formal statutes during the Reich. And if formal statutes were passed according to established procedure, they were valid regardless of their substantive content. Caldwell, *Popular Sovereignty*, 13–16, 36–39. Trans.]

5 [Following common practice, the term "Rechtsstaat" will remain in the original German. Much of German legal and political theory concerns the meaning of this term and its significance for law, politics, and society in Germany. This is also true of the present work. Offering an awkward locution might cause confusion, as Schmitt seeks to define the term himself.

Like the Anglo-American idea of the rule of law, the Rechtsstaat entails legal limitations on the conduct of government. An important difference is that the rule of law involves the consent of the governed in some form, whether expressed in terms of democratic control of the state or more implicitly, such as in the tacit acceptance of common-law principles. The Rechtsstaat concept, by contrast, did not always necessarily entail consent of the governed at all. Limitations on the conduct of state action in early nineteenth-century Germany, for example, were conceived as acts of grace by monarchs and their governments. Though the monarchs need not have granted political and civil rights, once conferred on the citizenry these legal limitations were genuine restraints on state action. Over the course of the nineteenth century, Germans received significant degrees of legal protection from arbitrary state action, even though they often did not have full rights of political participation in a democratic government. Because the state could define itself only through law, it expanded the sphere of law as it extended the reach of its own authority, perfecting the Rechtsstaat idea without ever becoming fully democratic.

For leading nineteenth-century understandings of the concept, see Robert von Mohl, *Das Staatsrecht des Königreich Württemberg* (Tübingen, 1829), 1:8; and Friedrich Julius Stahl, *Die Philosophie des Rechts* (1837), vol. 2, sec. 36. Konrad Hesse, "Der Rechtsstaat im Verfassungssystem des Grundgesetzes," in *Staatverfassung und Kirchenordnung: Festgabe für Rudolf Smend zum 80 Geburtstag am 15 Januar 1962*, ed. Konrad Hesse, Siegfried Reicke, and Ulrich Scheuner (Tübingen: J. C. B. Mohr [Paul Siebeck], 1962), is an influential contemporary account of the more directly legal aspects of the Rechtsstaat. On its history, see E. W. Böckenförde, "Entstehung und Wandel des Rechtsstaatsbegriffs," in *Recht, Staat, Freiheit*; and Ingeborg Maus, "Entwicklung und Funktionswandel der Theorie des bürgerlichen Rechtsstaats," in *Rechtstheorie und Politische Theorie im Industriekapitalismus* (Munich: Wilhelm Fink, 1986). Trans.]

6 [The concept of state types also figures prominently in *Der Hüter der Verfassung*. But Schmitt's claim in *Hüter* that one can categorize states according to the institutional center of their activity is somewhat fuller there than his reduction of state types to the institutional source of commands in the present work. In *Hüter*, for example, Schmitt argues that the state in the medieval period, the early *Ständestaat*, was a jurisdiction state in that it was primarily concerned with defining and enforcing jurisdictional boundaries among rival centers of power, whereas the absolutist state was a governmental state because its legitimacy was based on its capacity to establish circumstances under which norms could be valid (HV 74–76). In *Hüter*, in other words, state types were defined by the purpose of state action, not by the institutional means through which state action occurs. On Schmitt's use of state types,

see Renato Cristi, *Carl Schmitt and Authoritarian Liberalism: Strong State, Free Economy* (Cardiff: University of Wales Press, 1998), 179–93; and Jeffrey Seitzer, *Comparative History and Legal Theory: Carl Schmitt in the First German Democracy* (Westport, Conn.: Greenwood, 2001), 104–10. Trans.]

7 [Along with Anschütz, Thoma edited the influential *Handbuch des Deutschen Staatsrecht* and authored a number of important scholarly essays on different aspects of the Weimar Constitution, such as the role of courts in politics. He also wrote an influential review of Schmitt's essay *The Crisis of Parliamentary Democracy* (*Die geistesgeschichtliche Lage des heutigen Parlamentarismus*, 1923). Thoma criticized Schmitt for seeking out the "moral underpinnings" of parliamentary government in works, such as those by Rousseau and John Stuart Mill, written long ago in response to significantly different problems. Thoma suggested that Schmitt would do better to examine works of those actually involved in the establishment of the current system, such as Hugo Preuß, Friedrich Naumann, and Max Weber, in order to discern the "purpose" of parliamentary government, because they were responding directly to prevailing conditions. Thoma, "On the Ideology of Parliamentarism (1925)," in CPD, 77–83.

Thoma's criticisms obviously struck a nerve. For not only does Schmitt formally respond to Thoma in the preface to the second edition of *Crisis* (1926), but also in both *Verfassungslehre* (1928) and *Hüter der Verfassung*. Schmitt also bitterly recounts Thoma's charge that he wrongly focuses on the "moldy greats" of political theory in addressing the problems of parliament (e.g., v 313 and HV 89). In these later works, moreover, changes in Schmitt's method suggest that he is responding to Thoma's insistence on the need for a more pragmatic, context-sensitive approach. In *Verfassungslehre*, for example, Schmitt examines the actual history of parliamentary government in Europe, in order to address the distinctive problems of the Weimar Republic, while in *Hüter* he supplements analysis of constitutional structure with consideration of the political implications of long- and short-term developments in economy and society.

For contrasting views on this shift in approach, compare Seitzer, *Comparative History*, 44–50, with Reinhard Mehring, "Carl Schmitt's Lehre von der Auflösung des Liberalismus: Das Sinngefüge der Verfassungslehre als historisches Urteil," *Zeitschrift für Politik* 38 (1991): 206; and William Scheuermann, "Is Parliamentarism in Crisis? A Response to Carl Schmitt," *Theory and Society* 24 (1995): 142. Trans.]

8 [Schmitt distinguished between a "quantitative" and a "qualita-

tive" total state. Both types of state intervene so deeply in society, Schmitt argues, that in principle nothing lies beyond their reach. Their interventions in society, however, take a different form and stem from a different source. A quantitative total state responds to calls for assistance from any group that can exert the necessary pressure through established political institutions, providing more or less anything demanded of it, such as welfare benefits, economic regulation, business subsidies, cultural aid, and so forth. The quantitative total state, therefore, is a weak state in that it cannot resist pressure from the various elements that compose it. In fact, it merely reflects the diverse desires of the myriad social groups striving for political power.

A qualitative total state has an altogether different relationship to society, according to Schmitt. Guided by a substantive vision of social order, a qualitative total state intervenes in society in order to reshape it fundamentally, as in fascist Italy. Compelling social groups to conform to its substantive vision, rather than responding indiscriminately to the desires of social groups, the qualitative total state stands over and above society, as did the German state of the nineteenth and early twentieth centuries. The traditional state, however, intervened in society only to the extent necessary to ensure a relatively free social sphere.

The Weimar Republic, in Schmitt's view, is a quantitative total state. In order for the Weimar state to function effectively, Schmitt believes it is necessary to reduce the number and extent of the demands placed on it. Schmitt's solution is to limit state protection to a very restricted set of traditional civil and political rights, such as free speech and assembly, which can then be abrogated on a one-time basis, if the President deems this necessary to preserve the state. The panoply of economic and social rights meant to express the Republic's commitment to social justice would be sacrificed to the cause of effective government.

Schmitt's position on the total state is elaborated in "Die Wendung zum totalen Staat" (1931), in *Positionen und Begriffe im Kampf mit Weimar-Genf-Versailles, 1923-1939* (1940; reprint, Berlin: Duncker und Humblot, 1988), 146-57. On Schmitt's concept of the state, see Cristi, *Carl Schmitt and Authoritarian Liberalism*, 188-99; and John P. McCormick, *Carl Schmitt's Critique of Liberalism: Against Politics as Technology* (Cambridge: Cambridge University Press, 1997), 249-89. Seitzer, *Comparative History*, examines Schmitt's understanding of the institutional basis of the Weimar state crisis. Trans.]

9 [Prior to World War I, the Reich government was not the primary institutional locus for regulation of the economy and the pro-

vision of welfare services. That locus was primarily municipalities operating under the law of "local self-government" (*Selbstverwaltung*), which stemmed from the Prussian reforms of the early nineteenth century and became quite common throughout Germany in the nineteenth and early twentieth centuries. The law of local self-government provided local communities considerable autonomy from central (then Land, later Land and Reich) control because, it was thought, local government did not involve "state action." Rather, local government was merely "society" managing the "technical" details of everyday life that did not impinge on "political" affairs, such as the underlying purpose of the state itself. Under this system, however, cities operated businesses, regulated industry and commerce, and provided extensive social welfare services, anticipating the twentieth-century welfare and administrative states.

During World War I, the Reich government became more actively involved in regulating the economy and engaging in economic activities. On the basis of an enabling act, the Bundesrat issued hundreds of decrees covering almost every conceivable area of productive activity and economic exchange. The wartime government by decree clearly violated prewar understandings of the priority of the statute and enabled the Reich to attain a level of authority not possible in peacetime, more or less circumventing the complex constitutional arrangements under Bismarck's Reich Constitution. But the general sense was that such actions were temporary deviations from accepted practice necessitated by the war effort.

Schmitt's concern is that the trend toward active intervention in the economy and the provision of welfare services at the Reich level became ever more pronounced in the Weimar period. For Schmitt, this posed a problem not merely because the regulation of the economy and provision of welfare services threatened to overburden the German state. It was also a problem because the Reichstag could not issue decrees with the necessary specificity without violating what Schmitt considered the Rechtsstaat principle of the generality of statutes. Schmitt's critics charged that his concern for the generality of statutes was merely a means of depriving legislatures of the legal means necessary to retain a pivotal political role in the Weimar constitutional system.

On local self-government in the German state, see Hans Herzfeld, *Demokratie und Selbstverwaltung in der Weimarer Epoche* (Berlin: Kohlhammer, 1957). For Schmitt's critique of local self-government's role in the tendency toward the quantitative total state, see HV 92–93. Seitzer, *Comparative History*, 41–71, argues that Schmitt's position on local self-government misunderstands the nature of the independent state in the Reich period. On the issue of the changing role of law in the emerging welfare and administrative state in interwar Germany, see William E. Scheuerman, *Between the Norm and the Exception: The Frankfurt School and the Rule of Law* (Cambridge, Mass.: MIT Press, 1994). For a survey of the wartime administrative measures and the contemporary reaction to them, see Michael Stolleis, *Geschichte des öffentlichen Rechts in Deutschland*, vol. 3, *Staats- und Verwaltungsrechtswissenschaft in Republik und Diktatur, 1914–1945* (Munich: C. H. Beck, 1999), 67–71. Trans.]

10 [I have not located the source of this quotation. A likely one is his most important work, *Geschichte der socialen Bewegung Frankreichs von 1789 bis auf unsere Tage*, 3 vols. (1850). The principal claim in this work is that the dominant classes must use state power to ameliorate the condition of the dependent classes, for example, through the extension of legal equality and provision of social welfare programs. Otherwise, the dependent classes will be compelled to resort to social revolution. On Stein's understanding of the relation of state and society and its importance for German law and legal theory, see E. W. Böckenförde, "Lorenz von Stein als Theoretiker der Bewegung von Staat und Gesellschaft zum Sozialstaat," in *Recht, Staat, Freiheit: Studien zur Rechtsphilosophie, Staatstheorie und Verfassungsgeschichte* (Frankfurt am Main: Suhrkamp, 1991). Trans.]

11 [Max Weber, *Economy and Society: An Outline of Interpretive Sociology*, ed. Guenter Roth and Claus Wittich, trans. Ephraim Fischoff et al. (Berkeley: University of California Press, 1978), 2:220–23.

On Schmitt's relation to Weber, see Wolfgang J. Mommsen, *Max Weber and German Politics 1890–1920*, trans. Michael S. Steinberg (Chicago: University of Chicago Press, 1984), 332–89, esp. 381–93; Rune Slagstad, "Liberal Constitutionalism and Its Critics: Carl Schmitt and Max Weber," in *Constitutionalism and Democracy*, ed. Jon Elster and Rune Slagstad (Cambridge: Cambridge University Press, 1988); Reinhard Mehring, "Politische Ethik in Max Weber's 'Politik als Beruf' und Carl Schmitt's 'Der Begriff des Politischen," *Politische Vierteljahresschrift* 31, no. 4 (1990): 608–26; G. L. Ulmen, *Politische Mehrwert: Eine Studie über Max Weber und Carl Schmitt* (Weinheim: VCH Acta Humaniora, 1991); McCormick, *Schmitt's Critique*, 31–82, 206–12; and Seitzer, *Comparative History*, 22–35.

12 ["Decisionism" refers to what Schmitt considers the centrality to any system of authority of personal decisions unbounded by

norms. By making clear the unavoidability and productive value of decision, Schmitt argues, counterrevolutionary thinkers like Louis Boland, Joseph de Maistre, and Juan Donoso-Cortés expose the hollow core of Enlightenment political theory, which seeks to eliminate sovereignty and personal rule from law and politics. Contemporary liberals suffer from the same myopia about personal authority. The legal positivist Hans Kelsen, for example, views law and the state as a complete system of norms, in which sovereignty and personal rule are not necessary. Without the concept of decision, however, Kelsen and other legal positivists cannot account for the origin of this system of norms or how it is enforced, for Kelsen's basic norm cannot be traced to an anterior norm. It stems, rather, from the actions of concrete persons, who either develop legal and political orders from scratch or work within established institutions to bring about fundamental changes in the existing system. Similarly, with the application of legal norms, individual judges must decide how norms apply in concrete cases, and often this requires merely deciding how the norm applies to the case at hand. In many cases, in other words, the legal norms themselves do not provide judges sufficient guidance to settle a dispute authoritatively.

For Schmitt, recognizing the necessity of decisionism is essential for addressing the Weimar Republic's chronic governmental crisis. The Weimar Constitution, in Schmitt's view, did not represent a clear decision on the nature of the Republic's legal and political systems, as it gave expression to rival understandings of politics and society and established a highly democratic political system through which opposing groups could seek to realize their political and social visions at one another's expense. The result, according to Schmitt, was political chaos. The overtaxed Weimar state could no longer mediate effectively among opposing groups and render their conflict nondebilitating. By understanding the Weimar Constitution as a clear decision of the sovereign German people for a particular and limited form of political and social order, the German state could more effectively contain rising political and social conflict. The President would serve the essential purpose of deciding how to intervene in contemporary conflicts, resolving them such that the system overall would be preserved, even though for this purpose particular aspects of the system, such as individual rights, must be sacrificed at least temporarily.

Decisionism figures prominently in Schmitt's works throughout the Weimar period. Besides the present work, several particularly important landmarks in the development of the concept are

Gesetz und Urteil: Eine Untersuchung zum Problem der Rechts-praxis (1912; reprint, Munich: C. H. Beck, 1969), *Political Theology: Four Chapters on the Concept of Sovereignty* [*Politische Theologie: Vier Kapitel zur Lehre von der Souveränität*, 1922], trans. George Schwab (Cambridge, Mass.: MIT Press, 1985), and *Verfassungslehre*, esp. v 75–99. On the character of Schmitt's decisionism and its importance for his understanding of the political problems of interwar Germany, compare Renato Cristi, *Carl Schmitt and Authoritarian Liberalism*, and George Schwab, *The Challenge of the Exception: An Introduction to the Political Ideas of Carl Schmitt between 1921 and 1936*, 2d ed. (Westport, Conn.: Greenwood Press, 1989), on the one hand, with Hasso Hofmann, *Legitimität gegen Legalität: Der Weg der politischen Philosophie Carl Schmitts*, 2d ed. (Berlin: Duncker und Humblot, 1992); Christian Graf von Krockow, *Die Entscheidung: Eine Untersuchung über Ernst Jünger, Carl Schmitt, Martin Heidegger* (Stuttgart: F. Enke, 1958); and McCormick, *Schmitt's Critique*, on the other. Trans.]

13 [Like Schmitt, Rudolf Smend was a prominent opponent of legal positivism. Both Schmitt and Smend rejected legal positivism's concern with legal formality, and in response they each developed understandings of the state stressing substantive factors that were mostly devoid of content. Nonetheless, their respective understandings of state sovereignty differed significantly. In contrast to Schmitt's understanding of the Weimar Constitution as a decision of the people in its collective capacity, which then serves as the authoritative reference point in subsequent debates about the nature and limits of state action, Smend's concept of sovereignty was borrowed from Ernest Renan's idea of a daily plebiscite to stress the continuous formation of the character and purpose of collective life. The state, for Smend, was not a distinct body standing over against the society, as in Schmitt's ideal understanding. Rather than citizens being integrated into the existing state, as under the nineteenth-century understanding of the relation of state and society that Schmitt favored, Smend argued in his "integration theory" that state and society were elements in a complex mixture, which redefined itself in symbolic and empirical terms on an ongoing basis. In elaborating his idea of the state as an organic totality, Smend displayed some admiration for Italian fascism because of its capacity to mobilize symbols and political and social action in the service of developing and reinforcing a common purpose for the collective. At the same time, however, he made some halting attempts to defend the Weimar Constitution. And in the post–World War II era, Smend's "inte-

gration theory" emphasizing the fluid, never-finished nature of political and social unity again became quite influential. Smend's most influential work from the Weimar era is *Verfassung und Verfassungsrecht* (1928), in *Staatsrechtliche Abhandlungen und andere Aufsätze*, 3d ed. (Berlin: Duncker und Humblot, 1994). For an example of Smend's influence in the postwar era, see the important essay by Horst Ehmke, "Grenzen der Verfassungsänderung" (1953), in *Beiträge zur Verfassungstheorie und Verfassungspolitik*, ed. Peter Häberle (Königstein: Athenäum, 1981). Caldwell, *Popular Sovereignty*, 121–26, reviews Smend's Weimar-era work and his role in the Republic. Trans.]

14 [I have not found the exact quotation in Weber. What eventually became Weber's sociology of law is the most likely source. See Weber, *Economy and Society*, 2:641–900, esp. 654–58, 809–15, 880–95. Trans.]

15 [See Kirchheimer, "Legalität und Legitimität" (1932), which appears as "Legality and Legitimacy" in *Social Democracy and the Rule of Law: Otto Kirchheimer and Franz Neumann*, ed. Keith Tribe, trans. Leena Tanner and Keith Tribe (London: Allen and Unwin, 1987). A member of the early Frankfurt School, Otto Kirchheimer was a participant in Schmitt's seminars in the early 1930s. He initially adopted a left Schmittian view of the Weimar Constitution, criticizing its failure to represent a clear decision in favor of the right or the left and arguing that it was essential to develop the socialist elements of the constitution, not the bourgeois ones championed by Schmitt. See, for example, a book frequently cited by Schmitt, though not in this context, *Weimar—und was dann?* (1930), which appears as "Weimar—And What Then?" in *Politics, Law and Social Change: Selected Essays of Otto Kirchheimer*, ed. F. Burin and Kurt Schell (New York: Columbia University Press, 1969). Three years later, however, he wrote, with Nathan Leites, an extensive, critical review of the present work, arguing first that empirical evidence contradicts Schmitt's claim that democracy requires substantial social homogeneity; Schmitt also misunderstands the compromise character of constitutions, according to Kirchheimer. See "Remarks on Carl Schmitt's *Legalität und Legitimität*," in *Social Democracy and the Rule of Law*. Scheuerman, *Between Norm and Exception*, considers the relationship of Kirchheimer and Schmitt. Trans.]

16 [Late in the Republic, the Nazis and Communists cooperated to produce "negative majorities," the sole purpose of which was to stymie any positive action in the Reichstag. For Schmitt, the mere fact that a coalition of parties can muster a majority on a particular issue does not justify permitting it to bring down the current

government. If a majority is composed of parties with diametrically opposed positions, and if this temporary majority supports a vote of no confidence under Article 54 merely as a means of obstruction, rather than as a way of furthering a positive governmental program, then there is no duty of the government to step down, particularly when the President has already ordered the dissolution of the Reichstag (v 345).

Schmitt's concern about negative majorities was widely shared during the Weimar era. See, for example, Heinrich Herrfahrdt, *Die Kabinettsbildung nach der WRV* (1927), the most likely inspiration for Article 67 of the Basic Law (the current German Constitution), which provides for a "constructive vote of no confidence." Under the postwar provision, a vote of no confidence is only permissible when a majority opposed to the current government can itself agree on a successor government. Trans.]

17 [Weber's understanding of bureaucracy is elaborated in *Economy and Society*, 2:956–1005, while that of parliament as a means of leadership selection is developed in "Parliament und Regierung im neugeordneten Deutschland," in Max Weber, *Gesammelte Politische Schriften*, ed. Johannes Winckelmann (Tübingen: J. C. B. Mohr [Paul Siebeck], 1988), 306–443. Trans.]

18 [Schmitt refers to his famous definition of the "political" as the ability to distinguish between friend and enemy: "The political is the most intense and extreme antagonism, and every concrete antagonism becomes that much more political the closer it approaches the most extreme point, that of the friend-enemy grouping"; Carl Schmitt, *The Concept of the Political*, trans. George Schwab (Chicago: The University of Chicago Press, 1996), 29. Of Schmitt's works from the Weimar period, *The Concept of the Political* is arguably the most influential. Not surprisingly, the secondary literature on the work defies citation. See, for example, Ernst Wolfgang Böckenförde, "Der Begriff des Politischen als Schlüssel zum staatsrechtlichen Werk Carl Schmitts," in *Complexio Oppositorum: Über Carl Schmitt*, ed. Helmut Quaritsch (Duncker und Humblot, 1988); and Heinrich Meier, *Carl Schmitt und Leo Strauss: The Hidden Dialogue*, trans. J. Harvey Lomax (Chicago: The University of Chicago Press, 1995). Trans.]

19 [The first President, Friedrich Ebert, was elected twice by the Reichstag. After 1925, however, the President was directly elected for seven-year terms in a national vote under universal suffrage. Former Field Marshall Paul von Hindenburg was elected twice to the position under the new provision. On the President in Weimar generally, see Carl J. Friedrich, "The Development of Executive Power in Germany," *American Political Science Review* 27, no. 2

(1933): 185–203; Harlow J. Heneman, *The Growth of Executive Power in Germany* (Minneapolis, 1934); and F. M. Marx, *Government in the Third Reich* (New York, 1936), 53–61. Trans.]

20 [The term "Parteienstaat" (party state) is not translated to emphasize its important place in German political life. The term reflects the ambivalence of Germans toward the role of organized political parties in democratic government. In the Weimar period, political parties were not recognized by the constitution as such, though they were a central organizing feature of parliamentary government. Schmitt and many others had a decidedly negative view of parties, to which they attributed the lack of political unity and, therefore, instability. Schmitt argued in *The Crisis of Parliamentary Democracy* that parliamentary representatives were merely delegates sent by party officials to register decisions made outside parliament. With such control over the actions of representatives, parliament could no longer serve as a means to reach compromise and forge a unified political will. By contrast, the current constitution, the Basic Law, accords political parties a protected position in the process of the formation of the state will (Article 21), and the "so-called" decline of parties, the inability of established parties to shape political life, is considered a fundamental challenge to democratic government in Germany.

On the Parteienstaat in twentieth-century Germany, see Gerhard Leibholz, "Volk und Partei im neuen deutschen Verfassungsrecht," in *Strukturprobleme der modernen Demokratie* (Karlsruhe: C. F. Müller Verlag, 1967), 71–77; Michael Stolleis, Heinz Schaeffer, and René A. Rhinow, *Parteienstaatlichkeit: Krisensymptome des demokratischen Verfassungsstaats?* (Berlin: de Gruyter, 1986); and Klaus von Beyme, *Die politische Klasse im Parteienstaat* (Frankfurt am Main: Suhrkamp, 1993), 39–98. Trans.]

21 [During the Republic's two extended political crises, the President and the Reich government responded to problems of political instability and economic collapse by issuing presidential emergency decrees under Article 48. An enduring point of controversy is what, if any, role did Article 48 play in the failure of the Weimar Republic? In other words, did Article 48 ensure the survival of the Republic as long as it lasted, or did the presidential government made possible by Article 48 undermine democratic institutions, hastening or perhaps even ensuring the demise of the Republic?

Schmitt is at the center of this controversy, not only because he was an important adviser to key governmental officials late in the Republic, but also because his writings on constitutional dictatorship provided a theoretical foundation for the presidential government of the Republic's second crisis. Interestingly, Schmitt's first major work on constitutional dictatorship, *Die Diktatur: Von den Anfängen des modernen Souveränitätsgedankens bis zum proletarischen Klassenkampf* (1922), 5th ed. (Berlin: Duncker und Humblot, 1989), was not written in explicit reference to Article 48. Schmitt distinguishes between two forms of dictatorship, sovereign and commissarial. The Roman dictator was of the commissarial type in that he was not empowered to make permanent changes in the Roman Constitution. Rather, the dictator's sole purpose was to restore the Roman Constitution, even though some actions in pursuit of this goal violated particular aspects of the constitutional order, such as the rights of particular citizens. A sovereign dictator, by contrast, brings about a fundamental change in the existing order or establishes a new order under his own authority.

A 1924 essay, "Die Diktatur des Reichpräsidenten," later included as an appendix to *Die Diktatur*, is arguably Schmitt's most important explication of the legal basis of presidential government under Article 48. The first principal question, Schmitt argues, is the relation to one another of the first two sections of Article 48. Schmitt argues that until the passage of supplementary legislation under Section 5 (which never occurred), Section 1 is an independent grant of authority to the President to issue measures with the force of law, which is subject to only two limitations. First, the President cannot issue measures that involve permanent, general, and fundamental changes in the established constitutional order. In other words, his authority is commissarial, not sovereign. The National Assembly that promulgated the Weimar Constitution exercised a sovereign dictatorship, but this lasted only until the constitution took effect. Second, the Reichstag retains the right to demand the suspension or abrogation of any presidential action taken under Section 1. Section 2's enumeration of the Basic Rights that the President can suspend during an emergency, by contrast, is not a limitation on the general authority of Section 1, according to Schmitt. This listing of the Basic Rights does not indicate that these are the only provisions of the Weimar Constitution the President can suspend during a state of emergency. The drafting history of the Article indicates that if anything, Section 2 was intended to reinforce the authority granted under the first section. Moreover, Schmitt continues, the widely accepted practice of the exercise of presidential emergency powers under Article 48 indicates that the President's authority extends to all provisions of the Weimar Constitution, so long as it does not violate the previously two mentioned limitations.

On presidential emergency decrees in Weimar generally, see Frederick Watkins, *The Failure of Constitutional Emergency Powers under the German Republic* (Cambridge, Mass.: Harvard University Press, 1939); Clinton L. Rossiter, *Constitutional Dictatorship: Crisis Government in Modern Democracies* (Princeton: Princeton University Press, 1948), 31–73; Ulrich Scheuner, "Die Anwendung des Art. 48 der Weimarer Reichsverfassung unter den Reichspräsidentschaften von Ebert und Hindenburg," in *Staat, Wirtschaft und Politik in der Weimarer Republik: Festschrift für Heinrich Brüning*, ed. Ferdinand A. Hermens and Theodor Schieder (Berlin: Duncker und Humblot, 1967), 249–86; Heinrich Oberreuter, *Notstand und Demokratie* (Munich: Vögel, 1978), esp. 43–71; Ernst Rudolf Huber, *Deutsche Verfassungsgeschichte seit 1789*, vol. 6, *Die Weimarer Reichsverfassung* (Stuttgart: W. Kohlhammer, 1981), 434–50; Hans Boldt, "Der Artikel 48 der Weimarer Reichsverfassung: Sein historischer Hintergrund und seine politische Funktion," in *Die Weimarer Republik: Belagerte Civitas*, ed. Michael Stürmer (Königstein: Verlagsgruppe Athenäum, Hain, Scriptor, Hanstein, 1980), 288–309; Michael Frehse, *Ermächtigungsgesetzgebung im Deutschen Reich, 1914-1933* (Pfaffenweiler: Centaurus-Verlagsgesellschaft, 1985); John E. Finn, *Constitutions in Crisis: Political Violence and the Rule of Law* (New York: Oxford University Press, 1991), 139–78; and Peter Blomeyer, *Der Notstand in den letzten Jahren von Weimar* (Berlin: Duncker und Humblot, 1999).

For a critical evaluation of the use of emergency powers by the Republic's two Presidents, Friedrich Ebert and Paul von Hindenburg, see Gotthard Jasper, "Die verfassungs- und machtpolitische Problematik des Reichspräsidents in der Weimarer Republik: Die Praxis der Reichspräsident Ebert und Hindenburg im Vergleich," in *Friedrich Ebert und Seine Zeit: Bilanz und Perspektiven der Forschung*, ed. Rudolf König, Hartmut Söll, and Hermann Weber (Munich: R. Oldenburg, 1997).

On Schmitt's understanding of emergency powers and his role in late Weimar, compare Schwab, Bendersky, and Berthold, on the one hand, with McCormick and Dyzenhaus, on the other: Schwab, *Challenge of the Exception*, 80–89; Joseph W. Bendersky, *Carl Schmitt: Theorist for the Reich* (Princeton: Princeton University Press, 1983), 107–91; Berthold, *Schmitt und der Staatsnotstandsplan*, 32–77; McCormick, *Schmitt's Critique*, 121–56; Dyzenhaus, *Legality and Legitimacy*, 70–85. Trans.]

1. Legislative State and the Concept of Law

1 [Both *Gesetz* and *Recht* can be translated simply as "law." Doing
so, however, would obscure the rich texture of German legal ter-
minology. Moreover, since part of Schmitt's purpose is to render
more fluid some of the boundaries among traditional legal concepts, it is necessary to distinguish among types of law and administrative instruments to the extent possible without violating
accepted English usage.

Law in the formal sense (*Gesetz im formellen Sinn*) refers to statutes produced by legislatures through formal lawmaking procedures. Law in the substantive sense (*Gesetz im materiellen Sinn*)
refers to forms of law containing legal rules. The latter form of Gesetz can include customary law (*Gewohnheitsrecht*), which is not
written law, as well as some administrative instruments that have
the force of law (e.g., *Rechtsverordnungen*). Recht, by contrast,
refers to laws generally, whether written or unwritten, formal or
substantive, but it can also mean justice. For a brief overview
of the sources of the law in Germany, see Nigel Foster, *German
Legal System and Laws* (London: Blackstore Press, 1996), 51–53.

Often, however, Schmitt does not make explicit reference to the
classic formulations of law in the formal or substantive sense. It
is necessary to discern from the context whether he is referring
to statutes in the narrow formal sense or legal instruments containing a legal rule that are not the product of the formal lawmaking procedures of parliament. Even in these instances, however,
a clear distinction is often not available. Schmitt is calling attention to what he considers a fundamental, and detrimental, change
in the understanding of statutes under the Weimar Constitution.
A statute, in Schmitt's view, should not merely be a product of
the formal lawmaking procedures of parliament, in this case the
Reichstag. It should also meet certain other criteria, most notably
the generality requirement. In other words, a statute should not
apply to individuals or to a particular instance, as would typically be the case with an administrative law instrument. Rather,
it should be applicable generally and beyond the immediate instance. Schmitt's preferred understanding of a statute, therefore,
combines the formal and substantive concepts outlined above.

Schmitt's argument also involves myriad administrative law
terms. *Maßnahmen*, or measures, is a general term that can
refer to any one of several administrative law instruments, such
as decrees (*Verordnungen*) and orders (*Anordnungen*). Article 48,
for example, which empowers the President to take extraordinary action under certain conditions, refers to Maßnahmen,

even though presidential action under Article 48 typically took the form of decrees (Verordnungen) and, less frequently, orders (Anordnungen). Mostly, however, the term measures (Maßnahmen) is meant to refer to administrative law instruments that do not apply beyond the particular case. As noted, decrees under certain conditions can have the force of law in that they contain a legal rule that applies beyond the particular case (Rechtsverordnungen). Keeping in mind that there is no hard-and-fast rule, one can set up a hierarchy of administrative law instruments, proceeding from the highest potential level of generality to the lowest: decrees with the force of law (Rechtsverordnungen); simple decrees (Verordnungen), which may or may not have the force of law; orders (Anordnungen) and rulings or judgments (Verfügungen), both of which tend to apply to a particular instance, though these might have more lasting consequences; and instructions (Anweisungen), which are usually merely internal administrative directives.

Finally, idiomatic English usage requires deviating from literal renderings at times. I have used "law" or "act," for example, when referring to a particular statute passed by parliament, and "law" in the phrases "rule of law" (Herrschaft des Gesetzes) and "concept of law" (Begriff des Gesetzes), among others, unless Schmitt is attempting to emphasize the term "statute" in a specific instance. Also, the terms "substance" or "substantive," as in substantive due process or substantive legal rules, better capture what is meant by the German term materiel than the English "material." Trans.]

2   [Prior to the founding of Bismarck's Reich Constitution in 1871, many political reformers looked to law as a means of unity short of full political unification. The civil codes promulgated under the reigns of absolute monarchs in Prussia and Austria certainly provided some basis for legal unity in their domains. But these codes did not fully satisfy nationalist sentiment, partly because the codes did not sufficiently address the full gamut of legal questions encountered on an everyday basis, but also because many opposed the right of monarchs to legislate in this way.

It is in this context that the Historical School of Law became the dominant form of legal theory in the first half of the nineteenth century. Legal scholars such as Friedrich Karl von Savigny sought to compensate for these unsuccessful attempts at unity by discerning a Volksgeist, or national spirit, behind the mass of legal rules from diverse sources that constituted German law in a large number of separate legal jurisdictions. While they disagreed on the source of legal rules and their application, the scholars of the

Historical School of Law believed that this Volksgeist, made evident from careful scholarly analysis of German customs, provided an absolute grounding to legal transactions throughout Germany. A good introduction in English to Savigny's views is his lecture *Of the Vocation of Our Age for Legislation and Jurisprudence* (1814), trans. Abraham Hayward (London: Littlewood, 1975). Ernst Wolfgang Böckenförde, "Die Historische Rechtsschule und das Problem der Geschichtlichkeit des Rechts," in *Staat, Gesellschaft, Freiheit: Studien zur Rechtsphilosophie, Staatstheorie und Verfassungsgeschichte* (Frankfurt am Main: Suhrkamp, 1991), offers an interesting discussion of theoretical problems with the Historical School approach. James Q. Whitman, *The Legacy of Roman Law in the German Romantic Era: Historical Vision and Legal Change* (Princeton: Princeton University Press, 1990), provides an excellent study of the role of the professoriat, including Savigny, in German law in the nineteenth century. Trans.]

3 [The Reichsgericht was the only national court during the Reich period. Established in 1877, it had appellate jurisdiction in civil and criminal cases. The Reichsgericht was retained under the Weimar Constitution, though it took a decidedly different posture. Reflecting the German tradition of a judiciary deferential toward state authority, the Reichsgericht did not question the constitutionality of Reich laws prior to the Weimar Republic. In the post–World War I era, the Reichsgericht, along with the other newly established high courts, the *Reichsfinanzgericht* (Federal Tax Court) and the *Reichsarbeitsgericht* (Federal Labor Court), claimed the power of judicial review. Article 13 of the Weimar Constitution permitted high courts to review cases of conflicts between Reich and Land laws. As was the case in the United States, such issues of federal supremacy provided courts the opportunity to consider the constitutionality of laws, but this did not constitute an explicit grant of the authority of judicial review. Nonetheless, the President of the Reichsgericht from 1922 to 1929, Walter Simons, advocated a role for the Reichsgericht in German politics comparable to that exercised by the U.S. Supreme Court. The Reichsgericht did find a number of laws in violation of the constitution. Despite this newfound judicial assertiveness, however, the Reichsgericht never attained the position in German politics envisioned by Simons, remaining most of the time quite careful not to challenge state authority directly.

On the history and institutional ·features of the Reichsgericht prior to Weimar, see Kai Müller, *Der Hüter des Rechts: Die Stellung des Reichsgerichts im Deutschen Kaiserreich, 1879–1918*

(Baden-Baden: Nomos, 1997). The personnel and institutional features of the Reichsgericht in the Weimar period are covered extensively in Adolf Lobe, ed., *Fünfzig Jahre Reichsgericht* (Berlin: Walter de Gruyter, 1929). On judicial review during the Weimar period, see Knut Wolfgang Nörr, *Richter zwischen Gesetz und Wirklichkeit: Die Reaktion des Reichsgerichts auf die Krisen von Weltkrieg und Inflation, und die Entfaltung eines neuen richterlichen Selbstverständnisses* (Heidelberg: C. F. Müller, 1996); Gertrude Lübbe-Wolff, "Safeguards of Civil and Constitutional Rights — The Debate on the Role of the *Reichsgericht*," in *German and American Constitutional Thought: Contexts, Interaction and Historical Realities*, ed. Hermann Wellenreuther (New York: Berg, 1990); and Peter C. Caldwell, *Popular Sovereignty and the Crisis of German Constitutional Law: The Theory and Practice of Weimar Constitutionalism* (Durham, N.C.: Duke University Press, 1997), 145–70. Johannes Mattern, *Principles of the Constitutional Jurisprudence of the German National Republic* (Baltimore: Johns Hopkins Press, 1928), 249–56, examines the jurisdictional grant of Article 13 and the decisions reached on the basis of it. Trans.]

4 Cf. RGZ 134, p. 19, and the decisions presented there, especially RGZ 125, p. 422.

5 [A leading authority on the Weimar Constitution, Gerhard Anschütz was the author of an authoritative commentary that ran to fourteen editions, one, more or less, for every year of the Weimar Republic; see *Die Verfassung des Deutschen Reichs vom 11. August 1919*, 14th ed. (Berlin: Georg Stilke, 1933). Along with Richard Thoma, he also edited the *Handbuch des deutschen Staatsrechts* (1930–32), which contains contributions by the leading authorities on various aspects of German public law. Anschütz did not formulate an elaborate theoretical framework for defining law and its relationship to politics and the state, as was the case with some other legal positivists, most notably Hans Kelsen, or nonpositivist legal theorists such as Rudolf Smend and Erich Kaufmann. Instead, Anschütz insisted on a strict interpretation of statutory law as a means of determining the meaning and limits of valid law. Anschütz's focus on statutory law, narrowly understood, brought him into conflict with others, especially Schmitt, who insisted that in some instances, such as a state of emergency, one must look to the overall spirit of the law, rather than its letter. In particular, Schmitt and Anschütz were at loggerheads in regard to the issue of constitutional amendment, with the latter stressing the formal procedural requirements for constitutional changes (two-thirds of the Reichstag or a majority vote in a ref-

erendum); Schmitt believed that there were substantive limitations to the substance and scope of constitutional amendments that again were rooted in what he thought was the overall purpose of the constitution, that is, protection of the bourgeois order of rights and liberties and a certain institutional minimum. After the Nazi ascension to power, Anschütz retired from teaching with the justification that he could not in good conscience teach law under the Nazi regime.

On Anschütz and his place in German law and legal theory, see E. W. Böckenförde, "Gerhard Anschütz (1986)," in *Recht, Staat, Freiheit*, and Caldwell, *Popular Sovereignty*, 70–77. Trans.]

6 [The reference is to Paul Laband, a leading legal positivist of the Reich era. I have not identified the quotation, but the likely source is Laband's most famous and influential work, *Das Staatsrecht des Deutschen Reiches*, 3 vols. (Tübingen, H. Laupp, 1876–82). On Laband, see Michael Stolleis, *Public Law in Germany, 1800–1914* (New York: Berghahn Books, 2001), 323–30. Trans.]

7 [The French legal tradition has never accepted the form of judicial review of constitutionality practiced in the United States, where ordinary courts review the constitutionality of laws in the course of resolving an actual legal dispute. Even today, the French Constitutional Council is actually part of the legislative branch, and it reviews laws before they are promulgated. During the Third Republic, however, there was a debate on the appropriateness of American-style judicial review for French circumstances. For leading participants in this debate, cf. Raymond Carré de Malberg, *La Loi, expression de la volonté générale* (1931; reprint, Paris: Economica, 1984), and Edouard Lambert, *Le gouvernement des juges et la lutte contre la législation sociale aux État-Unis: L'Expérience américaine du controle judiciare de la constitutionalité des lois* (Paris: Marcel Giard, 1921). On the importance of the controversy for French constitutionalism generally, see Alec Stone, *The Birth of Judicial Politics in France: The Constitutional Council in Comparative Perspective* (New York: Oxford University Press, 1992), 33–40. Trans.]

2. Legality and Equal Chance

The word *chance* remains untranslated here. It belongs particularly to the way of thought and speech of a liberal era of free competition and of *expectation*, and it concerns the mixture of fortunate occurrence and conformity with law, freedom and calculability, arbitrariness and culpability, that is characteristic of this era. Other such words are, for example, ideology, risk, and, moreover, the "obligation" with its collective "implications," as well as all the possible types of "validity." Such words are better left unchanged, so that the mark of their intellectual origin remains visible. "Chance" occurs frequently in Max Weber's sociology.

1 [Schmitt refers to a debate over the meaning of Article 109 of the Weimar Constitution. Section 1 guarantees all citizens equality before the law. During the Reich period, equality before the law applied only to the administration, not the legislature. Under this understanding, for example, the Reichstag legitimately passed legislation singling out Social Democrats and Catholics for discriminatory treatment in the Reich period, because they did so through a formal statute, to which the equality requirement does not apply. If, however, administrative officials had discriminated against such groups without an explicit statutory grant of authority, these actions would have been invalid. The question in Weimar was whether Article 109, 1, also applied to the legislature, as Schmitt claimed. Aligned against Schmitt were legal positivists, such as Gerhard Anschütz, who placed no limitations on legislative action through statute, as well as others like Richard Thoma and Hermann Heller, who were concerned about empowering the democratic legislature. The issue had considerable practical import, because such a generality requirement, it was claimed, hindered the Reichstag from passing legislation necessary to manage and direct the ever more complex industrial society. This is because such actions might require legislation directed at particular individuals or economic organizations. Only the President, according to Schmitt, could act in this way through the use of his decree power, giving him another important institutional advantage over the legislature.

Schmitt's position on Article 109 is presented in summary form in v 155–56. See also "Grundrechte und Grundpflichten (1932)," in *VRA*, 181–231. For leading contemporary views, see Fritz Stier-Somlo, "Art. 109. Die Gleichheit vor dem Gesetz," in *Die Grundrechte und Grundpflichten der Reichsverfassung: Kommentar zum zweiten Teil der Reichsverfassung* (Berlin: Reimar Hobbing, 1929), 1:158–218; and Gerhard Leibholz, *Die Gleichheit vor dem Gesetz: Eine Studie auf rechtsvergleichender und rechtsphilosophischer Grundlage*, 3d ed. (Berlin: Otto Liebmann, 1966). See also Franz L. Neumann, "Die soziale Bedeutung der Grundrechte in der Weimarer Verfassung" (1930), in *Wirtschaft, Staat, Demokratie: Aufsätze, 1930–1954*, ed. Alfons Söllner (Frankfurt am Main: Suhrkamp, 1978), for a contemporary treatment focusing on the political consequences of the generality requirement. Trans.]

2 [The Austrian legal theorist Hans Kelsen was one of Schmitt's major opponents. A leading legal positivist, Kelsen was at the center of debates about the nature of law and the relation of law and politics in the interwar period. He argued for a strict separation of *sein* and *sollen*, facts and norms, and, relatedly, of law and politics. Rejecting preexisting norms like those of natural law theories, Kelsen argued that law was the product of an established and accepted system of lawmaking. The resulting laws might be considered immoral from some perspective. However, if they did not violate the appropriate procedural means for forming law, they were legally valid.

Schmitt considered Kelsen's understanding of legality problematical, because it did not account for the effectiveness of norms. The important consideration, for Schmitt, was not how norms came about, but rather whether and to what extent there are people and institutions willing and able to ensure that they are obeyed. Moreover, Kelsen's legal positivism, in Schmitt's view, could not respond effectively to the most pressing challenges to the Republic, specifically, the use of the established institutions and procedures to change fundamentally or even destroy the established system, because such actions would be legal in a narrow procedural sense. Only an understanding of law that in some circumstances subordinates procedure to substantive considerations can effectively defend the constitutional system under the sort of conditions prevailing in Weimar, according to Schmitt.

Schmitt and Kelsen also debated the role of courts in politics. Kelsen was the principal architect of the Austrian Constitutional Court, the world's first true constitutional court, and served as judge on the court until 1930, when he left for political reasons. In *Hüter der Verfassung* (HV 12–70), Schmitt claims that by rejecting laws clearly in conflict with the Weimar Constitution, courts could help ensure that the constitution is "respected." However, no court, particularly not one conceived along Continental lines, as was the Austrian Constitutional Court, could be an effective guardian of the constitution. This is because such a court could not deviate from the letter of the law in responding to opponents of the system, who sought to use the established system of legality to change the system fundamentally or destroy it altogether. Kelsen responded that Schmitt deliberately mischaracterizes the process of adjudication as properly involving mere "subsumption" of facts under established norms, in order to unfairly discredit constitutional adjudication. In reality, Kelsen argues, all legal application, even in the simplest cases, requires some judicial discretion, so one cannot disqualify constitutional adjudication as an illegitimate form of adjudication on this ground alone. See "Wer soll Hüter der Verfassung sein?" in *Die Wiener rechtstheoretische Schule*, ed. Hans Klecatsky, René Marcic, and Herbert Schambeck (Vienna: Europa-Verlag, 1968).

Among Kelsen's other major works from the period, see especially *Das Problem der Souveränität und die Theorie des Völkerrechts: Beitrag zu einer reinen Rechtslehre* (Tübingen: J. C. B. Mohr [Paul Siebeck], 1920), *Allgemeine Staatslehre* (Berlin: Springer, 1925), and *Vom Wesen und Wert der Demokratie*, 2d ed. (Tübingen: J. C. B. Mohr [Paul Siebeck], 1929). On Kelsen's legal and political theory, see Horst Dreier, *Rechtslehre, Staatssoziologie und Demokratietheorie bei Hans Kelsen* (Baden-Baden: Nomos, 1990). For comparisons of Kelsen and Schmitt, see Manfred Prisching, "Hans Kelsen und Carl Schmitt: Zur Konfrontation zweier staatstheoretischer Modelle," in *Reine Rechtslehre im Spiegel ihrer Fortsetzer und Kritiker*, ed. Ota Weinberger and Werner Krawietz (Vienna: Springer-Verlag, 1988); and David Dyzenhaus, *Legality and Legitimacy: Carl Schmitt, Hans Kelsen, and Hermann Heller in Weimar* (Oxford: Clarendon Press, 1997). On Schmitt's relation to Kelsen in the period 1933–34, when Kelsen was dismissed from university service and sent into exile, see Bernd Rüthers, "On the Brink of Dictatorship: Hans Kelsen and Carl Schmitt in Cologne 1933," in *Hans Kelsen and Carl Schmitt: A Juxtaposition*, ed. Dan Diner and Michael Stolleis (Gerlingen: Bleicher Verlag, 1999). Trans.]

3 [Schmitt is referring to the Pact of Paris, initially signed by fifteen states on August 27, 1928, and later approved by almost all remaining states. It is known as the Kellogg-Briand Pact because it was initially conceived of as a bilateral treaty between France and the United States and was thus named for the American and French secretaries of state at the time. The pact formally outlawed war as " 'an instrument of national policy.' " It permitted defensive wars, however, and was subject to a number of reservations and "interpretations" by signatory states. Thomas A. Bailey, *A Diplomatic History of the American People*, 10th ed. (Englewood Cliffs, N.J.: Prentice-Hall, 1980), 649–51. Trans.]

4 [The Staatsgerichtshof differed from the other high courts in the Weimar Republic in that it was only convened on occasion to address particular questions brought to it by governmental officials, with its composition varying according to the issue at hand. Moreover, the fact that Article 19 constituted an explicit grant of authority to consider a range of constitutional questions in the

area of federalism, while Article 59 established a complaint procedure allowing the Reichstag to challenge actions by the President, the Reich government, and its ministers, together suggest
the Staatsgerichtshof was meant to function like a constitutional
court. Though the Staatsgerichtshof decided a number of very important cases, it never exercised significant control over governmental action, rarely challenging state action, particularly that
taken under Article 48.
  For Schmitt's position on the Staatsgerichtshof, see esp. HV 48–
70. A good example of the prevailing contemporary opinion on
the Staatsgerichtshof is Ernst Friesenhahn, "Die Staatsgerichts-
barkeit," in *Handbuch des deutschen Staatsrecht*, ed. Gerhard
Anschütz and Richard Thoma (Tübingen: J. C. B. Mohr [Paul
Siebeck], 1930–32), 2:523–45. For an analysis of the Staatsgerichtshof's jurisdiction and a review of its decisions, see Johannes Mattern, *Principles of the Constitutional Jurisprudence of the German National Republic* (Baltimore: Johns Hopkins Press, 1928),
266–304. Peter C. Caldwell, *Popular Sovereignty and the Crisis of
German Constitutional Law: The Theory and Practice of Weimar
Constitutionalism* (Durham, N.C.: Duke University Press, 1997),
160–68, examines the Staatsgerichtshof's decisions on the question of presidential emergency powers. Trans.]

3. Extraordinary Lawgiver *Ratione Materiae*

1 [The Weimar Constitution contained a dizzying array of rights
   provisions. With some traditional political and civil rights, such
   as free speech and a right of assembly, together with a number
   of then less conventional economic and social rights, the Catalogue of Rights represented an impressive vision of a compromise
   social order spanning the political spectrum. There was considerable controversy, however, over the legal status of these rights
   provisions. Were they directly enforceable by courts, as is the case
   with many contemporary constitutions, or did they merely express goals for further legislative action, as was the case with
   rights under Länder constitutions prior to Weimar? Also, were
   those provisions containing legislative-reservation clauses subject to restriction by simple legislation, while those without such
   clauses somehow immune from parliamentary interference?
     Schmitt was at the center of the debate over the rights provi-
   sions. He argued that traditional political and civil rights should
   be given primacy over economic and social rights. He also argued
   that the equality provision of Article 109 applied to the legisla-

ture as well as to the administration. Finally, Schmitt contended that any legislative or executive action restricting a right could not completely deprive the right of its substance.

In some senses, Schmitt's insistence on a strict generality requirement and an inviolable core of a more limited range of rights provisions anticipated important features of the system of rights protection in the Federal Republic. See Reinhard Mußgnug, "Carl Schmitts verfassungsrechtliches Werk und sein Fortwirken im Staatsrecht der Bundesrepublik Deutschland," in *Complexio Oppositorum: Über Carl Schmitt*, ed. Helmut Quaritsch (Berlin: Duncker und Humblot, 1988). But Schmitt's position is controversial due to its perceived political implications. Besides denying the important compromise character of the Catalogue of Rights, as emphasized by the principal drafter of the constitution, Hugo Preuß, Schmitt's reading of the legal status of the rights provisions, particularly that regarding the important principle of the equality before the law, was seen as a roundabout way of limiting the powers of the legislature. Moreover, while Schmitt denied the executive the formal power of eliminating rights altogether, he gave the executive sweeping powers in regard to all aspects of the constitutional order, which far exceeded those of the legislature.

For Schmitt's position on the Catalogue of Rights, see v 157–82; "Freiheitsrechte und institutionelle Garantien der Reichsverfassung (1931)" and "Grundrechte und Grundpflichten (1932)," both in VRA; and "Inhalt und Bedeutung des zweiten Hauptteils der Reichsverfassung," in *Handbuch des deutschen Staatsrechts*, ed. Gerhard Anschütz and Richard Thoma (Tübingen: J. C. B. Mohr, 1930–32), 2:572–606. For a good overview of the Basic Rights in the politics of the Weimar Republic, see Detlev J. K. Peukert, *The Weimar Republic*, trans. Richard Deveson (London: Penguin Books, 1991), 129–46. Hans Carl Nipperdey, ed. *Die Grundrechte und Grundpflichten der Reichsverfassung: Kommentar zum 2 Teil der Reichsverfassung*, 3 vols. (1930; reprint, Berlin: Hobbing, 1975), is the authoritative commentary on the legal status of the various provisions of the Catalogue of Rights. Richard Thoma was a leading contemporary critic of Schmitt's. See "Das System der subjektiven öffentlichen Rechte und Pflichten," in *Handbuch des deutschen Staatsrechts*, ed. Anschütz and Thoma, 2:607–23. For Preuß's position on the compromise character of the constitution, particularly of the rights provisions, see "Begründung des Entwurfs einer Verfassung für das deutsche Reich," in Hugo Preuß, *Staat, Recht und Freiheit, aus vierzig Jahren deutscher Politik und Geschichte*, with an introduction by

Theodor Heuss (Hildesheim: Georg Olms, 1964). On rights in the nineteenth century, see Ulrich Scheuner, "Die rechtliche Tragweite der Grundrechte in der deutschen Verfassungsentwicklung," in *Festschrift für Ernst Rudolf Huber*, ed. Ernst Forsthoff, Werner Weber, and Franz Wieacker (Göttingen: Otto Schwarz, 1973); Rainer Wahl, "Rechtliche Wirkungen und Funktionen der Grundrechte im deutschen Konstitutionalismus," *Der Staat* 18 (1979): 321–48; and Gertrude Lübbe-Wolff, "Das wohlerworbene Recht als Grenze der Gesetzgebung im neunzehnten Jahrhundert," *Zeitschrift der Savigny-Stiftung für Rechtsgeschichte, Germanistische Abteilung* 103 (1986): 104–39. Rainer Wahl, "Der Vorrang der Verfassung," *Der Staat* 20 (1981): 485–516, considers the difficult transition from mere statutory legal rights of the Reich period to the directly enforceable constitutional rights in the Federal Republic. Trans.]

2 [Schmitt did not claim that pluralism was new to the Weimar Republic. In the prewar era, he concedes, German society was deeply divided along cultural, political, religious, and social lines. But because of the political dominance of the conservative Land Prussia, these differences did not destabilize the political system. The Weimar Constitution, by contrast, provided much greater opportunity for groups with narrowly defined interests to use the system to exhort concessions from the state, even if doing so threatened the stability of the overall system (HV 73–74).

Schmitt's emphasis on organized groups at all levels of the political system seeking to influence the process of will formation to their own advantage calls to mind the postwar American version of the concept. For American pluralists, however, the state does not have an identity apart from the amalgam of private groups participating in government, whereas Schmitt adheres to the traditional German notion of the state as independent of society, even under the Weimar Republic. Insofar as Schmitt's model understands pluralism as social groups seeking to influence the state, all the while remaining independent of it, one can trace that model's roots to the older English understanding of the concept.

For a concise analysis of the role of pluralism in the governing problems of the Weimar Republic, see Michael Geyer, "The State in National Socialist Germany," in *Statemaking and Social Movements: Essays in History and Theory*, ed. Charles Bright and Susan Harding (Ann Arbor: University of Michigan Press, 1984), 199–203. On the difference between the English and American understandings of pluralism, see Paul Hirst, ed., *The Pluralist Theory of the State: Selected Writings of G. D. H. Cole, J. N. Figgis, and H. J. Laski* (London: Routledge, 1993), 2–4. David Runciman, *Pluralism and the Personality of the State* (Cambridge: Cambridge University Press, 1997), offers an extended analysis of English pluralists, which, because of its focus on Hobbes and the state, is particularly illuminating for understanding Schmitt's view of pluralism. Trans.]

3 [Johannes Popitz was a career civil servant who developed important financial reforms and advocated enhanced state centralization. After serving as State Secretary for Finance from 1925 to 1929, he was the Reich Minister and Reich Commissioner for the Prussian Ministry of Finance in the Papen and Schleicher cabinets. He was executed after being implicated in the 1944 plot against Hitler.

Schmitt utilized Popitz's concept of "polycracy" to help describe what he considered to be the underlying structure of the Weimar state crisis (HV 71–94, esp. 91–94). Polycracy refers to a large number of organizations that are relatively autonomous from the state in a formal legal sense and yet are responsible for important public functions. The most obvious example is the large number of firms implementing social policy for the state, such as health insurance organizations. But polycracy also includes firms granted autonomy from the state in varying degrees, because they play a role in fulfilling state responsibilities, such as reparations payments. Finally, polycracy includes firms that are taken over and/or organized by governments but function otherwise like private companies. The common element among these diverse forms of economic organization and public/private partnership is the fact that they retain a degree of independence from the state. The dependence of the state on autonomous private organizations to provide an expanding array of government services, in Schmitt's view, contributed significantly to the Weimar Republic's governing problems, particularly because of the concessions the private organizations were able to extract from the state in return for providing state services. Hildemarie Dieckmann, *Johannes Popitz: Entwicklung und Wirksamkeit in der Zeit der Weimar Republik* (Berlin-Dahlem: Colloquium Verlag, 1960), 130–42; Lutz-Arwed Bentin, *Johannes Popitz und Carl Schmitt: Zur wirtschaftlichen Theorie des totalen Staates in Deutschland* (Munich: C. H. Beck, 1972), 13–18 (esp. 13–14), 123–41 (esp. 129–31); and Jeffrey Seitzer, *Comparative History and Legal Theory: Carl Schmitt in the First German Democracy* (Westport, Conn.: Greenwood, 2001), 43, 55, 58, 66–67. Trans.]

4 [Schmitt's insistence that there must be substantive limits on the power of amendment sparked heated controversy. Anschütz,

Thoma, W. Jellinek, and others argued that the formal, procedural limitations outlined in Article 76 were the only limits to constitutional amendment. If one followed proper procedures, one could change any part of the constitution or the constitution in its entirety.

Schmitt and others, such as Heinrich Triepel and Carl Bilfinger, argued that the constitution contained immanent limits on the power of constitutional amendment. Granting any group an "equal chance" to amend the constitution, even those committed to abolishing the system altogether and replacing it entirely, was tantamount to permitting constitutional or system suicide, as Schmitt puts it here. Instead of seeing the constitution as a mere assemblage of unrelated parts, the constitution, in Schmitt's view, represented a unified whole, the product of the German people's sovereign decision for a particular type of political existence, in this case a parliamentary democracy protecting bourgeois civil and political liberties. Considering the constitution as a unified whole meant that the Reichstag could not pass constitutional amendments changing the essential features of this collective, sovereign decision for a particular political form.

According to Horst Ehmke, Schmitt's critique of positivism laid bare the inadequacy of a strictly positivist approach to constitutional amendment; "Grenzen der Verfassungsänderung" (1953), in *Beiträge zur Verfassungstheorie und Verfassungspolitik*, ed. Peter Häberle (Königstein: Athenäum, 1981), 134. Article 79 of the Basic Law of the Federal Republic reflects this fundamental dissatisfaction with positivism, as it does not permit constitutional amendments that eliminate the federal structure of the system, deny the participation of Länder in the legislative process, or infringe on the guiding principles of the system established in Articles 1 and 20, specifically, the principles of human dignity and rights as well as the rights of the democratic and social federal state. At the same time, however, the particular principles exempted from the political process, even from the reach of supermajorities, diverge from Schmitt's more narrowly bourgeois proposals for the Weimar Constitution.

Schmitt's distinction between constitution and constitutional law as an immanent limit on the substance and scope of legislation, both ordinary and constitutional, is elaborated principally in part 1 of his *Verfassungslehre*, esp. v 20–36 and 102–112, respectively. For Schmitt's reaction to the Basic Law, see Dr. Haustein (alias Carl Schmitt), "Das Grundgesetz der Bundesrepublik Deutschland" (1949), reprinted in Hansen and Lietzmann, *Carl Schmitt und die Liberalismuskritik*. Michael Stolleis,

Geschichte des öffentlichen Rechts in Deutschland, vol. 3, *Staats-und Verwaltungsrechtswissenschaft in Republik und Diktatur, 1914–1945* (Munich: C. H. Beck, 1999), 113–14, surveys the positions on the question of the limits of constitutional amendment during the Weimar period. On Article 79 of the Basic Law, see Horst Dreier, "Art. 79," in *Kommentar zum Grundgesetz*, 2 vols., ed. Horst Dreier (Tübingen: J. C. B. Mohr [Paul Siebeck], 1998). Trans.]

5 [Schmitt's insistence that the constitutional system not be permitted to undermine itself by allowing all parties an equal chance to obtain and use political power calls to mind the Federal Republic's principle of "militant democracy" (*streitbare Demokratie*), under which individuals or groups forfeit their rights and privileges if they make use of the existing system and its legal protections to undermine the system or its basic values. There is an important institutional difference between Schmitt's position and that of the current system, however. Under Schmitt's understanding, the President of the Weimar Republic exercised this authority, whereas in the Federal Republic it falls to the Federal Constitutional Court, even during a state of emergency. Another important difference is that the Basic Law is quite explicit about the basic values to be protected and the means used to protect them, whereas Schmitt exempted a contested view of the legitimate social and political order from political struggle.

See Donald P. Kommers, *The Constitutional Jurisprudence of the Federal Republic of Germany*, 2d ed. (Durham, N.C.: Duke University Press, 1997), 37–38 and 217–37, on the concept of militant democracy. On Schmitt's understanding of denying an equal chance to all political parties as a means of preserving the Weimar Republic, see George Schwab, *The Challenge of the Exception: An Introduction to the Political Ideas of Carl Schmitt between 1921 and 1936*, 2d ed. (Westport, Conn.: Greenwood Press, 1989), 94–97. A historical treatment of Schmitt's position is found in Joseph W. Bendersky, *Carl Schmitt: Theorist for the Reich* (Princeton: Princeton University Press, 1983), 145–91. Hermann Heller, a leading contemporary critic of Schmitt, was to exert an influence in the postwar era equal to Schmitt's, particularly on the issue of maintaining the overall integrity of the constitutional order. On Heller, see Christian Müller and Ilse Staff, ed., *Staatslehre in der Weimarer Republik, Hermann Heller zu ehren* (Frankfurt am Main: Suhrkamp, 1985); and David Dyzenhaus, *Legality and Legitimacy: Carl Schmitt, Hans Kelsen, and Hermann Heller in Weimar* (Oxford: Clarendon Press, 1997), 161–258. Trans.]

6 [The legislative-reservation clauses (Gesetzesvorbehalte) reflect

the German understanding of the role of the legislature in rights protection prior to the Federal Republic. Under absolutist monarchies of the seventeenth and eighteenth centuries, the German state was understood as an impersonal entity with a purpose independent of the strivings of the individuals and groups that constituted society. The concept of the independent state remained vibrant into the Weimar Republic, though in modified form, and was particularly important to Schmitt. The most important change concerned the institutional connections between state and society. Specifically, the liberal reforms of the nineteenth century in many parts of Germany instituted what is commonly termed "constitutional dualism," under which the state and its executive retained a considerable degree of independence from society. However, for certain actions, specifically, those that interfered with the freedom and property of citizens, the state required the consent of society represented in the legislature. In contrast to Americans, therefore, who viewed both the executive and the legislature as potential threats to citizens' rights, nineteenth-century Germans looked to the legislature as the primary guarantor of rights against an overbearing executive. The people's representatives in parliament, it was thought, would not infringe on their own liberties, so German rights provisions typically proclaimed that a right could not be infringed "unless by law." Such provisions are explicit grants to parliament to enact restrictions on rights. Article 118 of the Weimar Constitution, for example, permits statutory exceptions to the right of freedom of opinion.

4. Extraordinary Lawgiver *Ratione Supremitatis*

1   [A referendum (*Volksentscheid*) is a popular vote on action taken by the duly constituted state authorities, whereas an initiative (*Volksbegehren*) is a petition for a referendum on a legislative proposal drafted by the petitioners themselves. A referendum might come about in a number of ways under Articles 73–76 of the Weimar Constitution. Through an initiative, one-tenth of enfranchised voters could call for a referendum on their own proposed legislation. If the Reichstag refused to accept the proposed legislation unchanged, then a referendum was called, which had to be decided by a majority of those casting ballots. If, however, the initiative involved a constitutional change, then a majority of enfranchised voters had to decide. The President or the Reichsrat could also call a referendum to challenge legislation passed by the

Reichstag. In order to set aside a provision of the Reichstag, however, a majority of enfranchised voters had to have participated in the referendum. Though the subject of heated controversy, referendums were seldom called and never successful. Detlev J. K. Peukert, *The Weimar Republic*, trans. Richard Deveson (London: Penguin Books, 1991), 40.

Schmitt's critical view of referendums is presented in *Volksentscheid und Volksbegehren: Ein Beitrag zur Auslegung der Weimarer Verfassung und zur Lehre von der unmittelbaren Demokratie* (Berlin: Walter de Gruyter, 1927). For a discussion of several referendums from the Weimar period, see Otmar Jung, *Direkte Demokratie in der Weimarer Republik: Die Fälle "Aufwertung," "Fürstenenteignung," "Panzerkreuzerverbot," und "Youngplan"* (Frankfurt am Main: Campus, 1989). Trans.]

2 [The term *Aufhebung* is usually rendered elimination or destruction. Here, however, it has the more uncommon meaning associated mostly with Hegel of something being eliminated yet preserved in another form. On Hegel's use of Aufhebung, see Charles Taylor, *Hegel* (Cambridge: Cambridge University Press, 1975), 119. Schmitt's relation to Hegel is treated in Jean-François Kervégan, *Hegel, Carl Schmitt: Le Politique Entre Spéculation et Positivité* (Paris: Presses Universitaires de France, 1992). Trans.]

3 [Article 31 of the Weimar Constitution established an Electoral Review Commission (*Wahlprüfungsgericht*) to settle electoral disputes. It was to function procedurally somewhat like an administrative court, though it was to be composed of an unspecified number of the members of the Reichstag, who were chosen for the duration of the current session and of members of the anticipated National Administrative Court (*Reichverwaltungsgericht*), which was never established. Instead, judges were selected from the Reichsgericht. Three members from the Reichstag and two from the Reichsgericht formed a quorum necessary for judgment, which could be rendered only after a public hearing. When the Commission was not conducting a hearing prior to a judgment, a National Commissioner appointed by the President led its proceedings. For an overview of the Commission's history, composition, jurisdiction, and procedure, see Georg Kaisenberg, "Die Wahlprüfung," in *Handbuch des deutschen Staatsrechts*, ed. Gerhart Anschütz and Richard Thoma (Tübingen: J. C. B. Mohr, 1930–32), 1:400–407; and Johannes Mattern, *Principles of the Constitutional Jurisprudence of the German National Republic* (Baltimore: Johns Hopkins Press, 1928), 428–29.

"Electoral Review Court" would be a more literal rendering of *Wahlprüfungsgericht*. The term "commission," however, better captures the combination of adjudication and administration characteristic of the administrative state in the United States. Trans.]

5. Extraordinary Lawgiver *Ratione Necessitatis*

1 [Because they were passed with a two-thirds majority of the Reichstag, enabling acts *(Ermächtigungsgesetze)* met the requirements of a constitutional amendment. They granted certain organs, typically the Reich government or the President, the power to issue decrees with the force of law (Rechtsverordnungen), which, in some cases, could deviate from express constitutional provisions *(Verfassungsdurchbrechungen)*. This decree power was subject to time limitations as well as restrictions on the content and object of the decrees issued.

Enforcement legislation *(Ausführungsgesetze)*, by contrast, were supplementary acts meant to fill out the details of legislation previously enacted. While one might disagree over whether the provisions of enforcement legislation constitute a change in the previously established principles, enforcement legislation is conceptually not meant to affect a substantive change in the parameters of the previous legislation.

Enabling acts played a very large role in the early years of the Weimar Republic and at the outset of the Nazi regime. Enabling acts in both periods broadly conformed to the features outlined above. Nonetheless, though the enabling acts in the Ebert era granted sweeping powers to the executive that allowed deviations from express constitutional provisions, they aimed at substituting for parliamentary government until the governmental crisis passed. The enabling act passed in March 1934 in the aftermath of the Reichstag fire, by contrast, effectively displaced democratic institutions and introduced permanent constitutional changes, specifically, the *Führerprinzip* (leadership principle) as a governmental form.

On the enabling acts under Ebert and Hitler, see Ludwig Richter, "Das präsidiale Notverordnungsrecht in den ersten Jahren der Weimarer Republik: Friedrich Ebert und die Anwendung des Artikels 48 der Weimarer Reichsverfassung," in *Friedrich Ebert als Reichspräsident: Amtsführung und Amtsverständnis*, ed. Eberhard Kolb (Munich: Oldenbourg, 1997), 248–53; and Hans Rein, *Weimar, rechtsgeschichtlickh dokumentiert* (Stuttgart: Richard Boorberg, 1991), 127–29, respectively. Trans.]

2 RGZ 134 1931, Anhang [appendix] pp. 12 and 26.

3 [Both the Reichsgericht and the Staatsgerichtshof sanctioned extensive executive discretion under Article 48. The Reichsgericht granted wide latitude to military officials under Prussian law during World War I. At the height of the Republic's first extended crisis, however, the Reichsgericht threatened to nullify actions taken by the Reich government under Article 48 and an enabling act to stabilize the currency. Generally, though, the Reichsgericht granted the President and the Reich government wide-ranging discretion in their exercise of presidential emergency powers. Peter Blomeyer, *Der Notstand in den letzten Jahren von Weimar: Die Bedeutung von Recht, Lehre und Praxis der Notstandsgewalt für den Untergang der Weimarer Republik und die Machtübernahme durch die Nationalsozialisten* (Berlin: Duncker und Humblot, 1999), 89–90, 95 n. 44, 229. This was also true of the Staatsgerichtshof. It was not until the important 1932 case on the Reich takeover of the Prussian government, the so-called sacking of Prussia, that the Staatsgerichtshof placed limits on executive discretion under Article 48. Even here, though, the Staatsgerichtshof sanctioned the Reich action where it mattered most, exercising governmental authority. The court merely refused to permit the Reich to completely and permanently replace the Prussian government. Peter C. Caldwell, *Popular Sovereignty and the Crisis of German Constitutional Law: The Theory and Practice of Weimar Constitutionalism* (Durham, N.C.: Duke University Press, 1997), 160–70, esp. 167. Trans.]

4 [Late in the Weimar Republic, several Länder governments, most notably Prussia, established general clauses empowering the police to provide for public safety. Combined with an ever more diffident judiciary, these new provisions circumvented to a great extent the extensive legal controls of police activity in the form of administrative law that had been built up since the early nineteenth century. See Michael Stolleis, *Geschichte des öffentlichen Rechts in Deutschland* (Munich: C.H. Beck, 1999), 3:365. Trans.]

5 Verordnung des Reichspräsident zur Sicherung der Staatsautorität, 13 April 1932 and 3 May 1932, RGBl 1932, 1:175. [Also in Ernst Rudolf Huber, ed., *Dokumente zur Deutschen Verfassungsgeschichte*, vol. 4, *Deutsche Verfassungsdokumente, 1919–1933*, 3d ed. (Stuttgart: W. Kohlhammer, 1992), 524–25. Trans.]

6 RGBl 1932, 1:185.

7 Decision of the 1st Senate of the Reichsgericht, October 6, 1931, in *Juristische Wochenschrift* (1931): 3603.

8 Verordnung des Reichspräsident über die Spar und Girokassen sowie die kommunalen Giroverbände und kommunalen Kredit-

institute, August 5, 1931, RGBl 1931, 1:429. [Schmitt's page reference is incorrect. It is actually p. 50. Trans.]

9 Gesetz über Aufnahme von Auslandskrediten durch Gemeinden und Gemeindenverbände, March 27, 1925, RGBl 1925, 1:11, 27. [The official date of the statute is March 27, not March 21, the date that Schmitt uses in the text. Trans.]

10 RGZ 134 1931, Anhang [appendix] pp. 12 and 26.

11 Justification of the Draft of the National Law concerning Retirement of Debt and Grants of Credit of May 12, 1932, in RGBl 1932, 1:191. On this, see Anschütz and Jellinek (1932).

12 [Negotiations in the Committee of State Representatives of February 5-8, 1919, *Bericht und Protokolle des Achten Verfassungsausschußes über den Entwurf einer Verfassung des Deutschen Reichs* (Berlin: Carl Heymann, 1919). Trans.]

13 Prussian Cameral Court, Decision of March 22, 1932, in *Deutsche Juristen-Zeitung* (1932): 534.

14 Verordnung des Reichspräsidenten v. Hindenburg über die Darmstädter und Nationalbank, July 13, 1931, RGBl 1931, 1:361. [Schmitt's page reference is incorrect. It is actually p. 359. Also in Huber, *Verfassungsdokumente*, 492. Trans.]

15 RGZ 134 1931, Anhang [appendix] pp. 24 and 43.

16 [*Staatsrechtslehre* is often translated as "legal and political theory." But like Staatsrecht, which is rendered above as "public law," Staatsrechtslehre has a restricted range of meaning in the Weimar context. Legal and political theory, for example, might involve normative arguments about the organization and operation of state organs, which is properly the subject of Staatsrechtslehre, though this is not necessarily the case. In fact, legal and political theory often considers topics outside the realm of Staatsrechtslehre, such as the nature of man and society. Trans.]

Conclusion

1 [Bismarck's Reich Constitution forged a national government from numerous independent states by permitting the Länder to retain a good deal of their former sovereignty. After the collapse of the Reich system, there was substantial support for a fundamental reform of the federal system. In the end, however, the Weimar Constitution preserved the traditional system with some modifications. Reich authority increased significantly, particularly in regard to taxation, but the Länder were still relatively autonomous governing units, with their own parliaments and court systems.

Moreover, as under the traditional system, the Länder retained control over much of the administrative apparatus needed to enforce Reich laws. Finally, though the Länder governments had a high degree of autonomy from the Reich, they could exert considerable influence at the Reich level. For example, they could hinder the full implementation of Reich laws through opposition in the Reichsrat or through half-hearted administration at the regional or local levels. Also, because parties with a narrowly local or regional orientation could gain representation in the closely divided Reichstag, more parochial interests could force concessions from hard-pressed parliamentary majorities that were detrimental to the national interest. So the problem of political pluralism so destructive at the Reich level, in Schmitt's view, was duplicated at the regional and local levels, complicating the already difficult task of governing (HV 72, 92–93).

On failed efforts to reform the federal system, see Ernst Rudolf Huber, *Deutsche Verfassungsgeschichte seit 1789* (Stuttgart: W. Kohlhammer, 1984), 7:668–79; and Gerhard Schulz, *Zwischen Demokratie und Diktatur: Verfassungspolitik und Reichsreform in der Weimarer Republik* (Berlin: Walter de Gruyter, 1963), 3:486–515, 564–612. On the complex changes in the tax system, see Huber, *Verfassungsgeschichte*, 6: 486–504; and Mabel Newcomer, *Central and Local Finance in Germany and England* (New York: Columbia University Press, 1937), 42–97. The impact of local and regional parties and interests on the Reich level is discussed in Huber, *Verfassungsgeschichte*, 6:498–99; and William L. Patch Jr., *Heinrich Brüning and the Dissolution of the Weimar Republic* (Cambridge: Cambridge University Press, 1998), 94–95. Jeffrey Seitzer, *Comparative History and Legal Theory: Carl Schmitt in the First German Democracy* (Westport, Conn.: Greenwood, 2001), 41–71, examines Schmitt's critique of German federalism. Trans.]

2 [The French Third Republic did not have a constitution as such. After the collapse of the Second Empire, there was an ongoing debate over the character of the successor regime, though no clear consensus formed. The Republic itself was established almost inadvertently as the by-product of an amendment to an ordinary piece of legislation. Several other pieces of ordinary legislation served as the Republic's constitution by stipulating the powers of the three primary institutions of government, the president, the senate, and the chamber of deputies. Though the laws were obviously of greater importance than ordinary legislation, they could be amended almost as easily, marking an important difference between these acts and the Weimar Constitution. Jean-

Marie Mayeur and Madeleine Réberioux, *The Third Republic from its Origins to the Great War, 1871–1914*, trans. J. R. Foster (Cambridge: Cambridge University Press, 1989), 5–41, esp. 23–27. Trans.]

3   Cf. Das Volksbegehren gegen den Young-Plan: Entwurf eines "Gesetzes gegen die Versklavung des deutschen Volkes" (September 11, 1929), *Verhandlungen des Reichstags*, vol. 438, no. 1429, appendix 1; with the Reichsgesetz über die Haager Konferenz vom 13. März 1930, RGBl 1930, 2:45. [The former was an unsuccessful initiative against the Young Plan of 1929 reorganizing German reparations that was sponsored by the Nazis, Conservatives, the Stahlhelm, and the Reichslandbund. The latter document is a Reich statute approving the revised Young Plan in 1930. The initiative, along with official pronouncements by the Reich government and the President, are reprinted in Ernst Rudolf Huber, ed., *Dokumente zur Deutschen Verfassungsgeschichte*, vol. 4, *Deutsche Verfassungsdokumente, 1919–1933*, 3d ed. (Stuttgart: W. Kohlhammer, 1992), 447–51. Trans.]

4   [Schmitt is referring here to an offshoot of institutions mentioned in Article 165, which envisioned a set of "workers' councils" at the local, regional, and national levels, Workers' Labor Councils, District Workers' Councils, and Reich Workers' Councils, respectively. The first two, along with a number of other organizations, were to form District and Reich Economic Councils, which were to have some administrative powers in the economy, particularly regarding socialization plans. Moreover, the Reich Economic Council was to have an important screening function, with proposed Reich laws concerning the economy and society presented to it for approval before being submitted to the Reichstag. The Reich Economic Council could also introduce draft laws, even if the Reich government disagreed with them, and assign one of its members the task of representing its draft law before the Reichstag.

The grand vision of Article 165 was never fully realized. A Workers' Councils Law was passed in 1920 mandating worker representation in the management of firms of a certain size, and, in the same year, a provisional Reich Economic Council was established by decree. Verordnung der Reichsregierung über den vorlaüfigen Reichswirtschaftsrat, May 4, 1920," RGBl 1920, 1:858. Also in Huber, *Verfassungsdokumente*, 188–92. In regard to the President's Economic Advisory Board mentioned by Schmitt (1958/337), it mostly only served as an advisory body of the Reich government, with no real legislative or administrative power. Charles Maier, *Recasting Bourgeois Europe: Stabili-*

zation in France, Germany, and Italy in the Decade after World War I (1975; reprint, Princeton: Princeton University Press, 1988), 207–8.

Throughout the Weimar era, however, Article 165 was the subject of intense debate. Believing that democratic political institutions were unable to provide genuine social equality, many socialists sought an "economic constitution" ensuring genuine worker representation and participation in economic policymaking and administration at all levels of the system and in both the private and public sector. Schmitt was a vocal opponent of such plans, arguing that one must focus on the Weimar Constitution's core political institutions and a select number of individual freedoms associated with the liberal Rechtsstaat.

Keith Tribe, ed., *Social Democracy and the Rule of Law: Otto Kirchheimer and Franz Neumann*, trans. Leena Tanner and Keith Tribe (London: Allen and Unwin, 1987), 200–201, contains an English translation of Article 165. Schmitt elaborates his position on Article 165 in *Hüter der Verfassung* (HV 98). For a contemporary critique of Schmitt's position, see Franz Neumann, "On the Social Significance of the Basic Laws" and "On the Conditions and Legal Concept of an Economic Constitution," both in Tribe, *Social Democracy and the Rule of Law*. Trans.]

5 [Emmanuel-Joseph Sieyès was the author of pamphlet *Qu'est-ce que le tiers état?* (1789), which was highly influential during the French Revolution. Early in the revolution, it was not clear what role the traditional estates and their institutions would have in founding a new constitution. Sieyès argued that a radical break with the past was necessary and that only an act of political will by the French nation could legitimately found a new order. For a brief account of Sieyès's role in the French Revolution, see Keith M. Baker, "Sieyès," in *A Critical Dictionary of the French Revolution*, ed. François Furet and Mona Ozouf (Cambridge: Harvard University Press, 1989), 313–23.

In *Verfassungslehre* (V 77–78) Schmitt relies on Sieyès's understanding of the nation as the *pouvoir constituant* in order to elaborate his theory of constitution-making as a decision of the people to create a new type of political existence. More specifically, he credits the French via Sieyès with discovering the true basis of constitution-making in a decision by the people in its collective capacity that is not bound by preexisting norms or institutions. For critical readings of Schmitt's appropriation of Sieyès, see Stefan Breuer, "Nationalstaat und pouvoir constituant bei Sieyès und Carl Schmitt," *Archiv für Rechts- und Sozialphilosophie* 70 (1984): 495–517; William Scheuerman, "Carl Schmitt's Critique of Liberal Constitutionalism," *Review of Politics* 58 (1996): 309; and Seitzer, *Comparative History*, 18, 20–21. Trans.]

6 Verordnung des Reichspräsidenten über die Auflösung des Reichstags, June 4, 1932, RGBl 1932, 1:255. [Schmitt's page citation is incorrect. It should be 297. Trans.]

7 [In *Hüter der Verfassung* (HV 60–70), Schmitt argues that features of the Weimar Constitution, such as its extensive catalogue of basic rights and the expansion of the specialized system of courts, encourage the use of courts for political purposes. Individuals, groups, and even governmental organs may use court challenges as a means of obtaining through the judiciary what they fail to gain via the political process, according to Schmitt. He points out, for example, that even the Reich government itself was not above seeking to use the Staatsgerichtshof to circumvent its own policies, when it was politically expedient (HV 59).

Schmitt's critique of the potential politicization of the German judiciary anticipated the current scholarly interest in the political role of courts. See, for example, Donald Kommers, *Judicial Politics in West Germany* (Beverly Hills, Calif.: Sage Publications, 1976); Christine Landfried, *Bundesverfassungsgericht und Gesetzgeber*, 2d ed. (Baden-Baden: Nomos, 1984); and Alec Stone, *The Birth of Judicial Politics in France: The Constitutional Council in Comparative Perspective* (Oxford: Oxford University Press, 1992). Contemporary social science treatments stress the significant influence of courts on policymaking, with legislative deliberations actually coming to reflect the legal discourse of courts. Alec Stone, "Constitutional Dialogues: Protecting Rights in France, Germany, Italy, and Spain," in *Constitutional Dialogues in Comparative Perspective*, ed. Sally Kenney, John Reitz, and William Reisinger (London: Macmillan, 1999), 8–41. Schmitt, by contrast, argued that "a juridification of politics" in this sense would not occur. Rather, the judiciary would merely become another pluralist battleground, but without effectively resolving any of the contentious issues brought before the courts (HV 22). Finally, contemporary treatments chart actual developments, whereas Schmitt was postulating that certain trends were possible given various conditions, even though, as he pointed out, courts were only willing to make the most tentative steps toward addressing major constitutional questions (HV 62–70, 102–3).

Schmitt's critique of the judiciary in German politics is considered in Seitzer, *Comparative History*, 73–127. Trans.]

8 ["Supplements" is a literal rendering of the German term *Supplementen*. What Schmitt means here, however, might be better expressed by the English term "payoffs" or perhaps "side payments."

Notes to Conclusion 153

The rule of a monarch, according to Schmitt, typically has a claim to legitimacy independent of elections or governmental performance. Governments in the pluralist Parteienstaat, by contrast, are legitimate in the eyes of the electorate to the extent that, and only so long as, they can deliver the goods, so to speak. That is, do particular groups benefit tangibly from their rule? Pluralist parties, in Schmitt's view, are forced to pay off supporters and even opponents in order to continue to hold the reins of state power.

Much the same can be said of the German term *Ergänzungen* [1932/94], rendered in this translation as "extensions." By using their temporary hold on state power to supply lukewarm supporters or outright opponents with some benefit, political parties are able to maintain their grip on power, if only for a time. Trans.]

9 [For Schmitt, the Weimar Republic's electoral law is a primary defect of the political system, because it reinforces the position of political parties. The shift from single-member district elections in the Reich period to strict proportional representation in the Weimar period, more specifically, encouraged the fragmentation of the party system, which, in turn, contributed to the Republic's governability problems (HV 85–90).

While proportional representation works to the advantage of small parties, at least in comparison to most systems of single-member district elections, it is difficult to attribute the fragmentation of the party system to proportional representation. First, there was significant continuity between the party system of the Reich period and that of Weimar, even though representation in the Reich was determined in single-member district elections, suggesting other factors produced the splintering of the party system. Also, the fragmentation of the party system did not become a serious problem until 1928, when splinter parties first appeared with 17.1 percent of the vote. There were major changes in vote totals prior to this, but these shifts were best attributed to reactions to important events at the time. In the 1920 election, for example, disappointment over the peace settlement and lack of progress on socialization fueled a significant shift toward the right and left, respectively, reducing the share of the vote of the Weimar Coalition (Social Democrats, Democrats, and Catholic Center) from over 75 percent to just shy of 42 percent.

These shifts, moreover, did not benefit splinter parties. In 1920, the existing parties, such as the Conservatives, the German People's Party, the Independent Socialists, and the Communists, divided among themselves many of the Coalition's lost votes. The defection of much of its Bavarian wing into the newly formed Bavarian People's Party (4.2 percent) mostly accounted for the Center Party's decline in votes. With the exception of the absorption of the Independent Socialists by the Social Democrats and the Communists and the increase in support for the Conservatives mostly at the expense of the bourgeois parties, the German Democratic Party and the German People's Party, there was very little change in the vote totals in 1924 and 1928.

Finally, Nazi electoral fortunes illustrated that the possible negative impact of the splinter parties was short-lived. After losing support between 1924 and 1928, dropping from 6.5 to 2.6 percent of the vote, the Nazi electoral breakthrough first came in 1930 with 18.3 percent of the vote, mostly at the expense of the Conservatives and the bourgeois parties. For the remaining three "free" elections, that in March 1933 being influenced by Nazi control of the police, the vote totals for the combined left and the Center Party remained mostly constant. In July 1932, however, the Nazis drew its largest vote total, 37.3 percent, pulling support from the bourgeois parties, the Conservatives, and the splinter parties. In the next election the following November, the splinter party share increased slightly, from 6.2 to 6.5 percent of the total, while the Nazi share dropped to 33.1 percent, mostly to the benefit of the Conservatives.

Thus splinter parties only became a significant feature of the electoral landscape after almost a decade of democratic practice and then only for two elections. Perhaps a threshold requirement like that of the current Federal Republic might have discouraged the formation of these parties initially. Nonetheless, the timing and duration of their appearance suggest that the system of proportional representation alone was not responsible for the fragmentation of the party system.

On the continuity between the two party systems, see M. Rainer Lepsius, "Parteiensystem und Sozialstruktur: Zum Problem der Demokratisierung der deutschen Gesellschaft," in *Demokratie in Deutschland: Soziologisch-historische Konstellationsanalysen: Ausgewählte Aufsätze* (Göttingen: Vandenhoeck und Ruprecht, 1993), 31–38. Detlev J. K. Peukert, *The Weimar Republic*, trans. Richard Deveson (London: Penguin Books, 1991), 38, analyzes the political implications of the proportional representation system. For an exhaustive study of parliamentary elections in the Weimar Republic, see Richard F. Hamilton, *Who Voted for Hitler?* (Princeton: Princeton University Press, 1982). Appendix A contains a summary analysis of Reichstag elections. Trans.]

10 [Friedrich Naumann, a prominent Christian social theorist and politician, believed that the collapse of the Imperial system of-

fered the opportunity to establish a new type of system combining features of the capitalist West and socialist East. The Second Principal Part of the Weimar Constitution reflects Naumann's vision in that it contains a wide array of rights provisions, including traditional political and civil as well as economic and social rights. The economic and social rights lent constitutional status to the extensive social legislation of the Reich. In practical terms, therefore, the inclusion of these rights provisions represented mostly only a symbolic change from the previous era, though not an altogether insignificant one in Schmitt's view.

While Schmitt in this context praises what he considers Naumann's preference for substantive constitutional provisions over procedural ones, he was quite critical of the Second Principal Part of the Weimar Constitution, labeling it a "bottomless pit of doubts" and "differences of opinion" about the constitution (HV 49). Leaving aside the difficult question of the legal status of these rights provisions, their inclusion in the Weimar Constitution signaled that the system was not the sole preserve of one end of the political spectrum. This indecisiveness regarding the overall purpose of the system, in Schmitt's view, had disastrous consequences for the Weimar Republic (V 157–82, esp. 181–82). By lending apparent constitutional status to multiple and often competing claims for state action, the Basic Rights provisions, in Schmitt's view, encouraged competing groups to seek special treatment, exacerbating rather than moderating the social tensions that caused political instability.

Class conflict was, indeed, a major factor in the unstable politics of the era, with disputes over civil servant salaries and worker contributions to unemployment insurance greatly complicating the task of governing the Republic. But it is difficult to say that the Basic Rights provisions further exacerbated already tense social relations. Various groups would have agitated for their causes, even without constitutional provisions supporting their claims. Peukert, *Weimar*, 132–47.

On Naumann generally, see Peter Theiner, *Sozialer Liberalismus und deutsche Weltpolitik: Friedrich Naumann im Wilhelminischen Deutschland (1860–1919)* (Baden-Baden: Nomos, 1983). The politics of the welfare state is considered in Young-Sun Hong, *Welfare, Modernity, and the Weimar State, 1919–1933* (Princeton: Princeton University Press, 1998); and David Crew, "The Ambiguities of Modernity: Welfare and the German State from Wilhelm to Hitler," in *Society, Culture, and the State in Germany, 1870–1930*, ed. Geoff Eley (Ann Arbor: University of Michigan Press, 1996). On the difficulties of governing due to poor economic conditions, see David Abraham, *The Collapse of the Weimar Republic: Political Economy and Crisis*, 2d ed. (New York: Holmes and Meier, 1986); and Jürgen von Kruedener, "Die Überforderung der Weimarer Republik als Sozialstaat," in *Geschichte und Gesellschaft* 11, no. 3 (1985): 358–76.

Afterword (1958)

[I have deleted Schmitt's reference to the original essay's date of completion. Also, Schmitt's comments include many references to the 1958 edition of *Legality and Legitimacy* as well as to other essays and addendums included in *Verfassungsrechtliche Aufsätze aus den Jahren 1924–1954* (VRA). Schmitt's references to specific pages of this essay collection, which he places in parentheses in the body of the text, might be confused with the page numbers to the 1958 edition that I have placed in brackets in this essay and in the main text of *Legality and Legitimacy*. To avoid any possible confusion, I have removed Schmitt's references from the main text and included them in translator's notes. Trans.]

1 [See VRA 286. Trans.]
2 [See VRA 302–3. Trans.]
3 [See VRA 344–45. Trans.]
4 [For further evidence, see VRA 301f. Trans.]
5 [A Social Democrat, Radbruch was a member of the Reichstag from 1920 to 1924 and Justice Minister in the Wirth and Stresemann cabinets in 1921/22 and 1923, respectively. During his tenure as Justice Minister, there were a number of significant legislative actions, such as the admission of women to the practice of law and the passage of a law to protect the Republic (*Reichschutzgesetz*). His scholarly work on criminal law reform had some impact during his time in office, but it became more influential in the postwar period. For an overview of Radbruch's life and work, see M. Kayßer, "Gustav Radbruch," in Michael Stolleis, ed., *Juristen: Ein biographisches Lexikon von der Antike bis zum 20. Jahrhundert* (Munich: C. H. Beck, 2001). Trans.]
6 [In 1932, Kirchheimer published four essays in the journal *Die Gesellschaft*, all of which discussed Schmitt to varying degrees, but one of which was a review of *Legality and Legitimacy* that marked a more critical turn in his relationship with Schmitt. Kirchheimer ([1932] 1987). On Schmitt's relation to the Frankfurt School, cf. William E. Scheuerman, *Between the Norm and the Exception: The Frankfurt School and the Rule of Law* (Cambridge, Mass.: MIT Press, 1994), esp. 80–99; and Ellen Kennedy,

"Carl Schmitt and the Frankfurt School," *Telos* 71 (Spring 1987): 37–66. Trans.]

7 [On the controversy over Kautsky's position on the Russian Revolution, see Dick Geary, *Karl Kautsky* (Manchester: Manchester University Press, 1987), 73–85. Trans.]

8 [Cf. VRA 452f. Schmitt is referring to the first page of the essay "Rechtstaatlicher Verfassungsvollzug (1952)," where he quotes in full Article 41 of the Hessian Constitution. Among the provisions in that constitution were the transferral to public property of mining, iron and steel producers, and energy companies and the regulation or administration by the Land of large banks and insurance companies. These were generally stated provisions, and details about them were to be "settled by statute." Trans.]

9 [See VRA 278 and 300f. Trans.]

10 [Article 19(1) reads: "Insofar as a basic right may, under this Basic Law, be restricted by or pursuant to a statute, such statute shall apply generally and not solely to an individual case. Furthermore, such statute shall name the basic right, indicating the Article concerned." Federal Ministry of Justice and Ministry of Finance, *The Basic Law of the Federal Republic of Germany* (Bonn: Press and Information Office of the Federal Government, 1989), 21–22. Trans.]

11 [Article 80 reads in part: "The Federal Government, a Federal Minister or the Land governments may be authorized by statute to issue ordinances (Rechtsverordnungen). The content, purpose, and scope of the authorization so conferred shall be laid down in the statute concerned. This legal basis shall be stated in the ordinance. Where such a statute provides that such authorization may be delegated, such delegation shall require another ordinance." Ibid., 49–50. Trans.]

12 [Article 14 reads:
(Property, right of inheritance, taking of property)
(1) Property and the right of inheritance shall be guaranteed. Their content and limits shall be determined by statute.
(2) Property imposes duties. Its use should also serve the public weal.
(3) The taking of property shall only be permissible in the public weal. It may be effected only by or pursuant to a statute regulating the nature and extent of compensation. Such compensation shall be determined by establishing an equitable balance between the public interest and the interests of those affected. In case of dispute regarding the amount of compensation, recourse may be had to the courts of ordinary jurisdiction. Ibid., 20. Trans.]

13 [Article 2 reads:
(Rights of liberty)
(1) Everyone shall have the right to the free development of his personality insofar as he does not violate the rights of others or offend against the constitutional order or against morality.
(2) Everyone shall have the right to life and physical integrity. The liberty of the individual shall be inviolable. Intrusion on these rights may only be made pursuant to a statute.
Ibid., 14. Trans.]

14 [Article 9 reads:
(Freedom of association)
(1) All Germans shall have the right to form associations, partnerships, and corporations.
(2) Associations, the purposes or activities of which conflict with criminal statutes or which are directed against the constitutional order or the concept of international understanding shall be prohibited.
(3) The right to form associations to safeguard and improve working and economic conditions shall be guaranteed to everyone and to all occupations. Agreements which restrict or seek to impair this right shall be null and void; measures directed to this end shall be illegal. Measures taken pursuant to Article 12a, to paragraphs (2) and (3) of Article 35, to paragraph (4) of Article 87a, or to Article 91 may not be directed against any industrial conflicts engaged in by associations within the meaning of the first sentence of this paragraph in order to safeguard and improve working and economic conditions.
Ibid., 16–17. Trans.]

15 [Article 12 reads:
(Right to choose an occupation, prohibition of forced labour)
(1) All Germans shall have the right to freely choose their occupation, their place of work and their place of study or training. The practice of an occupation may be regulated by or pursuant to a statute.
(2) No person may be forced to perform work of a particular kind except within the framework of a traditional compulsory community service that applies generally and equally for all.
(3) Forced labour may be imposed only on persons deprived of their liberty by court sentence.
Ibid., 18. Trans.]

16 [See VRA 283f. Trans.]

17 [See VRA 107. Schmitt is referring to the essay "Das Reichsgericht als Hüter der Verfassung (1929)." Trans.]

18 [On this, see VRA 305. Trans.]

19 [See VRA 448–51. Schmitt is referring to comments on the essay "Das Problem der Legalität (1950)." Trans.]
20 Prelate Kass to Schleicher, January 26, 1933, *Reichskanzlei*, R-43-I, 1865, 403–5. Reprinted in *Das Jahrbuch des öffentlichen Rechts* 21 (1933/1934): 141–42.
21 [On the dispute between Schmitt and Kaas, see Olivier Beaud, *Les derniers jours de Weimar: Carl Schmitt face à l'avenèment du nazisme* (Paris: Descartes, 1997), 186–90. Trans.]
22 [Cf. remark 2 at VRA 357. Schmitt is referring to comments on the essay "Die Stellvertretung des Reichspräsidenten (1933)." Trans.]
23 [Cf. remark 1 at VRA 365. Schmitt is referring to comments on the essay "Weiterentwicklung des totalen Staats in Deutschland (1933)." Trans.]
24 [Cf. the essay at VRA 367–71. Schmitt is referring to the essay "Machtpositionen des modernen Staates (1933)." Trans.]
25 [See note 5 at VRA 450. Schmitt is again referring to the essay "Das Problem der Legalität (1950)." Trans.]

WORKS CITED BY CARL SCHMITT

in *Legality and Legitimacy*

———

Anschütz, Gerhard. 1901. *Die gegenwärtigen Theorien über den Begriff von der gesetzgebenden Gewalt.* 2d ed. Tübingen: J. C. B. Mohr.

———. 1912. *Die Verfassungs-Urkunde für den preußischen Staat vom 31. January 1850: Ein Kommentar für Wissenschaft und Praxis.* Berlin: O. Häring.

———. 1932. *Die Verfassung des Deutschen Reiches vom 11. August 1919.* 14th ed. Berlin: Georg Stilke.

Anschütz, Gerhard, and Walter Jellinek. 1932. *Reichskredite und Diktatur: Zwei Rechtsgutachten.* Tübingen: J. C. B. Mohr (Paul Siebeck).

Anschütz, Gerhard, and Richard Thoma, ed. 1930–32. *Handbuch des deutschen Staatsrechts.* 2 vols. Tübingen: J. C. B. Mohr.

Ballerstedt, Kurt. 1957. "Über wirtschaftliche Maßnahme-gesetze." *Festschrift zum 70. Geburtstag von Walter Schmidt-Rimpler.* Edited by Rechts- und Staatswissenschaftlichen Fakultät der Rheinischen Friedrich-Wilhelms Universität. Karlsruhe: C. F. Müller.

Burdeau, Georges. 1949–57. *Traité de science politique.* 7 vols. Paris: Librairie générale de droit et de jurisprudence.

Eisele, Fridolin. 1885. *Unverbindlicher Gesetzesinhalt.* Freiburg: Lehmann.

Forsthoff, Ernst. 1955. "Über Maßnahme-Gesetze." *Forschungen und Berichte aus dem öffentlichen Recht, Gedächtnisschrift für Walter Jellinek.* Edited by Otto Bachof et al. Munich: Isar.

Fraenkel, Ernst. 1931. "Die Krise des Rechtsstaats und die Justiz." *Die Gesellschaft* 2 (October): 327–41.

Gerber, Hans. 1932. "Entwicklung und Reform des Beamtenrechts." *Veröffentlichungen der Vereinigung der Deutschen Staatsrechtslehrer* 7:1–52.

Grau, Richard. 1932. "Die Diktaturgewalt des Reichspräsidenten." In *Handbuch des Deutschen Staatsrechts.* Vol. 2. Edited by Gerhard Anschütz und Richard Thoma. Tübingen: J. C. B. Mohr (Paul Siebeck).

Häntzschel, Kurt. 1932. *Die Verordnungen gegen politische*

Ausschreitungen und über die Auflösung der kommunistischen Gottlosenorganisationen. 3d ed. Berlin: Stilke.

Hauriou, Maurice. 1925. *Précis élémentaire de droit constitutionnel.* Paris: Tenin.

Jacobi, Erwin. 1929. *Die Reichsgerichtspraxis im deutschen Rechtsleben: Festgabe der juristischen Fakultäten zum fünfzigjährigen Bestehen des Reichsgerichts.* Berlin: de Gruyter.

Jellinek, Walter. 1927. *Verfassung und Verwaltung des Reichs und der Länder.* 3d ed. Leipzig: B. G. Teubner.

Kautsky, Karl. 1919. *Terrorismus und Kommunismus: Ein Beitrag zur Naturgeschichte der Revolution.* Berlin: Neues Vaterland.

Kelsen, Hans. [1928] 1949. "Natural Law Doctrine and Legal Positivism." In *General Theory of Law and State.* Translated by Wolfgang Herbert Kraus. Cambridge, Mass.: Harvard University Press.

Kirchheimer, Otto. [1932] 1987. "Legality and Legitimacy." In *Social Democracy and the Rule of Law: Otto Kirchheimer and Franz Neumann.* Edited by Keith Tribe. Translated by Leena Tanner and Keith Tribe. London: Allen and Unwin. Originally published as "Legalität und Legitimität," *Die Gesellschaft* 9 (July 1932): 8–26.

———. 1957. "Vom Wandel der politischen Opposition." *Archiv der Rechts- und Sozialphilosophie* 43:59–80.

Koellreutter, Otto. 1932. "Parteien und Verfassung im heutigen Deutschland." In *Festgabe für Richard Schmidt.* Edited by Hans Gmalen and Otto Koellreuter. Leipzig: Aalen.

Kühnemann, Max. 1931. "Können Reichstat und Reichskredite diktorisch geregelt werden? Ein Beitrag zur Lehre vom Ausnahme zustand." *Reichsverwaltungsblatt* 52:745–52.

Lammers, Hans-Hermann, and Walter Simons, eds. 1929. *Die Rechtsprechung des Staatsgerichtshofs für das Deutsche Reichsgerichts auf Artikel 13 Absatz 2 der Reichsverfassung.* 2 vols. Berlin: Georg Stilke.

Leuthold, Carl Edwin. 1884. *Annalen des Deutschen Reiches für Gesetzgebung, Verwaltung und Volkswirtschaft.* Munich: Schweitzer.

Loewenstein, Karl. 1931. "Die Verfassungsmässigkeit der Notverordnungen vom Juli und August 1931." *Archiv des öffentlichen Rechts* 21:124.

Malberg, Raymond Carré de. 1931. *La loi, expression de la volonte générale.* Paris. Mayer, Otto. 1924. *Deutsches Verwaltungsrecht.* 3d ed. Leipzig: Duncker und Humblot.

Poetzsch-Heffter, Fritz, and Richard Grau. 1932. "Der Spruch des Staatsgerichtshofes." *Deutsche Juristen-Zeitung* 37:1373–78.

Popitz, J. 1929. "Verfassungsrecht und Steuervereinheitlichungsgesetz." *Deutsche-Juristen-Zeitung* 34.

Radbruch, Gustav. 1932. *Rechtsphilosophie.* 3d ed. Leipzig: Quelle und Meyer.

Schmitt, Carl. [1922] 1989. *Die Diktatur: Von den Anfängen des modernen Souveränitätsgedankens bis zum proletarischen Klassenkampf.* 5th ed. Berlin: Duncker und Humblot.

———. 1931. "The staatsrechtliche Bedeutung der Notverordnung, insbesondere ihre Rechtsgültigkeit." In *Notverordnung und öffentliche Verwaltung.* Berlin: Industrieverlag Späth und Linde. Reprinted in *Verfassungsrechtliche Aufsätze aus den Jahren 1924-1954.* 3d ed. Berlin: Duncker und Humblot, 1985.

———. [1931] 1985. *Der Hüter der Verfassung.* 3d ed. Berlin: Duncker und Humblot.

———. 1932. "Grundsätzliches zur heutigen Notverordnungspraxis." *Reichsverwaltungsblatt und Preußisches Verwaltungsblatt.* 53, no. 9:161–65.

———. [1958] 1985. *Verfassungsrechtliche Aufsätze aus den Jahren 1924-1954: Materialien zu einer Verfassungslehre.* 3d ed. Berlin: Duncker und Humblot.

Schneider, Hans. 1953. "Das Ermächtigungsgesetz vom 24. März 1933." *Vierteljahreshefte für Zeitgeschichte* 1 (July).

Smend, Rudolf. [1928] 1994. "Verfassung und Verfassungsrecht." In *Staatsrechtliche Abhandlungen und andere Aufsätze.* 3d ed. Berlin: Duncker und Humblot.

Starosolskyj, W. 1916. *Das Majoritätsprinzip.* Vienna: F. Deuticke.

Triepel, Heinrich. 1922. *Quellensammlung zum deutschen Reichsstaatsrecht.* 3d ed. Tübingen: J. C. B. Mohr.

Wacke, Gerhard. 1957. *Staatsrechtliche Prüfung der Zusatzsteuer: Kritische Untersuchungen zu abs. 8 des Umsatzsteuergesetzes.* Cologne: O. Schmidt.

Weber, Max. 1978. *Economy and Society: An Outline of Interpretive Sociology.* 2 vols. Edited by Guenther Roth and Claus Wittich. Berkeley: University of California Press.

Wolzendorff, Kurt. 1915. *Staatsrecht und Naturrecht.* Breslau: M. und H. Marcus.

Ziegler, Heinz O. 1932. *Autoritärer oder totaler Staat.* Tübingen: Mohr.

INDEX

Aristotle: regime types in, 6, 8
Article 48 (Weimar Constitution), 13, 67, 69, 74, 80–83, 97; and fundamental rights, 71–73, 75, 77–79; and the Nazis, 71; organizational minimum under, 75; Prelate Kaas and, 100; and separation of powers, 70–71; and the Staatsgerichtshof, 74; in state of exception, 78. *See also* Decree; Dictator

Civil service, 11–14, 18, 91–92
Constitutional change: Article 76 (Weimar Constitution), 39, 47–49, 51–52; Article 79 (Basic Law), 95; by formal amendment, 39, 53–54; via referendum, 64; by statute, 44, 57, 63
Constitutional monarchy, 12–13, 17, 23, 25, 76
Constitution-making, 99

Decisionism, 9, 21, 56, 85, 89. *See also* Positivism
Decree: administrative, 5, 22, 23; with force of law, 25–26, 67, 73, 75–76, 80–82, 97; under Article 48(2), 13, 75, 87
Dictator, 70, 78–79, 81–83; and parliament, 86
Direct democracy, 39, 59–61

Equal chance, 28–36, 47, 88, 94, 98

Friend and enemy distinction, 95

Homogeneity (of the people), 24, 27–28, 40–43, 45, 88

Identity, 28
Initiative, 62, 86. *See also* Referendum

Law: administrative, 20–21; concept of, 10, 20–21, 24–25, 27, 30, 72, 76, 79, 82, 86, 97–98; formal, 17; procedural, 39; statute, 20, 22–23, 27, 43–44, 53, 56–57, 62–63, 68, 80; in substantive sense, 21–22
Legality, 9, 12, 14, 27, 29, 30, 34, 36, 40, 87, 93–94, 96, 98, 100; concept of, 3, 10, 28–29, 30, 40, 88, 101; system of, 6, 13, 19, 24, 25, 51, 54, 59–60, 62, 65–66, 69–70, 73, 76, 80, 85, 88; system suicide and, 48
Legal revolution, 95
Legislative-reservation clause, 19, 56–57, 68, 72–73
Legitimacy, 6, 12, 94, 96–97; dynastic, 7, 13; liberal, 6; monarchical, 9, 12; plebiscitory or democratic, 9, 12, 13, 60, 65–66, 88–90, 93
Liberalism. *See* Legitimacy

Majority, 14, 30, 87, 89, 98; negative, 100; principle of, 36; qualified, 40–41, 43–45, 51–53, 64; simple, 41, 44–45, 51–52, 64, 73, 86, 99
Measure, 11, 14, 68–70, 73, 97–98. *See also* Decree; Law, statute

Monarchy, constitutional, 12, 13, 17, 23, 25, 76

Neutrality, 25, 27, 47–50, 53, 59, 85, 93–94, 96

Norms: conditions for, 69; hierarchy of, 41, 54–55; and rights, 97; statutory, 80, 82–83

Pluralism, 87–88, 98–99; Parteienstaat, 92–93

Political, the, 13, 87–88

Political premiums, 13, 50, 88, 98–99, 100

Positivism: as decisionism, 21; legal, 96–97

Rechtsstaat, 3, 5, 12, 14, 18, 21, 22, 23, 57, 68, 70, 72–73, 79, 82, 97, 99

Referendum, 59–62, 64, 89; and initiative, 62, 86

Rights: to resistance, 29, 31, 87; substantive guarantees for, 39–40, 45–46, 52–53, 56–57, 59–60, 77–78, 99. *See also* Norms; Weimar Constitution

Separation of powers, 86. *See also* Article 48

Sovereignty, 5, 60, 65

State: administrative, 5, 6, 7, 8, 9, 10, 11, 14, 55, 58, 83, 89, 97; authoritarian, 90; economic, 6–7; governmental, 5, 7, 8, 9, 11, 55, 58; jurisdiction, 5, 7, 8, 11, 53, 55, 58–59, 67, 85, 86, 89; legislative, 3–14, 17, 19–20, 24–26, 27, 29, 33, 36, 40, 45, 51, 53–54, 56–63, 67, 71–72, 75–83, 85–89, 97; and society, 23; total, 6, 35, 92–93

Weimar Constitution, 39–40, 50, 53, 58, 76–79, 94–95. *See also* Article 48; Constitutional change; Rights

Will, 52, 61, 86–88

CARL SCHMITT (1888–1985) was a leading political and legal theoretician of the twentieth century. Among his many works, the following have been translated into English: *State, Movement, People: The Triadic Structure of the Political Unity: The Question of Legality* (2001); *Land and Sea* (1997); *The Leviathan in the State Theory of Thomas Hobbes: Meaning and Failure of a Political Symbol* (1996); *Roman Catholicism and Political Form* (1996); *The Tyranny of Values* (1996); *The Idea of Representation: A Discussion* (1988); *Political Romanticism* (1986); *Political Theology: Four Chapters in the Concept of Sovereignty* (1985); *The Crisis of Parliamentary Democracy* (1985); *The Concept of the Political* (1976); *The Necessity of Politics; and Essay on the Representative Idea in the Church and Modern Europe* (1931).

JOHN P. McCORMICK is an associate professor of political science at the University of Chicago. He is the author of *Carl Schmitt's Critique of Liberalism: Against Politics as Technology* (1997) and editor of *Confronting Mass Democracy and Industrial Technology: Political and Social Theory from Nietzsche to Habermas* (Duke, 2001).

JEFFREY SEITZER is the author of *Comparative History and Legal Theory: Carl Schmitt in the First German Democracy* (2001). He has also translated Schmitt's *Constitutional Theory* (*Verfassungslehre* [1928]).

Library of Congress Cataloging-in-Publication Data

Schmitt, Carl
Legality and legitimacy / Carl Schmitt ; translated and edited by Jeffrey Seitzer ; with an introduction by John P. McCormick.
p. cm.
Includes bibliographical references and index.
ISBN 0-8223-3161-6 (cloth : alk. paper) — ISBN 0-8223-3174-8 (pbk. : alk. paper)
1. Legitimacy of governments—Germany. 2. Legislative power—Germany. 3. Rule of law—Germany. I. Seitzer, Jeffrey. II. McCormick, John P., 1966– III. Title.
KK4713.S3613 2004
340'.11—dc22   2003022709